D1592658

The Sunday School Movement

Studies in the Growth and Decline of Sunday Schools

STUDIES IN CHRISTIAN HISTORY AND THOUGHT

A full listing of all titles in this series
appears at the close of this book

STUDIES IN CHRISTIAN HISTORY AND THOUGHT

The Sunday School Movement

Studies in the Growth and Decline of Sunday Schools

Edited by Stephen Orchard and John H.Y. Briggs

Paternoster:
thinking faith

MILTON KEYNES · COLORADO SPRINGS · HYDERABAD

Paternoster is an imprint of Authentic Media
9 Holdom Avenue, Bletchley, Milton Keynes, Bucks, MK1 1QR
1820 Jet Stream Drive, Colorado Springs, CO 80921, USA
OM Authentic Media, Medchal Road, Jeedimetla Village,
Secunderabad 500 055, A.P., India
www.authenticmedia.co.uk
Authentic Media is a division of IBS-STL UK, a company limited by guarantee
(registered charity no. 270162)

13 12 11 10 09 08 07   7 6 5 4 3 2 1

British Library Cataloguing in Publication Data
A catalogue record for this book is available from the British Library

ISBN 978-1-84227-363-0

Typeset by A.R. Cross
Printed and bound in Great Britain
for Paternoster
by Nottingham AlphaGraphics

STUDIES IN CHRISTIAN HISTORY AND THOUGHT

Series Preface

This series complements the specialist series of *Studies in Evangelical History and Thought* and *Studies in Baptist History and Thought* for which Paternoster is becoming increasingly well known by offering works that cover the wider field of Christian history and thought. It encompasses accounts of Christian witness at various periods, studies of individual Christians and movements, and works which concern the relations of church and society through history, and the history of Christian thought.

The series includes monographs, revised dissertations and theses, and collections of papers by individuals and groups. As well as 'free standing' volumes, works on particular running themes are being commissioned; authors will be engaged for these from around the world and from a variety of Christian traditions.

A high academic standard combined with lively writing will commend the volumes in this series both to scholars and to a wider readership.

Series Editors

Contents

Contributors

Clyde Binfield Professor Associate in History, University of Sheffield

Faith Bowers Sub-Editor, *Baptist Quarterly*

John H.Y. Briggs Professor Emeritus, The University of Birmingham, Senior Research Fellow in Ecclesiastical History and Director of the Centre for Baptist History and Heritage, Regent's Park College, University of Oxford

Grayson Ditchfield Reader in Eighteenth-Century History, University of Kent

Hugh McLeod Professor of Modern History, University of Birmingham

Stephen Orchard URC Minister, Principal of Westminster College, Cambridge, and Honorary Professor, Brunel University

Jack Priestley Honorary Research Fellow, Exeter School of Education and Lifelong Learning

Geoff Robson retired Her Majesty's Inspector

Doreen Rosman retired Senior Lecturer, School of History, University of Kent

Martin Wellings Methodist Minister, Convenor of the Association of Denominational Historical Societies and Cognate Libraries

Preface

The Association of Denominational Historical Societies and Cognate Libraries (ADHSCL) came into being in October 1993. The Association brings together twelve societies and seven libraries, including Baptists and Congregationalists, Methodists and Unitarians, the Society of Friends and the 'New Church', the United Reformed Church and the Huguenots, the Welsh Presbyterians and The Chapel Society, with libraries in Oxford, Cambridge and London. Since its inception the Association has sought to encourage research into the several traditions represented by its members, with special reference to projects which relate to more than one tradition. This aim has been pursued through an annual lecture, a publishing programme and occasional conferences.

Given the tremendous significance of the Sunday School movement across the denominations in the period from the late eighteenth century to the mid-twentieth century, a bicentenary retrospective on the National Sunday School Union offered a welcome opportunity to reassess a major phenomenon in British church life. The Association was, therefore, delighted to support the conference 'The National Sunday School Union. An anniversary retrospective', held at Westminster College, Cambridge, from 21-23 September 2004. The papers given there, and published in the present volume, ranged from surveys of the Sunday School movement in the eighteenth and twentieth centuries via denominational and local explorations to biographical, architectural and thematic studies. The detailed primary research underpinning the papers both challenged accepted interpretations of Sunday Schools and identified the need for further work in this neglected field.

On behalf of the ADHSCL I am glad to welcome this volume, and to congratulate the editors, the contributors and the publishers on the outcome of their labours. It is a particular pleasure to record the Association's thanks to Margaret Thompson for organizing the conference, to thank Westminster College for its hospitality and The Jerusalem Trust, the Westhill Endowment Trustees and the British and Foreign Schools Society for their financial support.

Martin Wellings,
Kidlington

Sunday Schools: Some Reflections

Stephen Orchard

One thing which soon became apparent when these papers were shared in conference was the enormous affection in which Sunday Schools were held by that older generation who had experienced them at first-hand. This was evident both among participants and the anecdotal evidence collected by those who presented papers. Sunday School Outings, Whit Walks, Anniversaries, banners, even the humble star card which recorded attendance at Sunday School, were all recalled with great nostalgia. There was also a recognition of years of disinterested service to other people's children given by Sunday School teachers. All this was on a scale which gives it great significance in the national life of the nineteenth and early twentieth centuries. There is work for the oral historians to do, in gathering up the memories of the older generation who are the last survivors of the mass Sunday School movement. This is especially emphasised because research for the conference papers revealed how little is formally recorded of the experience of children in Sunday Schools. History tends to be written from the point of view of the powerful, in this case, the adult concerns about running Sunday Schools.

The depths of feeling which were stirred are related to that most potent area of human experience, early childhood. It is notable that the understanding of children's experience and needs shifted significantly over the life of the Sunday School movement. Although not directly involved in Sunday School work as notable a theologian as P.T. Forsyth made imaginative attempts to enter the world of childhood as something set apart from adult experience. His Protestant rationality is modified by appeal to story and emotion, such as one might experience in a great medieval cathedral. This change of tack by the preacher who wishes to communicate with children is matched by the educationalist G.H. Archibald, supported by the philanthropist George Cadbury. Having lost a role as primary educators in skills and knowledge Sunday Schools and their sponsoring churches moved into the area of religious development, with a particular emphasis on exploring childhood experience. This was to spread from Sunday Schools to general education, especially through one of Archibald's successors as Principal of Westhill College, Basil

Yeaxlee. Yeaxlee brought the new discipline of educational psychology to bear in schools as well as churches and popularised the notion of 'lifelong learning'. Yeaxlee's work on strengthening religious education in schools after 1944 may well have contributed to the eventual decline of Sunday Schools. It is persuasively argued in Doreen Rosman's paper that parents came to regard school provision of religious education as an adequate substitute for Sunday School, especially as Sunday Schools became more focused on religious formation and shifted their meeting times to fit around services of worship.

The strength of the National Sunday School Union (NSSU) in the late nineteenth century was due to its essentially auxiliary nature as a supporter of local action and a sharer of good practice. Although theories of teaching were discussed and methodologies compared the life-blood of the NSSU was business, albeit not for profit in the usual sense. A study which instantly suggests itself, once the papers here are read, is the role of the business man in promoting Sunday Schools. In any locality in the country larger numbers of children were gathered together in voluntary educational enterprises which were, by and large, efficiently run. The governance and bureaucracy required in any one community to organise 300 children and their teachers in adequate accommodation with appropriate resources was not only found but replicated again and again. The NSSU was a way of sharing this expertise rather than providing the direction. As Faith Bowers observes, the wonder is that the leaders of the NSSU found time for business alongside their commitment to its workings. The obverse side of this coin is that the leadership did not spend time envisaging how the Sunday School movement should develop; they brought together their experience of their local Sunday School and their business acumen and did the best they could. Their best was exactly what was needed, for publishing lesson materials, hymnbooks, stationery and so on met the needs of those who had local organisation in their hands. Moreover, holding great national or regional rallies was a way of improving and developing good practice by example rather than attempting a command structure. Command structures came later, with the various youth movements of the twentieth century, especially Brigades. And although kindly meant, it could be argued that an intellectual command structure began to emerge with Archibald's Westhill, which took the view that Sunday Schools needed to be changed.

Anxiety about Sunday School decline seems to have begun in the late nineteenth century alongside the fear that the churches were losing influence over the population at large. As one elderly Welshman put it to me in 1968, 'I grew up in a world where when you stepped out of your door on a Sunday evening to go to church you noticed those few doors on the street which remained closed. I now live in a world where you notice the few doors that open.' When it was reckoned that church attendance had dropped to 25% of the population in some parts of London in 1910 it was regarded as a crisis the churches needed to address. It is one thing to be anxious about decline; it is another thing to reverse it. The introduction of sport, the promotion of uniformed organisations, the introduction of a new philosophy by Archibald, these were all sincere attempts to reverse the trend. However, these energetic efforts probably obscure the real reasons for the decline—that the need for Sunday Schools was lessening. The anxiety to retain large numbers of children in Sunday School and to renew church membership from this pool of young talent is an entirely different motive from that which animated the work of Robert Raikes and his contemporaries. Rhetoric conceals the shift. The people who respond to an offer of teaching in basic skills against a religious background cannot be transmuted into eager catechumens.

Even if the NSSU had both correctly identified the cause of decline in Sunday Schools and found a remedy for it they were still unable to command local resources of either people or money. This was a voluntary movement, its capacity to change dictated by the constituency. Indeed, as the twentieth century wore on the NSSU found that the collapse of local activity restricted its own national resources just as it did that of all other national groupings of Christian youth and children's work. The strengths of the Sunday School movement were also its weakness.

Throughout their history Sunday Schools always existed in tension with ecclesiastical authority. Early Sunday Schools were often independent charities with their own funds and buildings. The rising denominationalism of the nineteenth century brought these independent enterprises to an end, to be replaced by local Sunday School auxiliaries where the representatives of the various schools met. The role of missionary societies and the YMCA in shaping the modern ecumenical movement has been studied but we know of no assessment of the significance of Sunday School unions in shaping local ecumenism. The Sunday School unions in Wales and Scotland may have a special role here. Lay leadership is critical in local ecumenism and may be both more radical and more conservative than that of transient ministers and clergy. It can be seen that the early moves towards assigning Sunday Schools to particular churches did not necessarily end their ecclesiological ambiguity. Sunday School leaders still saw themselves as answerable to the community they served rather than to church authorities. Much of this attitude survived into the modern era. Vicars or ministers and church councils were often at odds with their Sunday Schools. At the conference there was no shortage of anecdotes on this topic, a frequent problem being squabbles over the use of buildings or the horror with which clergy and ministers approached the Sunday School anniversary services, which had a liturgical shape alien to all they tried to inculcate on the other Sundays of the year. It is clear that Sunday Schools often became an alternative power base within church communities, particularly under the sponsorship of a prominent layman. Running with this was what the church authorities saw as a consistent failure of Sunday Schools to increase church membership. Only a very small proportion of Sunday School attenders became communicants. School leaving age was also Sunday School leaving age. Attempts to combat this by, for instance, a programme of sports for older pupils, had limited success and threw up other problems, such as defining who might play for a Sunday School team. These were issues for all churches, but especially for those Nonconformists who kept a strict discipline of church membership by admission to the church roll on profession of faith.

On the positive side, clergy and ministers promoting local ecumenism in the 1960s and '70s would often find that their lay leaders brought to the process long experience of inter-denominational collaboration through their local Sunday School auxiliary. In Wales a further dimension was added, for the Sunday School movement had always been a place for those who taught in the Welsh medium to consider educational matters at a time when the day-schools were promoting English medium teaching. It seems likely that these contributions to the modern ecumenical movement have been overlooked. Decline in the old Sunday School structures has coincided with a rise in local ecumenical activity, including churches co-operating to sponsor Christian education work with children.

Early Sunday Schools on an undenominational basis relied on the Bible as both a textbook for literacy and a sufficient religious curriculum. Denominational Sunday Schools introduced catechetical elements peculiar to themselves, though some deliberately avoided this in order to serve more widely. It could be argued that the shift to denominational Sunday Schools marks the first shift in objectives, a first step towards the major shift accompanying the educational changes of 1870. Geoff Robson indicates how the way for Archibald was in some sense prepared by Joshua Fitch. From the late nineteenth century onwards pedagogical reasons were found for supporting a Sunday School curriculum based on the telling of Bible stories. What was taken for granted in 1780 needed supporting by argument in 1880. The telling of Bible stories can be effective in developing religious imagination. However, by 1880 many Christians felt the Bible to be at odds with science and responded dogmatically. The Bible was not used to free the imagination but to defend the frontiers of traditional Christian belief against the scepticism encouraged by science. Add to this the fact that doctrinal teaching, especially at an early age, presents greater problems for both children and teachers. The decline in Sunday Schools coincided with the new attitudes to Bible stories, and this compounded the pedagogical difficulties.

One of the reasons for the resilience of Sunday Schools, given these ideological difficulties, was their extensive social role in the community, well beyond actual Christian teaching. Outings, lectures, concerts, publications, sport, temperance societies and so on were associated with the Sunday School. Until their collapse Sunday Schools provided the means and motivation for children to develop aptitude in debate and the performing arts. No modern government programme could possibly mobilise so many opportunities for children to act, sing or speak. It is possible that today's children have more opportunity to learn to play a musical instrument, but even this is questionable when one considers the vast number of pianists deployed when Sunday Schools were at their peak, not to mention bands and orchestras. It is a commonplace that Labour politicians were raised in Methodist chapels. More specifically, the Sunday School probably played a larger part in their political education than the chapel itself. It was the Sunday School which focused concern for others and which recruited for the Bands of Hope and other temperance organisations which had social improvement and personal advancement firmly within their sights. The Young Man's Bible Class fed the Wesley Guild or the Debating Society where humane learning was prized and cultural horizons lifted. It was the Sunday School, rather than the public house, which offered a reflection of Ruskin or an echo of Elgar. All Sunday Schools had their equivalent of the modern after-school clubs, where extra-curricular learning took place. The shift from the communal society to the privatised society in the 1960s and '70s, together with a shrinking of the child population, meant that the population at large would find less use for Sunday Schools, but they would also lose these social benefits.

There was, of course, always an overlap with weekday education. Sunday Schools sometimes shared premises with day schools and, as we keep on reminding ourselves, played a part until 1870 in the provision of elementary education in general. From 1870 Sunday Schools took on a more specialised role in what we might now term Further Education, part of which is embodied in the activities mentioned in the previous paragraph. The Sunday School curriculum has always been informed by general educational practice. In recent years it has tended to remain 'child-centred' in the face of changes in the day school curriculum. This is partly because the notion of 'school' has now been largely abandoned. In the population at large, parents now expect the day school to provide the basic Christian training which they looked to the Sunday Schools to provide up to the 1950s. They also look to schools for general spiritual and moral formation. It is sometimes noted by educationalists that the British differ from the rest of Europe in this respect. There, although the school is expected to be moral, it is principally a didactic institution. There is a greater public recognition of the role of the home and the church in shaping the lives of children. In Britain many more parents assign the school a pastoral role in the upbringing of their children. A minority secure supplementary education for their children in music or dance or other performing arts. A few children are still encouraged to go to meetings of children's and youth organisations. The majority of parents look to the school for the support and stimulus their children need beyond the home. The effect of the 1944 Education Act and subsequent legislation on religious education is germane here. Perhaps also one should study what parents expect from independent schools, especially those advertising their religious foundation.

The conference identified certain other historic enquiries which might usefully be made. We know of no detailed investigation into the collapse of Sunday School attendance in the decade 1960–70. The changing nature of society is one theme but the documentation of which we were aware showed considerable hostility within the churches to the old kind of Sunday School and the name itself, building in strength after 1945. This may have hastened the decline, given that Sunday Schools had always included a majority of children whose parents were not regular churchgoers. We need a study of auxiliary Christian organisations for children, such as Crusaders, CSSM, Christian Endeavour and so on. These papers have no specific study of an Anglican Sunday School as a distinct type, or of radically different interpretations of the Sunday School idea such as secularist schools. Sunday Schools were the means of introducing millions of children to the concept of overseas mission and worldwide Christianity and we know of no recent study of this phenomenon and its effects on the population at large. Is there any reinforcement or reduction of ethnic stereotyping as a result of Sunday School images of children in other parts of the world? There is also work to be done on the spin-off from Sunday Schools into Temperance, especially in the Band of Hope and its social effects. Was the image of teetotal killjoys a price worth paying to avoid the binge drinking culture of young people today? We have no papers here on Ragged Schools or on the role of music in Sunday Schools.

One more area which concerns modern historians and which eluded these papers and that is gender studies. It is almost certain that the majority of Sunday School teachers were women. Who were they and how did this activity relate to the rest of their lives and to their self-image? Sunday Schools reflected the social mores of their time, separating boys and girls by gender. Did their work contribute to the dissolving of such distinctions or reinforce them? In public education girls' schools commonly offered a curriculum meant to prepare them for their role in the home and family. Yet the very act of separating out girls sometimes released them to develop free from male dominance. It would be good to trace the impact of Sunday Schools on female emancipation, or the role of organisations such as the Girls' Life Brigade in developing self-confidence. The women who took on hitherto masculine jobs during the World Wars of the twentieth century had almost all been to Sunday School as children. At a time when women were still scarcely trusted to hold a collection plate in church some of them were leaders of large Sunday School departments and girls' organisations. Although most male clergy and ministers might express grave doubts about opening their vocation to women there were some who entertained an alternative vision, or even encouraged it. When Constance Coltman was ordained by Congregationalists in 1919, on the day before her marriage, it was done with the active encouragement of at least those men who laid their hands upon her head, seeking the gifts of the Holy Spirit for her. She then gave an emphasis in the pastoral ministry she shared with her husband to family concerns. It was she who carried out most infant baptisms in their churches. It may be that one of the unexpressed reasons for hostility between church and Sunday School is bound up with what we would now term 'gender issues'.

What comes home in the end after considering these papers is the extent to which the Sunday School movement has not been a central theme in the study of church history. It has been largely left to educational historians, especially ordained practitioners. This history needs to be brought in from the cold, as it were. The traditional topics of nineteenth century church history, such as the rise of Ritualism in the Church of England, or the growth of the missionary movement, do not take place in a world without Sunday Schools. On the contrary, public interest in these matters at the time is more likely to have been informed by what was learnt in Sunday School than in church services. Popular piety and that sentimental gloss which accompanies so much Victorian religion was rooted in a spirituality formed in childhood and early adolescence. The heroes of the Bible are matched by contemporary heroes, be they Grace Darling or Lord Shaftesbury. The touchstone of morality becomes 'the simple commands of Jesus' unqualified by dogma or apologetic. Childhood becomes sentimentalised as the time of greatest religious insight. On that ground alone it might be hoped that these essays will stimulate more study and research into both the history of Sunday Schools and their significance.

CHAPTER 1

From Catechism Class to Sunday School

Stephen Orchard

In his bi-centenary book on the Sunday School movement Philip Cliff pays tribute to his mentor, H.A. Hamilton.[1] Hamilton, a Congregational minister and advocate of what was termed 'Family Church', was part of a tradition of Christian Education at Westhill College, Birmingham, which traced its origin from G.H. Archibald. This liberal ecumenical tradition of Christian Education has been enormously influential in church and school around the world. From Cliff's standpoint the rise and development of the Sunday School movement takes us from some fairly incoherent reasons for gathering children in Sunday Schools through the highly organised mass movement of the Victorian era to the subtleties of maintaining Christian education in a secularising society. In this story Robert Raikes of Gloucester is celebrated as the populariser of Sunday Schools, whose origins lay as far as 200 years or more before his time. Cliff is following his sources. Leslie Stephen did the same a hundred years earlier in his *DNB* article on Raikes, where he wrote: 'It must no doubt have occurred to many people to teach children on Sunday. Among Raikes's predecessors are generally mentioned Cardinal Borromeo (1538–1584), Joseph Alleine, Hannah Ball, and Theophilus Lindsey.' This approach rates the day on which the activity occurred as being the determinative factor instead of asking what the activity was. Leslie Stephen was anticipated by the anonymous 1798 contributor to the *Evangelical Magazine* who attributed the first Sunday Schools to Alfred the Great.[2] Closer examination of what Raikes's so-called predecessors were actually doing on Sundays is necessary if we are to understand the

---

[1] Philip Cliff, *The Rise and Development of the Sunday School Movement in England, 1780–1980* (Birmingham, National Christian Education Council, 1986). Herbert Alfred Hamilton (1897–1977), a Congregational minister who developed the idea of Family Church in his period as Secretary of the Youth and Education Department of the Congregational Union in England and Wales from 1933–1945. He then became Principal of Westhill College, Birmingham from 1945–54 and after further ministerial service in Brighton worked for the World Council of Christian Education from 1963–65 and then the World Council of Churches.

[2] *Evangelical Magazine* 6 (1798), p. 15

significance of the rapid spread of the Sunday School movement between 1780 and 1800.

The problem of approaching the history of Sunday Schools by concentrating on the Sunday rather than the school is that this approach is misleading when dealing with the eighteenth-century evidence. What are already disparate scraps of information about educational activities on Sundays become even more confused when forced into this template. In particular, there needs to be a greater distinction than the standard historians of Sunday Schools make between the catechetical traditions of the church and the demand for popular education consequent upon the Industrial Revolution. By the time Cliff wrote Hamilton had established a view that Sunday School, or whatever was to replace it, was preparatory to church membership, essentially a catechetical model, though Hamilton shrank from catechising children in the traditional way. Hamilton could assume that on five other days of the week children were provided with a general education, including what we now call skills, such as numeracy. The Sunday Schools advocated by Robert Raikes from 1780 onwards were focused much more on general education which, in a religious age, included learning the catechism. The only question for the early Sunday Schools was in which version the catechism should be learned, Church or Dissent? Soon after Sunday Schools had begun there was a move among Evangelicals in Scotland to distinguish them from Sabbath evening catechetical schools. The Sunday School was regarded as a place principally designed to teach children to read. A Sabbath evening catechetical school was for religious instruction only. The Sunday School was designed for the poor and its teachers were hired. The Sabbath School was principally conducted by gentlemen and respectable tradesmen.[3]

In revisiting the question of how Sunday Schools began it will be necessary to re-examine the catechetical practices of the eighteenth century in England and to define Sunday Schools in that period with more exactness. 'Sunday School' has become a compound noun in the popular imagination. We must try and recapture the sense of it as describing a schooling process which happened on the one day of the week when children and young people were not working. Historically, the Church of England followed ancient practice and laid a requirement on incumbents that they should catechise children before confirmation. Similarly, parents and masters of apprentices were to send children for such catechising. The requirement can only exist when there are children unconfirmed and unprepared. It is also assumed that it is not a continuous exercise through childhood but what we would now call a course or even a module. It was time-limited and the Prayer Book

[3] *Evangelical Magazine* 7 (1799), p. 480.

specified Sunday as the day it should take place. Catechism within the Church of England had acquired a new rigour under Puritan influences. The Westminster Assembly produced a much fuller Shorter Catechism for parish use. It contained much more than the old Prayer Book catechism, though less than the supplementary scholarly catechisms produced by such Divines as Alexander Nowell, the Elizabethan Dean of St Paul's.[4] After 1662 Nonconformists continued to use the Westminster Shorter Catechism for the same purpose as Conformists used the Prayer Book catechism, that is, for the preparation of children and young people for communicant membership of the Church. However, because Dissenters set the bar higher than the Church of England by using the Westminster Shorter Catechism, with its greater length and more sophisticated vocabulary, they tended to admit young people to the Lord's Table at a slightly older age.

What are the differences between the Catechism found in the Book of Common Prayer from 1662 and the Westminster Shorter Catechism? The obvious one, already mentioned, is of that length. The Westminster Shorter Catechism is short only in comparison with the Westminster Longer Catechism. With its 108 questions and answers it far outstrips the Prayer Book catechism. One reason for this difference is in the context. Before 1661 the Prayer Book had included a catechism as part of the confirmation service. The bishop was expected to ask questions of those offering themselves for confirmation as part of the service. The 1662 Prayer Book takes the catechism out of the confirmation service but still places it in that section of the book, between the service for the baptism of adults and the confirmation service. Clergy were required to catechise during evensong, rather than out of service time as in the past. This looks like a compromise position between, on the one hand, making the confirmation service inordinately long and awkward by using the fuller catechism of 1662, and, on the other hand, taking the catechism out of any liturgical setting. The Westminster Assembly and subsequent Nonconformists viewed catechising as a teaching and learning activity practised out of service time. A child who could pass the test of the Shorter Catechism satisfied the minister that they knew enough of the faith to be received at the Lord's Table. Moreover, not just length but sophistication of language separated the two catechisms. In the Prayer Book the child is expected to learn from the eighth commandment, 'Thou shalt not steal', 'to keep my hands from picking and stealing'.[5] The Shorter Catechism operates beyond this directness in a world of ethical complexity. 'The eighth commandment requireth the lawful

---

[4] Alexander Nowell's catechism in Latin and English, with a Memoir, was published by the Parker Society, *A Catechsim written in Latin...* (Cambridge, 1853), XXXII.

[5] *Book of Common Prayer, 1662* (pagination dependent on edition).

procuring and furthering the wealth and outward estate of ourselves and others... The eighth commandment forbiddeth whatsoever doth or may unjustly hinder our own or our neighbour's wealth or outward estate.'[6] It is no wonder that commentaries on the Shorter Catechism began to be written, trying to make its meaning plain. On the other hand this amplification could actually do more justice to the subject. The Prayer Book catechism has a single answer to the question about the Lord's Prayer, which includes the phrase 'that he [i.e., God] will be merciful to us, and forgive us our sins'; The Shorter Catechism defines the Lord's Prayer in terms of six petitions and a conclusion, each with its own questions and explication. Thus we have 'In the fifth petition we pray, That God, for Christ's sake, would freely pardon all our sins; which we are the rather encouraged to ask, because by his grace we are enabled from the heart to forgive others.'

The differences of length and emphasis between the two catechisms should not obscure their similarities. Each is agreed that knowledge of the Lord's Prayer and the Ten Commandments is essential to Christian life. Where the Prayer Book requires the Apostles' Creed the Shorter Catechism sets out the basics of the faith at greater length in thirty-eight questions and answers, incorporating the Calvinist nuances one would expect. Each is agreed that there are two sacraments. The Prayer Book offers its famous definition of a sacrament as an outward and visible sign of an inward and spiritual grace. The Shorter Catechism avoids such a distinction and tells us that 'a sacrament is an holy ordinance instituted by Christ; wherein, by sensible signs, Christ, and the benefits of the new covenant, are represented, sealed, and applied to believers'. The use of 'represented' is what you might expect from the Zwinglian influences amongst the Puritans. 'Sealed, and applied' is perhaps more traditionally sacramental than we might expect. Neither Protestant source is going to give ground toward transubstantiation. Having allowed for its brevity, the chief distinguishing mark of the Prayer Book catechism is its beginning with the child and its godparents, rather than with a creed, and its failure, even allowing for its brevity, to elaborate on the fourth commandment, concerning the Sabbath. The Shorter Catechism, by contrast, is silent on the subject of godparents and fulsome on Sabbath keeping. The overall distinction remains the length and style, rendering the Prayer Book catechism a basic test of Christian competence and the Shorter Catechism a virtual syllabus of Christian instruction.

The inadequacy of the Prayer Book catechism, in its various forms, for fuller instruction was acknowledged by the Church of England. From 1570 the bishops had authorised the printing of Alexander Nowell's catechism for grammar schools. His catechism first appeared in Latin and

---

[6] *Westminster Shorter Catechism, 1646* (pagination dependent on edition).

was subsequently translated into English by Thomas Norton.[7] As in the Westminster Longer Catechism Nowell is able to use length to explore theological subtleties more fully. For him a sacrament is 'an outward testifying of God's good-will and mercifulness toward us, through Christ, by a visible sign representing an invisible and spiritual grace, by which the promises of God touching the forgiveness of sins and eternal salvation given through Christ, are, as it were sealed, and the truth of them is more certainly confirmed in our hearts'.[8] Nowell goes on to explore the outward and visible sign and the invisible grace at greater length. The Westminster Longer Catechism follows Nowell and other Puritan divines in saying that there are two parts of a sacrament, 'the one an outward and visible sign, used according to Christ's own appointment; the other an inward and spiritual grace thereby signified'.[9] Apart from style and content the other notable aspect of Nowell's catechism is that it was prepared for use in school, albeit a grammar school. Catechesis takes on a wider educational significance beyond the parish church and formal requirements. It is not that schools are formed as catechetical institutions but that the extension of catechesis to schools as part of the curriculum is a pragmatic consequence of the Church's role in education. However, since so small a part of the child population attended school the primary focus of catechising remained the parish church or dissenting meeting.

In the decades immediately preceding the emergence of the Sunday School movement ministers still largely relied on the Prayer Book catechism and the Westminster Shorter Catechism as the manuals for instructing children. Isaac Watts attempted to lighten the load for children by writing instructive verses and a catechism of his own. The verses, such as 'How doth the little busy bee improve the shining hour?', were used with children well into the nineteenth century, allowing Lewis Carroll to parody them in his own versions—'How doth the little crocodile improve his shining tail?' Carroll's joke at Watts's expense obscures the progressive trend of Watts' thinking. The attempt to address a child's imagination in simple language for the purpose of religious and moral growth was an advance on the rigidities of the Westminster Shorter Catechism with which the children of Dissenters were usually confronted.

Perhaps because catechising took place in thousands of churches and meeting-houses the length and breadth of England in the eighteenth century we know very little about how it was actually done. The commonplace is rarely recorded in detail. Derbyshire will serve as a representative county, since the records of bishops' visitations are easily

---

[7] See n. 4.
[8] Nowell, *A Catechism*, p. 205.
[9] Westminster Longer Catechism, A 163.

accessible.[10] In both the 1751 and 1772 visitations questions were asked about catechising. The basis for this was the rubric

> The Curate of every parish shall diligently upon Sundays and Holydays, after the Second Lesson at Evening Prayer, openly in the Church instruct and examine so many Children of his Parish sent unto him, as he shall think convenient, in some part of this Catechism.

> And all Fathers, Mothers, Masters, and Dames, shall cause their children, Servants, and Prentices (which have not learn'd their Catchism) to come to the Church at the time appointed, and be ordered by the Curate, until such time as they have learned all that is here appointed for them to learn.[11]

Rather more returns for 1772 survive than for 1751 with the result that the impression is created that incumbents were more diligent in catechising by the later date. Even allowing for that it is only the earlier returns which yield negatives. At Pinxton and South Normanton it is asserted that the incumbent had no time to catechise. At Glossop catechising happened once a year but few children were sent and at Castleton catechising only took place when the parents sent their children. Nevertheless, from both sets of returns it seems that Lent was the favourite season for catechising, though some waited until after Easter and everyone had concluded by Michaelmas. Catechising was a fair weather activity conducted when it was most likely that children and servants could come to a late afternoon activity in the parish church. The evidence from Dissent is even harder to trace, but in Derbyshire we have the diaries of James Clegg (1679–1755), Nonconformist minister at Chinley, and he regularly catechised, using the Westminster Shorter Catechism, from Easter to late summer each year, using the time between the morning and evening preaching services.[12] In 1772 the question was enlarged to enable incumbents to say what material they used for catechising. Newcome's[13] catechism was in use at Brailsford and Dronfield, Wake's[14] at Hucknall

---

[10] J. Beckett, M. Tranter and W. Bateman (eds), *Visitation Returns from the Archdeaconry of Derby 1718–1824* (Chesterfield: Derbyshire Record Society, vol. 29, 2003).

[11] *Book of Common Prayer* 1662.

[12] Vanessa S. Doe (ed.), *The Diary of James Clegg of Chapel en le Frith, 1708–1755, 1708–55* (3 vols; Matlock: Derbyshire Record Society, 1978–81), vols. 2, 3 and 5.

[13] Peter Newcome [1656–1738], *A catechetical course of Sermons for the whole year...* (London, 1702).

[14] William Wake [1657–1737, Bishop of Lincoln], *The principles of the Christian religion explained: in a brief commentary upon the church-catechism* (London, 3rd edition, 1708).

and Tibshelf, Secker's[15] at South Normanton and Pinxton where, after twenty years, a new enthusiasm had been discovered. Bates's Catechism[16] was used at Alvaston, Lewis'[17] at Hathersage, 'Marshall's'[18] at Mackworth, and Williams'[19] at Matlock. It is striking to see how venerable some of these texts were by 1772. Lawrence Bourne at Dronfield was moving from Newcome to the modern Secker but old Calvinism, admittedly of the moderate and episcopal kind, was still informing the instruction of the young in Derbyshire in the parish church. Given the decay of Dissent by 1772 it could be argued that the Church of England was the main guarantee of Calvinist orthodoxy for the rising generation.

These catechising activities account for some of the examples which purport to be early Sunday Schools. No less than fourteen proto-Sunday Schools, as it were, are listed in the bicentenary history of Robert Raikes published by the National Christian Education Council.[20] Take the case of the Nonconformist divine Joseph Alleine. The chief source of information about him is a biography by his widow, Theodosia.[21] We know that his wife kept a school to supplement the family income.[22] It may be that the school was in her name to protect him against prosecution as a Nonconformist minister keeping a school. Alleine had been imprisoned for his activities as a Nonconformist. He seems to have turned this to good account, for we are told

> And for the help of the Governours of Families, in the Weekly Catechizing those under their charge, he *explained the Assemblies Shorter Catechism*; to which he annexed an affectionate Letter, with Rules for their daily Examination, which were Printed and Dispersed into all their Houses by Order, while he was a Prisoner.[23]

---

[15] Thomas Secker [1693–1768], *Lectures on the catechism of the Church of England: with a discourse on confirmation...* (London, 1769).

[16] Bate was chaplain to the local squire, Sir Henry Harpur.

[17] John Lewis [1675–1747], *The Church catechism explained...* (London, 27th edition 1759).

[18] Thomas Marshall [1621–1685], *The Catechism set forth in the Book of Common-Prayer...* (Oxford, 1704).

[19] John Williams [1636?–1709], *A brief exposition of the church-catechism with proofs from Scripture* (London., 1689).

[20] Frank Booth, *Robert Raikes of Gloucester* (Birmingham: National Christian Education Council, 1980). Booth makes the same claims in his article 'Robert Raikes: Founder of the Sunday School Movement', in John Ferguson (ed.), *Christianity Society and Education* (London: SPCK, 1981).

[21] *The Life and Death of that Excellent Minister of Christ Mr Joseph Alleine* (London, 1672) [by Theodosia Alleine, his widow].

[22] *Joseph Alleine*, p. 41.

[23] *Joseph Alleine*, p. 72.

This enthusiasm for catechising was pursued in his house visits,[24] and in his distribution of catechisms to poor families.

> He was very forward to promote the Education of Youth, in the Town of *Ilchester*, and Country adjacent, freely bestowing Catechisms on those that were of poor Families, to instruct them in the Principles of Religion; stirring up the Elder to Teach, and incouraging the Younger to Learn.[25]

What may have confused the issue is another typical Puritan activity which the biography records.

> In the Even of the Lord's Day, his course was to repeat his Sermon again, in the publick Place of Worship, where abundance of People constantly resorted to hear him; which when he had done, several Youths were called forth, which did give him an Account of the Heads of all his Sermon by Memory.[26]

This is a pious activity but it bears no resemblance to what Robert Raikes and his associates were doing on Sundays a hundred years later except that it involved young people and Sundays. What is more, like every good Puritan, Alleine saw these activities as supplementary and supportive to the Christian education which all parents had a duty to provide. His distribution of catechisms and his catechetical questioning when making home visits testify to his belief that the home was the place to cultivate faith. Moreover, we are told he wrote a paper for the Somerset ministers on private Family Instruction,[27] not, let it be noted, Church Instruction. Either Alleine is not a pioneer of the Sunday School movement or all catechising ministers, conforming or nonconforming, somehow anticipated Robert Raikes. By the same token Theophilus Lindsey, whose name is also brought into play in these accounts of early Sunday Schools, was a diligent minister, in and out of the Church of England, who gave an emphasis to his catechetical responsibilities. His biographer, describing his Catterick ministry in the Church of England, notes his catechising of children between the Sunday services, his sabbatarianism and his promotion of charity schools, which were a weekday activity.[28] Lindsey's philanthropy does not make him a Sunday School pioneer in the way we associate with Raikes. Lindsey, moving from the Evangelical circles around Lady Huntingdon to friendship with Joseph Priestley has a different and fascinating significance in eighteenth-century church history.

---

[24] *Joseph Alleine*, p. 48.

[25] *Joseph Alleine*, p. 72.

[26] *Joseph Alleine*, p. 49.

[27] *Joseph Alleine*, p. 51.

[28] Thomas Belsham, *Memoirs of the late Reverend Theophilus Lindsey, M.A....* (London: Williams and Norgate, 1873), pp. 16-17.

Similarly, that John Wesley catechised children before every service in Savannah in 1736, or that the non-juror Robert Frampton, Bishop of Gloucester, explained the sermon to children on Sundays, or that the episcopalian Thomas Kennedy of Bright, County Down, held a singing class on Sundays, do not provide evidence of a long Sunday School history before the 1780s.[29] It is only as we near 1780 that it becomes arguable that the new institution of the Sunday School had a variety of begetters. James Hey at Little Lever, near Bolton, was teaching reading on a Sunday in 1775. David Simpson, of Christ Church, Macclesfield, was paying teachers to work with children on Sundays in 1778. John Marks Moffatt, of Forest Green Chapel, Gloucestershire, had been teaching children on Sundays for six years before Raikes publicised his own schools. Finally, Raikes' own account of his formation of Sunday Schools shares the credit with Thomas Stock, the Gloucester clergyman. In writing their hagiographies of Raikes, in which the divine inspiration of the Sunday School movement was a key assumption, the Victorians left little room for the Holy Spirit to act in several places at roughly the same time.

It is, however, those same hagiographies, that spell out to us the distinctiveness of the new Sunday Schools as against the old catechesis. The wonderful idea came to Raikes as he observed boys idling their time away on Sundays. In his classic account of Sunday Schools in *The Gloucester Journal* he specifically mentions that vandalism is concentrated on Sundays, which '...proceeds from the lawless state of the younger class, who are allowed to run wild on that day, free from every restraint'. Teaching reading and the catechism and conducting these 'younger persons' to church is designed to combat lawlessness by providing occupation.[30] Raikes shared the general view of the time that the Devil finds work for idle hands to do, especially children's hands. Not for him the Rousseau vision, embraced by Wordsworth, that children come into the world 'trailing clouds of glory' and that school and work are the prison-houses which close on childhood. For the overwhelming mass of Raikes' contemporaries children were sinners from their birth, in need of redemption. In 1790 an anonymous writer celebrates the glories of the town of Derby, 'fine, beautiful, and pleasant', rejoicing in the technology of the Silk Mill, which provides employment 'to the great relief and advantage of the poor'. The benefits of industrialisation are also evident in the china-manufactory. The gold and blue colours, the flowers and the general elegance of the wares are extolled. More than that, 'A great number of hands are employed in it, and happily many

---

[29] Booth, *Robert Raikes*, p. 74, lists these and other examples.
[30] *The Gloucester Journal,* 3 November 1783.

very young are enabled to earn a livelihood in the business.'[31] It is in that phrase 'happily very many young' that we need to understand the growth of the Sunday School movement. This is not the Carey Bonner world of the early twentieth century, in which small children sing of how happy they are to be standing in a ring, holding hands, in Sunday School. This is a world which puts a child to work as soon as possible and wishes to discourage idleness in the short period between weaning and employment. One of the benefits of Sunday Schools urged by their promoters was 'requiring the child's attendance only on the Lord's day, takes nothing from his earnings in the week'.[32] Sunday Schools in the beginning were far from being academies of faith; they were part of the church's mission to the poor, turning the idle moments of children and young people to good account by increasing their basic skills, but not too much, and, more importantly, instilling moral discipline and social compliance, reinforced by catechetical instruction and public devotions.

By 1786 Manchester had a Sunday School charity which served more than one parish and denomination and therefore several hundred children. The trustees had appointed visitors and the Sunday School also had the interest of various ministers. This was a charity to benefit the children of poor parents by providing some basic education ('useful Learning') together with spiritual and moral training. The church catechism was used. A form of prayer began and ended the Sunday School day, hymns were sung and the Bible read. The form of prayer used tells all that we need to know about the spirit and purpose of the charity.

> Almighty God, from whom all holy desires, all good counsels, and all just works do proceed, we bless thee for inclining the hearts of thy people to establish these Schools, for the Instruction of the Ignorant, and the advancement of thy true religion, and virtue.[33]

Amongst other petitions the Almighty is beseeched to 'Make the Parents of these Children duly thankful for this blessing.' Most importantly, the teachers pray 'that, whilst we are instructing them in useful Learning, we may sow that precious seed of thy word in their hearts'.[34] The pious language of prayer cannot obscure the new dynamic combination of useful and religious learning which will eventually mean that Sunday Schools displace traditional catechising in the life of English Protestantism. The Ten Commandments run with the need to stabilise

---

[31] *The Universal British Directory...* (London, 1791).

[32] *Evangelical Magazine* 6 (1798), p. 16.

[33] *Catechism, prayers and hymns, for the use of Sunday Schools in Manchester* (1786) p. 13.

[34] *Catechism, etc....Manchester*, p. 14.

social values in a world which is experiencing radical social and economic changes. The Manchester prayers underline Raikes' fundamental concern.

> May we influence them, whilst under our care, never to take God's name in vain; never to break the Sabbath; never to lie, or steal; but to be true and just in all their dealings; to love, honour, and succour their Parents; to order themselves, lowly and reverently, to all their Betters; to keep their bodies in temperance, soberness, and chastity; and, contentedly, to do their duties in that state of life, unto which it shall please God to call them.

> Enable us, particularly, to impress upon their minds, that thou art present in all places, and knowest their most secret thoughts; and hast, in thy wisdom, appointed a solemn day of Judgment, when the Wicked must go away into everlasting punishment, but the Righteous into Life eternal.[35]

In Nottingham on 21 October 1784 the mayor presided over a meeting to consider 'in what manner a Sunday school for the children of the poor might be established in Nottingham'.[36] A subscription charity was formed, the subscribers having the right to introduce children to the school. Although formed with broad guidelines the charity quickly restricted itself to boys aged between 8 and 11 and allowed for attendance at a customary place of worship. There was a large schoolroom in the Exchange Hall, but other rooms in homes and shops were used and most of the teachers paid at the rate of one penny per pupil. The children went from their schoolroom to a place of worship for the religious aspects of their learning. It would seem that the Methodists came to dominate the school at the Exchange Hall and that branches were established as Methodism divided and grew. By 1796 the Methodists were still paying four teachers on the grounds that a purely voluntary system was not reliable. As in Manchester, so in Nottingham, the Raikes system for providing a basic education and an ordered Sunday prevailed. The schools on Sundays were a charitable auxiliary to the life of the church. They might serve to bring children into the orbit of an Evangelical congregation but the work of conversion and commitment was a further step. Reporting a Calvinistic Methodist meeting at Aberystwyth in 1805 a correspondent remarked on the hundreds of children hearing the preaching, their faces bathed in tears. 'This work first began at Aberystwyth in the Sunday School there; in which two young men, under twenty years of age, were the teachers.'[37]

---

[35] *Catechism, etc....Manchester*, pp. 14, 15.

[36] What is said about Nottingham in this paragraph is taken from Rowland C. Swift, 'Methodist Sunday Schools in Nottingham', *Proceedings of the Wesley Historical Society* 33 (1961), pp. 17-20, pp. 36-40.

[37] *Evangelical Magazine* 13 (1805), p. 235.

A considered assessment of Sunday Schools was made by an unknown writer in the *Evangelical Magazine* in 1798.[38] It was acknowledged that some Sunday Schools had failed but the expansion of their numbers was urged on serious Christians. The first step was to raise subscriptions or arrange for the preaching of Charity Sermons. As many poor children as possible, aged 5 and upwards, should be admitted. Parents making application for their child could be given tracts and a useful word could be spoken to them. Boys and girls should be taught separately and young people kept apart from children. The ideal teacher pupil ratio was one to fifteen, though more could be managed with voluntary help. Houses or vestries, preferably near a place of worship should be used. Teachers should be paid no more than two shillings a day; good volunteers were preferable. It is the role of the visitors, respectable Christians, to attend to the spiritual life of the children within the school. The Nottingham practice of sending visitors to call on absentee scholars was commended. Classes should commence with some religious exercises but move on to reading and spelling until the time of public worship. In church the teachers were to watch the children to ensure that they kept their eyes closed for the prayers and fixed on the minister for the sermon. During the afternoon classes there would be opportunity to test the children on whether they remembered the text. The Stockport practice of visiting sick children was commended. 'But how encouraging to a teacher to see one of his pupils dying happy in the love of God, and to hear him breathe out his last prayer for his benefactors.'[39] By the standards of the day this was not a severe regime, indeed, it was reckoned that corporal punishment was unsuited to both the Lord's Day and the institution. Rewards, including money and clothing, were reckoned to be the best way of regulating discipline. The benefits of Sunday Schools were obvious. 'Peace and quietness is enjoyed in many a parish, where noise, riot and mischief before prevailed. Many thousands have already learned to read the scriptures, who would otherwise have remained in heathen darkness.'[40] Religious conversion might also follow but it is not claimed that this is the sole purpose of Sunday Schools, nor even their chief aim. Sunday Schools were useful and were commended much in the way that churches today advocate community ministries or social service projects as an aid to mission.

What were the actual processes of teaching and learning in these early Sunday Schools? Samuel Bamford describes his experiences in an early Methodist school as follows:

---

[38] *Evangelical Magazine* 6 (1798), pp. 15-18, pp. 52-59. Other similar accounts of early Sunday Schools are to be found in Cliff, *Rise and Development*.

[39] *Evangelical Magazine* 13 (1805), p. 57.

[40] *Evangelical Magazine* 13 (1805), p. 59.

A hymn was first read out and sung by the scholars and teachers. An extempore prayer followed, all the scholars and teachers kneeling at their places; the classes ranging from those of the spelling book to those of the Bible, then commenced their lessons, girls in the gallery above and boys below. Desks which could be either moved up or down, like the leaf of a table, were arranged all around the school, against the walls of the gallery, as well as against those below, and at measured distances the walls were numbered. Whilst the Bible and Testament classes were reading their first lesson, the desks were got ready, inkstands and copy books numbered, containing copies and pens, were placed opposite corresponding numbers on the wall; and when the lesson was concluded the writers took their places, each at his own number, and so continued their instruction. When the copy was finished, the book was shut and left on the desk, a lesson of spelling was gone through, and at twelve o'clock singing and praying again took place, and the scholars were dismissed. At one o'clock there was service in the chapel, and soon after two the school reassembled, girls now occupying the writing desks, as boys had done in the forenoon, and at four or half-past the scholars were sent home for the week.[41]

The significant aspects of this description for our purposes is that the Sunday School took place in a purpose-built room, distinct from the chapel; that the organization of the learning by numbers reflects the kind of pedagogical changes being promoted independently by the educational reformers Joseph Lancaster (1778–1838) and Andrew Bell (1753–1832); that the specific skills of writing and spelling were taught in this Methodist school, it already being a bone of contention amongst Sunday School promoters as to whether it was proper to do more than teach Bible reading on the Sabbath; and that although there were hymns and prayers and a break for public worship, the primary focus was clearly skills education. Limited as the curriculum and pedagogy may seem by modern standards, it is clearly different from the purely catechetical. What happened on Sunday was a truncated version of the new schools for the poor, not the old catechism class somehow supplemented.

Raikes published a *Sunday Scholar's Companion* for use as a primer. One striking feature of this is a catechism, almost certainly of Raikes' own devising.[42] This is a *credo* heavily laced with Raikes' own moral judgments and views of doctrine.

Q. Did the world make itself?
A. No; if that clock had a maker, much more the whole world had a maker.
Q. Why must you believe in God?

---

[41] Quoted in Asa Briggs, 'Innovation and Adaptation: The Eighteenth-Century Setting', in John Ferguson (ed.), *Christianity Society and Education* (London: SPCK, 1981), p. 24. Briggs gives no source for the quotation.

[42] *The Sunday Scholar's Companion* (1794). The source for this is the description in Guy Kendall, *Robert Raikes; a critical study* (London: Nicholson and Watson, 1939).

A. Because if I do not believe in him, I should deny and forget my Maker, and be
without God in the world, like those who spend their money in public houses while
their wives and children are without bread; and because such men shall be turned into
hell, with all the people who forget God.
Q. How do you prove that there is a God?
A. 1st, by common sense; 2ndly, by our conscience; 3rdly, by tradition; 4thly, by
the Sabbath; and 5thly, by the Scriptures.[43]

If ever we needed to be persuaded that Raikes was an Anglican and that
Sunday Schools were not simply an adaptation of traditional catechizing
we need look no further than this catechism.

Advocacy of Sunday Schools may be found in a variety of
publications. It was also strengthened by the founding of societies to
support them. Just as the Evangelical public rallied to the Missionary
Society, the Bible Society, or the Society for the Conversion of the Jews,
so they attended sermons and committee meetings to buttress the
development of Sunday Schools. Religious societies were not unknown
before the 1790s but their proliferation then is characteristic of the era.
Amongst the Evangelicals societies were a way of operating beyond the
diocese. This enabled conventional Church of England Evangelicals,
Methodists and Dissenters to combine to promote their common
concerns. The situation was always complex. The looseness of association
allowed Dissenters and Anglicans to work together but also to split apart.
The example of the Baptist Missionary Society was followed by the
creation of the Missionary Society (later known as the London
Missionary Society), embracing Calvinist paedobaptists of different
denominations, but then the Church Missionary Society was formed and a
Wesleyan one. So it was with Sunday Schools. The early growth of
Sunday School societies was dynamic rather than institutional. For
example, groups of Christians in London would form committees and
organize public meetings, sometimes on a confessional basis sometimes
acting across denominations. Similar groups might then be formed in
provincial cities and towns and they would affiliate to the London body.
Even when the National Sunday School Union (NSSU) emerged it was as
an affiliated rather than a monolithic organization.

The key word is 'Movement'. This was the way the Bible Society grew
and a generation later the societies associated with David Nasmith and
then the YMCA.[44] The first Sunday School Society which Cliff notes is
that formed by William Fox and Joseph Hanway in Clapton in 1786.[45]
This society was very much identified with Baptists. What distinguished it
from the local Sunday School charities which were springing up

---

[43] Kendall, *Robert Raikes*, pp. 85-86.

[44] See Clyde Binfield, *George Williams and the YMCA* (London: Heinemann, 1973).

[45] Cliff, *Rise and Development*, p. 47.

everywhere at the time was Fox's concern to link Sunday Schools in a common programme. Fox had property in Gloucestershire and told Raikes in 1785 that he had long wished to establish a system of universal education and had found little support.[46] This commitment to promoting a particular system, and the dominance of Baptists in the committee, may explain why his society did not win early acceptance. A similar process occurred when in 1802 the Wesleyans extended their London Sunday School Society to embrace corresponding members around the country. The distinctive feature of this society, apart from Methodism, was that all the teachers in its schools should be unpaid.[47] Within a generation these kinds of societies, certainly so far as Dissenters were concerned, were caught up within the NSSU. That body traced its foundation to yet another local beginning, the Sunday School Union formed at the Surrey Chapel by William Brodie Gurney, Thomas Thompson and James Nisbet in 1803.[48] Gurney was a Baptist, a parliamentary short-hand writer, and had opened his first Sunday School in Walworth with Joseph Fox in 1795.[49] The Surrey Chapel, non-denominational, served the poor on the South Bank of the river through various philanthropic societies, including one for Sunday Schools. Its minister was the Revd Rowland Hill, who by this time was beginning to take on the mantle of a senior leader within the Evangelical movement. What happened at the Surrey Chapel was influential amongst London Evangelicals and beyond. It is not surprising that a loose national association of Sunday Schools grew from local co-operation there. However, it was not obvious to the original founders that a long history of a national Sunday School union would be the outcome of their plans. Gurney was equally occupied in promoting the British and Foreign Bible Society, which also prospered, and the London Female Penitentiary, which is now almost unremembered. The latter body was formed to rescue very young women from the streets when they had been driven into prostitution. In its day it was as important to Gurney and his friends as Sunday Schools—all part of the redemption of the poor from the ignorance and vice which prevented their believing the gospel and securing eternal happiness. We cannot understand the first Sunday Schools out of that context.

In conclusion, the questions of whether Raikes was the founder of Sunday Schools and the origins of the National Sunday School Union are only profitable if we pursue them broadly. The Sunday School itself needs careful definition to distinguish it from catechetical or other religious exercises. The tendency of Evangelicals to look for distinctive evidences of providence in the lives of individuals predisposes the source

---

[46] *DNB.*

[47] *Evangelical Magazine* 10 (1802), p. 378.

[48] Cliff, *Rise and Development*, p. 74.

[49] *DNB.*

material towards looking for a specific start to Sunday Schools rather than allowing for the emergence of similar ideas in different places at roughly the same time. The informal way in which these ideas were transmitted does not lend itself to the same kind of enquiry as the specific data such as we find in the pages of the *Gloucester Journal*. In reviewing the history of the Sunday School movement what might we say are the distinctive characteristics of the early Sunday Schools? First, Sunday Schools were a natural product of an era when Christians were looking beyond the immediate circle of the worshipping community to explore their wider mission in the world. The declared objective of most Sunday Schools, to combat the idleness of youth and protect private property, complemented the anxieties of the magistracy and the government that Jacobinism should not find a foothold among the labouring classes and the poor. Second, the Evangelical culture which formed societies to promote religious ideas and corporate action served the Sunday School movement particularly well. Such societies mobilized the energies of leading lay people as well as clergy and ministers. Resources, in the form of subscriptions and management committees, which were dominated by the middle classes, were funnelled through paid teachers to the poorer parts of society. Sunday Schools are a classical model of how religious societies operated in the early nineteenth century. Third, as Sunday Schools developed, lay leadership, in contrast to ministerial control of catechesis, was a significant dimension. In time, Sunday Schools with strong lay leadership and their own buildings took on the character of para-churches. Fourth, Sunday Schools were precisely that; pieties were observed in conformity with the age in which they were founded, but the primary purpose was to school children on Sundays. The conventional view of education, which believed that children needed to be schooled in certain skills much as horses did, in order to be useful, was also supportive of Sunday Schools. A minimum of training, rather than education, was necessary. On Sundays it could be organized not to interfere with a child's capacity to work the other six days of the week. The provision of universal elementary education in the late nineteenth century removed this dimension and left only further education for the voluntary church movements, or extended Christian education whose object was formational, even catechetical. By the time the bi-centennial histories of the Sunday School movement came to be written such Sunday Schools as still survived were wholly concerned with the Christian formation of children and young people. This, in turn, led to certain problems of perception as educational researchers tried to chronicle the emergence of Sunday Schools and describe their character.

CHAPTER 2

English Rational Dissent and Sunday Schools[1]

G.M. Ditchfield

I

The necessity for a paper with a title such as this might seem rather surprising. The commitment to education of eighteenth-century English Rational Dissent and the Unitarianism into which it subsequently evolved is very well known. This, after all, was the religious tradition that produced educational theorists such as Lant Carpenter, celebrated ministers and teachers such as James Martineau and John Hamilton Thom, and one of the leading figures in the development of ragged schools, Mary Carpenter. Yet relatively little has been written about the Sunday Schools which were a significant feature of that denominational evolution. It is not a subject which has been a priority for historians of Unitarianism; Sunday Schools, for instance, occupy only six pages in R.V. Holt's rather whiggish *The Unitarian Contribution to Social Progress in England.*[2] One reason for this state of affairs has been the understandable emphasis given by such historians to moves for religious toleration[3] and to higher education and ministerial training, in the works, especially, of Herbert McLachlan and, much more recently, of Dr David

---

[1] I am grateful to my fellow-trustees of Dr Williams's Library, to the John Rylands University Library of Manchester, and to Shropshire Archives for permission to quote from manuscripts in their possession. This paper has benefited from the advice of Alan Ruston, David Turley and David Wykes.
[2] R.V. Holt, *The Unitarian Contribution to Social Progress in England* (London: Lindsey Press, 2nd edn, 1952), pp. 248-54. The same is true of older histories, such as H. McLachlan, *The Unitarian Movement in the Religious Life of England: I. Its Contribution to Thought and Learning 1700–1900* (London: George Allen and Unwin, 1934), which has lengthy sections on schools and universities but makes no mention of Sunday Schools.
[3] For instance G.M. Ditchfield, 'Anti-Trinitarianism and Toleration in Late Eighteenth-century British Politics: The Unitarian Petition of 1792', *Journal of Ecclesiastical History* 42.1 (January, 1991), pp. 39-67; F. Schulmann, '*Blasphemous and Wicked*'. *The Unitarian Struggle for Equality 1813–1844* (Oxford: Harris Manchester College, 1997).

Wykes.[4] The volume edited by Knud Haakonssen, entitled *Enlightenment and Religion: Rational Dissent in Eighteenth-century Britain*, published in 1996, has a distinguished chapter on dissenting academies, but does not mention Sunday Schools.[5] Nor do those schools figure prominently in the pages of the *Transactions* of the Unitarian Historical Society, except in articles dealing with the fortunes of individual congregations. The most recent specialist scholarly analysis of nineteenth-century Unitarian education, by Dr Ruth Watts, has a short and valuable section on Sunday Schools but devotes most of its attention to other forms of education.[6] A further reinforcement to the examination of an institution of higher education presented itself in 2004, when the 150th anniversary of the Unitarian College, Manchester, was commemorated with a celebratory volume with the unambiguous title *Unitarian to the Core.*[7]

Admittedly, the Unitarianism which owed its emergence primarily, albeit not exclusively, to Rational Dissent was always a minority affair. Returns to the Religious Census of 1851 indicated the existence in England and Wales of just 229 places of Unitarian worship (many of them still formally designated as Presbyterian or General Baptist), with a total attendance at morning, afternoon and evening worship on 30 March of that year of 50,061.[8] Whatever its flaws, the Census was probably not far wrong in its estimate of Unitarian adherents.[9] The number of Unitarian ministers in England in 1863, including those not attached to a congregation, has been estimated at 320.[10] But two justifications of this paper might be offered. Firstly, Unitarians in Britain, as has often been

---

[4] For example, H. McLachlan, *English Education under the Test Acts: Being the History of the Nonconformist Academies, 1662–1820* (Manchester: Manchester University Press, 1931); David L. Wykes, 'Manchester College at York (1803–1840): Its Intellectual and Cultural Contribution', *Yorkshire Archaeological Journal* 63 (1991), pp. 207-18; and David L. Wykes, 'Dissenting Academy or Unitarian Seminary? Manchester College at York', *Transactions of the Unitarian Historical Society* 19:2 (April, 1988), pp. 102-12.

[5] K. Haakonssen, *Enlightenment and Religion: Rational Dissent in Eighteenth-century Britain* (Cambridge: Cambridge University Press, 1996); the relevant chapter is by David L. Wykes, 'The Contribution of the Dissenting Academy to the Emergence of Rational Dissent' (pp. 99-139).

[6] Ruth Watts, 'The Unitarian contribution to Education in England from the late eighteenth century to 1853' (PhD thesis, Leicester University, 1987), pp. 314-34.

[7] Leonard Smith (ed.), *Unitarian to the Core: Unitarian College Manchester 1854–2004* (Manchester: Unitarian College, 2004).

[8] Figures from R. Currie, A. Gilbert and L. Horsley (eds), *Churches and Churchgoers: Patterns of Church Growth in the British Isles since 1700* (Oxford: Clarendon Press, 1977), p. 216.

[9] See, for instance, R.K. Webb, 'Views of Unitarianism from Halley's Comet', *Transactions of the Unitarian Historical Society* 18.4 (April, 1986), pp. 180-95.

[10] Currie, Gilbert and Horsley (eds.), *Churches and Churchgoers*, p. 207.

observed, were influential far beyond their numbers, especially in the political leadership of early nineteenth-century Dissent. Secondly, there has been a substantial body of published work on evangelicalism and Sunday Schools as well as a series of assumptions that those schools owed their inspiration almost entirely to evangelical impulses. According to P.B. Cliff, Sunday Schools belonged to a 'mainly evangelical milieu', while Malcolm Dick in 1980 claimed that 'generally Sunday schools were evangelical conservative institutions' which inculcated values 'inherited from conservative evangelicalism'.[11] On a note that was only slightly more qualified, K.D.M. Snell suggested that their teaching 'was often informed by the late eighteenth-century emphasis on salvation through faith, which owed so much to Methodist influence'.[12] So it might be useful, and perhaps salutary, to offer a study of the growth of Sunday Schools whose environment was markedly non-evangelical.

Several elements formed the umbrella of Rational Dissent—English Presbyterians, General Baptists (though not of course their post-1770 New Connexion), a very few Independents and even fewer Quakers, together with a small number of high-profile and influential secessionists from the Latitudinarian tendency of the Church of England. All of them were either by-passed by, or reacted strongly against, the phenomenon, or series of phenomena, known as the Evangelical Revival. Rational Dissent, an expression which, although much older in origin, came into common usage during the 1770s, elevated human reason as a divine gift and, following Locke, understood reason, and the spirit of inquiry which was its natural concomitant, to be reinforcements to biblical revelation. It rejected even the most moderate forms of Calvinism and replaced them not with a Wesleyan-style Arminianism of the heart but, in Geoffrey Nuttall's words, a much more rarefied 'Arminianism of the head'.[13] That development led those whom Richard Price in 1772 described as 'preachers of Christianity on the rational plan',[14] towards theological speculation, especially over the doctrine of the Trinity, which in turn led to Arian and, by the end of the century, increasingly to Socinian

---

[11] P.B. Cliff, *The Rise and Development of the Sunday School Movement in England, 1780–1980* (Birmingham: National Christian Education Council, 1986), p. 2; Malcolm Dick, 'The Myth of the Working-Class Sunday School', *History of Education* 9.1 (1980), pp. 36, 33.

[12] K.R.M. Snell, 'The Sunday-School Movement in England and Wales: Child Labour, Denominational Control and Working-Class Culture', *Past & Present* 164 (August, 1999), p. 129.

[13] G.F. Nuttall, *The Puritan Spirit: Essays and Addresses* (London: Epworth Press, 1967), p. 78.

[14] D.O. Thomas and W.B. Peach (eds), *The Correspondence of Richard Price* (3 vols., Durham, NC: Duke University Press/Cardiff: University of Wales Press, 1983–94), I, p. 142.

conclusions. When Joseph Priestley, perhaps its best-known eighteenth-century adherent, defined the term 'those more rational Dissenters' in 1769, he specified those deliberately excluded from the protection of the Toleration Act of 1689 and proscribed by the Blasphemy Act of 1698 on account of their heterodoxy over the doctrine of the Trinity.[15] With its reputation for involvement—sometimes dangerous—in the political agitation of the 1790s (Tom Paine was toasted in Hackney College), it is perhaps not altogether surprising that its political activities should have taken priority over its Sunday Schools in the works of recent and not so recent historians.[16]

Yet there is ample evidence of awareness on the part of Rational Dissenters and their Unitarian successors of the value and history of their own and other Sunday Schools. The Boy Monument at Essex Chapel commemorates eleven originators of Sunday Schools, beginning with St Charles Borromeo and with the founder of that chapel, Theophilus Lindsey, in the fourth place on the list.[17] Proposals for Sunday Schools in the 1780s came particularly easily to those Anglican clergymen who seceded to Unitarianism. William Robertson's 'Unitarian dissenting congregation' at Wolverhampton had in 1786, according to Lindsey, 'by voluntary subscription erected a Sunday School for 25 boys and the same number of girls, of different denominations', while William Frend had held Sunday catechism classes as Madingley.[18] The female members of their congregations sometimes took the initiative, as with the domestic and household Sunday Schools essayed by Catharine Cappe at Catterick and by Mary Hughes at Hanwood, Shropshire.[19] Lindsey himself, who in the 1780s described Sunday Schools as 'the only sure way of reformation', has been credited by the early twentieth-century church historians, J.H. Overton and Frederick Relton, with the establishment of 'the first Sunday

[15] Joseph Priestley, *An Essay on the First Principles of Government and on the Nature of Political, Civil and Religious Liberty*, in *The Theological and Miscellaneous Works of Joseph Priestley* (ed. J.T. Rutt; 25 vols in 26; Bristol: Thoemmes Press, 1999 [1817–32]), XXII, p. 96.

[16] E.M. Wilbur, *A History of Unitarianism* (2 vols; Cambridge, MA: Harvard University Press, 1947–52); J.E. Cookson, *The Friends of Peace: Anti-War Liberalism in England, 1793–1815* (Cambridge: Cambridge University Press, 1982); J. Graham, *The Nation, the Law and the King: Reform Politics in England 1789–1799* (2 vols; Lanham, MD, New York and Oxford: University Press of America, 2000).

[17] 'The Boy Monument' [no author named], *Transactions of the Unitarian Historical Society* 7.2 (October, 1940), pp. 208-209.

[18] Dr Williams's Library, London, MS 12.44 (45): Theophilus Lindsey to William Turner of Newcastle, 28 October 1786; F. Knight, *University Rebel: The Life of William Frend 1757–1841* (London: Victor Gollancz, 1971), p. 38.

[19] *Memoirs of the Life of the late Mrs Catharine Cappe. Written by herself* (London, 1822), pp. 120-21; R. Watts, *Gender, Power and the Unitarians in England 1760–1860* (London and New York: Longman, 1998), p. 76.

School, actually so called', while he was still a parish priest, at Catterick in 1765.[20]

What Lindsey did, in fact, was hardly unusual by the standards of the age. According to the sympathetic *Memoirs* of Catharine Cappe, he held a Sunday catechizing class for one hour in his church at two o'clock, immediately before the afternoon service, and, on alternate Sunday afternoons, conducted Bible classes for the boys of a nearby school.[21] He abbreviated for popular circulation some of the devotional tracts of the late seventeenth-century evangelist William Burkitt.[22] Lindsey frequently used the catechetical form in seeking to advance the Unitarian doctrines which had led him to resign from the Church of England in 1773, with *The Catechist*, published in 1779, and his *Conversations on Christian Idolatry* (1792). In the latter work he took the opportunity to demand a change in the Catechism as taught in Sunday Schools to eliminate the reference to God the Son.[23] Lindsey's reputation as a pioneer of Sunday Schools, however exaggerated, acquired subsequent importance because of his status as a patriarch of Unitarianism, whose Essex Street Chapel, described by Joseph Priestley in 1787 as 'the head-quarters of Unitarianism, the great mother-church', was the first self-proclaimed Unitarian place of worship in England. His reformed version of the *Book of Common Prayer* first published in 1774, came to be adopted by numerous Rational Dissenting congregations—a development of some significance in the light of the well-known Dissenting commitment to extempore prayer.

Already, however, amongst Old Dissent, from which, especially from English Presbyterianism, Unitarianism gradually emerged, there was much discussion of, and experimentation with, the theory and practice of Sunday Schools during the 1780s. They could hardly escape the wave of publicity that heralded their rise during that decade. Indeed they were a small part of the process whereby Sunday Schools became a national phenomenon. When the Presbyterian William Turner of Newcastle-upon-Tyne and the General Baptist Joshua Toulmin of Taunton both published tracts on the subject, they displayed considerable awareness of the burgeoning literature, which they were themselves augmenting. Turner not only established a Sunday School in association with his Hanover Square Chapel, but also drew favourable attention to the

---

[20] Dr Williams's Library, MS 12.44 (45); J.H. Overton and F. Relton, *The English Church: From the Accession of George I to the End of the Eighteenth Century (1714–1800)* (London: Macmillan, 1924), p. 300.

[21] *Memoirs of Catharine Cappe*, p. 118.

[22] John Rylands University Library of Manchester (hereafter JRULM), Lindsey letters, Vol. 1: Lindsey to William Tayleur, 1 December 1785.

[23] Theophilus Lindsey, *Conversations on Christian Idolatry, in the Year 1791* (London, 1792), pp. 64-65.

recommendations of Sunday Schools issued by a range of diverse figures. As well as Robert Raikes, they included the magistrate Thomas Butterworth Bayley who was a member of Cross Street Chapel, Manchester, Charles Moore, vicar of Boughton and Blean in Kent, the high churchman George Horne, Dean of Canterbury and the evangelically-minded Beilby Porteus, Bishop of Chester.[24] Toulmin praised the 'liberal spirit' of *An Essay on the Depravity of the Nation, with a View to the Promotion of Sunday Schools* (1788) by the rather unorthodox Catholic priest Joseph Berington.[25] In Bewdley, the Unitarian banker Samuel Kenrick thought in 1786 that 'Thousands & thousands to come will have reason to bless the name of Raikes in future generations.'[26] At Birmingham New Meeting, Joseph Priestley held what would soon come to be called Sunday School classes. After a visit to his friend and fellow-Unitarian in 1783, Theophilus Lindsey described Priestley's method, with an ironical reference to Edmund Burke, with whom Priestley was then, if not later, on fairly friendly terms.

> But Mr Burke did not see, and w[d]. not perhaps have relished his Sunday-work, which constitutes a chief part of his happiness. I was surprized on the Sunday afternoon in going into the Vestry for my hat, to see near 30 young ladies, some of em I was told married, seated to be instructed in the principles of christianity. This was the third class that had been before him that day. And this is his usual work every Sunday, added to his officiating to the whole congregation one part of it.[27]

The originator of catechetical classes at the Birmingham New Meeting seems to have been Priestley's ministerial predecessor but two, Samuel Bourn. But Priestley revived the practice and extended it to Sundays. His teaching was organized into three classes, in order of age. The youngest class studied the catechism and Isaac Watts's hymns; for the intermediate class, the fare was Watts's *Historical Catechism* and Priestley's own *Scripture Catechism*; while for the older class these works were supplemented by Priestley's rather more dogmatic *History of the Corruptions of Christianity*.[28] The social, as well as the devotional, motive

---

[24] William Turner, *Sunday Schools recommended in a Sermon preached before the Associated Dissenting Ministers in the Northern Counties, at their Annual Meeting, at Morpeth, June 13, 1786* (Newcastle, 1786), pp. 39-43, 56-59.

[25] Joshua Toulmin, *The Rise, Progress, and Effects of Sunday Schools, considered in a Sermon, preached at Taunton, March 28, 1789* (Taunton, 1789), p. 19 n. *.

[26] Dr Williams's Library, MS 24.157 (113); Samuel Kenrick to James Wodrow, 20 March 1786.

[27] Dr Williams's Library, MS 12.44 (38), Lindsey to William Turner of Wakefield, 1 September 1783.

[28] Full details of Priestley's Sunday classes may be found in Emily Bushrod, 'The History of Unitarianism in Birmingham from the Middle of the Eighteenth Century to 1893' (MA thesis, Birmingham University, 1954), pp. 22-24.

was apparent. A few years later, in 1794, Samuel Palmer of Hackney strongly defended the practice in Sunday Schools of teaching children to read and write, on the ground that it would be 'of the greatest benefit to the nation'.[29]

Concern over the state of the nation, indeed, dominated the deluge of works which advocated Sunday Schools in the 1780s. According to George Horne, the level of national decadence was such that foreigners asked 'how happens it, that under a constitution, of which you boast, as the glory of the world, monthly scenes are exhibited, which would shock the minds of Turks and Tartars?'[30] Berington wrote despairingly of a nation plunged into depravity and seized upon the Royal Proclamation against vice, issued in 1787, as a potential stimulus to the development of Sunday Schools.[31] This moral earnestness which characterized much of elite opinion in late eighteenth-century Britain owed something to the personal example of George III and Queen Charlotte (if not of the Prince of Wales). But it owed more to the impact of defeat in the American War of Independence, a war which Rational Dissenters had consistently opposed, and a consequent sense of divine punishment for the sin of overweening pride, and to a discernible humanitarianism derived from the diffusion of evangelical and Enlightenment values. However, for Rational Dissenters two further considerations were conducive to their interest in, and an appreciation of, the desirability, of Sunday schools.

The first was an uneasy sense of a numerical decline of their interest. In November 1780 Lindsey wrote, 'For these rational Dissenters as they are called are manifestly crumbling away every day, and they and their families sliding back into the Trinitarian worship of the C. of E..'[32] With even sharper relevance to the ability of their congregations to sponsor ancillary activities, Richard Price complained in October 1783, 'The truth is, that the Dissenting interest in London is declining, and that it is more than our charitable people can do to support the necessities of our own poor congregations and ministers, whose difficulties have been lately much increased by a load of new taxes.'[33] In 1786 William Turner of Newcastle observed, 'The decline of the Dissenting interest is a constant subject of complaint among us, and we see it, as much as any where, in the failure of subscriptions for the support of our charity schools.'[34] He

---

[29] *Protestant Dissenters' Magazine* I (1794), p. 286.

[30] G. Horne, *Sunday Schools recommended in a Sermon preached at the Parish Church of St Alphege, Canterbury, on Sunday December the Eighteenth 1785* (Oxford, 1786), p. 3.

[31] J. Berington, *An Essay on the Depravity of the Nation, with a View to the Promotion of Sunday Schools* (Birmingham, 1788), pp. 10-20.

[32] JRULM, Lindsey Letters, Vol. 2, Lindsey to William Tayleur, 29 November 1780.

[33] Thomas and Peach (eds.), *Price Correspondence*, II, p. 199.

[34] Turner, *Sunday Schools recommended*, p.25.

urged that the remaining funds of declining or defunct Dissenting charity schools be diverted to the support of Sunday Schools. Clearly, there was an understanding of a need for a new type of fund-raising for educational purposes, to reinvigorate Rational Dissent and to retain the allegiance of its younger generation. The short-term effects of the French Revolution, the Priestley riots of July 1791, and the emigration of some to North America and the transportation of others to Australia increased the sense of depression.

The second consideration was a realization that the ethos of Rational Dissent was marked by a rather arcane intellectual elitism, in which its anti-Trinitarian speculations, even when their heretical implications did not repel, were bound to be inaccessible to all but the smallest of minorities. This became apparent with the formation, on metropolitan initiatives, of the Society for Promoting Knowledge of the Scriptures (SPKS) in 1783 and the Unitarian Society in 1791, both designed to foster Unitarian doctrines by the diffusion of tracts. William Tayleur of Shrewsbury wrote in 1784 that the newly formed SPKS was 'by no means well adapted to render the gospel level to the capacities of the common people, which seems to be the great desideratum at present'.[35] As Lindsey himself acknowledged five years later, 'We want much to have the common people applied to, as enough has been done, and is continually doing, for the learned and higher ranks.'[36] The need to appeal to a broader audience and to counter the effects of propaganda against them helped to render Sunday Schools an attractive proposition to Rational Dissenters. The need was heightened as their disparate elements showed signs of evolving into something resembling a denomination, with the appearance of central bodies, notably the Unitarian Fund in 1805, the Christian Tract Society in 1809 and the Association for the Protection of the Civil Rights of Unitarians in 1819. This process was consolidated by the merging of these organizations into the British and Foreign Unitarian Association in 1825. Early in the nineteenth century, a further stimulus to their Sunday Schools was provided by the more popular preaching and missionary work of the former General Baptists Robert Aspland and Richard Wright.

Unitarian Sunday Schools developed on a more significant scale as the denomination itself became more clearly defined. Even before William Smith's Trinity Act of 1813 removed legal penalties against the public profession of Unitarianism, many leading congregations had organized such schools. In 1811 William Turner, in a published history of his Hanover Square Chapel, Newcastle-upon-Tyne, outlined the functions of

---

[35] JRULM, Letters of William Tayleur (unfoliated): Tayleur to Lindsey, 26 February 1784.

[36] Quoted in T. Belsham, *Memoirs of the Late Reverend Theophilus Lindsey, M.A.* (Centenary edition; London: Williams and Norgate, 1873), p. 204.

his chapel's two Sunday Schools, one for each sex, maintained by annual contributions of five shillings, and (in the case of the girls) subject to a quarterly examination.[37] Earlier, nascent Unitarian congregations at Coseley in 1781 and at Warwick, Derby and Stourbridge slightly later, had started Sunday Schools, contemporaneous with Priestley's efforts at New Meeting, Birmingham.[38] During the 1790s a Sunday School was founded by the Shrewsbury High Street Chapel. As the process continued, a Unitarian Sunday Schools Association, at the national level, was formed in 1833, it affiliated to the British and Foreign Unitarian Association and made book grants to individual Sunday Schools. The *Unitarian Chronicle* included Sunday Schools in the series of 'Unitarian statistics' which it published in 1832. Its survey revealed that of the 137 Unitarian congregations in England which provided details of their membership, day schools and vestry libraries, seventy-three, or just over 53%, also had a Sunday School. Those fifty-eight of the seventy-three schools that actually reported the numbers of pupils according to gender were teaching boys and girls in a proportion of approximately 55% to 45%.[39]

This survey was incomplete (it omitted, for instance, such important congregations as the Norwich Octagon and Cross Street Chapel, Manchester) and in some respects under-stated the extent of the prevalence of Sunday Schools among Unitarians at that time. A predictable geographical pattern can nevertheless be detected, with Lancashire, the old Presbyterian areas of the South-West of England featuring prominently, as did smaller congregations in Kent, reflecting the historic General Baptist strength in that county. The Sunday Schools sponsored by large urban congregations were over-represented in the survey: Birmingham New Meeting claimed 800 Sunday School pupils (560 boys, 240 girls), while Bolton and Nottingham High Pavement Chapel each claimed 200 pupils. But these figures also indicate that the process must not be exaggerated. Almost half of the relevant congregations did not possess a Sunday School. The deficiency caused anxiety in Unitarian circles. As a correspondent to the *Monthly Repository* put it in 1824:

> It is a fact, a lamentable fact, and to me no less a matter of regret than it is of surprise, that among Unitarian Christians there are to be found those, and I fear many, who, if not averse, are manifestly indifferent to the teaching of the poor, in other words, to Sunday-Schools... How is it that our public donation lists teem with

---

[37] William Turner, *A Short Sketch of the History of Protestant Nonconformity, and of the Society assembling in Hanover-Square Newcastle* (Newcastle, 1811), pp. 39-40.

[38] R.D. Woodall, *Midland Unitarianism and its Story* (Sutton Coldfield: Norman A. Tector, n.d.), pp. 20-21.

[39] *Unitarian Chronicle* 8 (September 1832), pp. 145-47; 197-99; 234-35.

items in favour of ministers and chapels, and almost every other praiseworthy
object, and not a solitary one applicable to that of Sunday-Schools?[40]

Significantly, the pseudonymous correspondent wrote from Bristol,
where Lant Carpenter at the Lewin's Mead Chapel had taken important
leads with Sunday Schools and allied charitable activity. Other letter-
writers to the *Monthly Repository* strongly disputed the diagnosis,[41] but
even by 1851, according to K.D.M. Snell's estimate, the proportion of
Unitarian congregations with a Sunday School was no more than 62%.
That compared with 72.3% for the Church of England, 67.6% for the
Independents, 83.3% for the New Connexion General Baptists and 77.1%
for the Methodist New Connexion.[42] Of the major Protestant
denominations, only the Presbyterian Church in England, Particular
Baptists, Wesleyan Methodists, and Primitive Methodists had a lower ratio.

Admittedly, the pattern changed after the first third of the nineteenth
century. A new generation of Unitarian ministers, led by James
Martineau, John Hamilton Thom and John Relly Beard, promoted
Sunday Schools from the outset of their careers. Martineau and other
students at Manchester College, York, in the 1820s taught at a Sunday
School attached to a small chapel in that city; many of them became
prominent Unitarian ministers later in the century.[43] Sunday Schools
subsequently became central to Martineau's work in London, notably at
the school associated with the congregation of Little Portland Street
Chapel,[44] as was recognized by the publication of a biography of him by
the Unitarian Sunday School Association in 1906. It became the general
expectation that a Unitarian church would be associated with a Sunday
School. At the annual meeting of the Unitarian Sunday Schools
Association in 1856 it was reported that 153 Sunday Schools employed
2,721 teachers and taught 17,251 children; and these figures take no
account of those congregations, which, true to the old spirit of
independency, would not affiliate to a central body.[45] From the
predictable urban initiatives, rural and suburban Sunday Schools had
developed; the Manchester Unitarian Village Missionary Society reported
in 1834 that the vast majority of villages in the area seen by its visitors

---

[40] *Monthly Repository* 19 (1824), pp. 201-202.

[41] For example, *Monthly Repository* 19 (1824), p. 549.

[42] K.D.M. Snell and Paul S. Ell, *Rival Jerusalems: The Geography of Victorian
Religion* (Cambridge: Cambridge University Press, 2000), p. 300.

[43] See Wykes, 'Manchester College at York', p. 215.

[44] See J.E. Carpenter, *James Martineau: Theologian and Teacher* (London: P. Green,
1905), p. 39; W.H. Burgess, 'James Martineau and Sunday School Work', *Transactions of
the Unitarian Historical Society* 4.4 (October, 1930), pp. 365-75.

[45] *Christian Reformer* n.s. 12 (1856), p. 370.

had Sunday Schools.[46] The process extended to smaller towns, for example Stockton-on-Tees (1850) and Chesham, where the Sunday School which came into existence in 1875 owed its birth to the financial failure of the local bowling club, which released the necessary land for purchase; by 1882 the school had 113 pupils.[47]

Not surprisingly, Unitarian Sunday Schools adopted many practices which were entirely consistent with those of other denominations. They included the publication of regular reports in the denominational periodical press, the *Monthly Repository* and *Christian Reformer*, and, later in the century, the *Christian Life and Unitarian Herald*, as well as in more specialist periodicals such as Travers Madge's *Sunday School Penny Magazine*. There was full appreciation of the importance of regular home visiting and of the symbolic resonance of the anniversary meeting with the star preacher, whose address was subsequently published. And at least some contribution was made to the economic impact exerted by Sunday Schools upon the producers and retailers of tea, biscuits, cakes and buns. But the main purpose of this paper is not one of narration, description or enumeration. It seeks instead to understand the nature of the Sunday Schools associated with Rational Dissent and to ask to what extent they possessed distinctive qualities. In so doing it is forced into a dismal recognition of problems familiar to all historians of Sunday Schools. Those problems include the overwhelming bias of the surviving evidence towards those in authority—ministers, benefactors and, to some extent, teachers (that is to say towards producers rather than consumers) and the consequent difficulty of assessing the extent to which performance matched aspiration. But, with these limitations in mind, the second section of this paper seeks to address the question under five headings. They are: the extent to which these schools were driven by distinctively theological considerations; their methods and objectives of teaching; their role as a branch of Unitarian philanthropy; the extent to which they facilitated a discernible working-class culture; and finally, their contribution to the growth of denominationalism.

II

The main distinguishing theological characteristics of Unitarianism were a rejection of the doctrine of the Trinity and an assertion of the simple humanity of Christ as the supreme exemplar and teacher of the divine will, but not the Son of God to whom worship should be accorded and prayers addressed. It denied the concept of original sin, and the belief

---

[46] Watts, 'Unitarian Contribution to Education', p. 316.

[47] [No author named], *Chesham Unitarian Congregation and Sunday School, Bury. A brief Historical Sketch* (Bury: Roberts and Spencer, 1902), pp. 1-2.

that the death of Christ represented atonement for human transgressions. Their preachers expressed considerable scepticism as to the notion of eternal punishment; both Priestley and the author from whom he derived much of his inspiration, David Hartley, affirmed that all persons, including the wicked, would ultimately achieve eternal happiness.[48] Their fundamental optimism as to human powers of self-improvement was neatly encapsulated by Jared Sparkes of Boston, Massachusetts, with words much quoted in England: 'We believe men have in themselves the power of being good or bad.'[49] It was a doctrine emphasized triumphantly by the self-professed theist Frances Power Cobbe in her address to the anniversary meeting of the Clerkenwell Unitarian Sunday School on 5 October 1873 which was published with the rather ironical title *Doomed to be Saved*.[50]

Such opinions placed Unitarians beyond the margins of orthodoxy. Anti-trinitarianism was widely regarded as irreligious, was nervously shunned by orthodox Dissenters afraid of the contamination of heresy, and was disadvantaged at law, while threats to Unitarian church property were not removed until the Dissenters' Chapels Act of 1844. Their opinions were likened to those of the Painite Deists of the stamp of Richard Carlile, whose trial on a charge of blasphemous libel in 1819 discredited all those of heterodox views: a 'rational' approach to religion could easily be depicted as a short step to Deism and infidelity.[51] Especially from the 1790s, Unitarians developed the mentality of the persecuted minority, a sect, in Priestley's well-known phrase, 'everywhere spoken against'.[52] That mentality involved an inward-looking sense of moral superiority over a purblind and corrupt external contemporary world. Addressing the first yearly meeting of the Unitarian Sunday Schools Association in 1834, Lant Carpenter attributed the growth of Unitarian Sunday Schools, especially in London and Bristol, to this very factor: 'Prejudice and parochial influence have been active against us; but this should stimulate our zeal. Whose zeal is not stimulated by being told we are not Christians?'[53] In the same year the dreadful prospect of the exposure of young minds to such heresy led a group of evangelical ladies

---

[48] David Hartley, *Observations on Man, his Frame, his Duty, and his expectations* (2 vols; London, 1749), II, pp. 419-37.

[49] Quotes in J. Manton, *Mary Carpenter and the Children of the Streets* (London: Heinemann, 1976), p. 26.

[50] Frances Power Cobbe, *Doomed to be Saved* (London: Williams and Norgate, 1874).

[51] See I. McCalman, 'Ultra-radicalism and Convivial Debating Clubs in London, 1795–1838', *English Historical Review* 102 (1987), p. 315.

[52] J. Priestley, *The Uses of Christianity, especially in Difficult Times* (London, 1794), p. 7.

[53] *Christian Reformer* 1 (1834), p. 496.

in Cheltenham to pay for children to be taught at an orthodox Sunday School rather than that run by the local Unitarian chapel.[54]

The experience of religious discrimination and prejudice gave to Unitarians a vested interest in political reform, organic and constitutional reform, as well as personal moral reformation. It was easy to adopt a questioning attitude towards structures of power, civil and ecclesiastical, which were perceived as hostile and threatening. The element of inquiry was something to be encouraged in a thoroughly optimistic spirit; through the inculcation of a critical attitude towards established practices there would develop an increasingly liberal political climate. As Lant Carpenter put it in his *Principles of Education* in 1820, 'Though religious belief must, in the early periods of life, be chiefly founded upon authority, yet we ought, as circumstances permit, to render it rational, by showing the grounds of it...in this age of inquiry'.[55] There was an equally optimistic expectation of material improvement, some of which was realized as a quite disproportionate number of Unitarian laymen achieved municipal office in the aftermath of the reform of urban local government in 1835. Hence Unitarian Sunday Schools tended to rely less upon 'enthusiasm' than upon immediate social and moral concerns and, rejecting the general depravity of mankind, upon the promotion of secular values and learning.[56] The engineer millwright Edwin Rose of Manchester left his Methodist Sunday School for its Unitarian counterpart in Lower Mosley Street because the latter taught reading and writing.[57] The association of Unitarianism with reforming causes is familiar; the future Chartist George Holyoake experienced his early education in mathematics and logic through a Unitarian Sunday School.[58] Moreover, a natural sympathy towards those whom it regarded as oppressed has led to the attribution to Unitarianism of a particular commitment to female advancement.[59] In the late eighteenth century John Jebb had written, 'Women are not dealt with justly by the law of the land.

---

[54] Watts, 'Unitarian Contribution to Education', p. 317.

[55] Lant Carpenter, *Principles of Education, intellectual, moral and physical* (London, 1820), p. 306.

[56] See, for example, Watts, 'Unitarian Contribution to Education', pp. 318-19; and L. Burney, *Cross Street Chapel Schools, Manchester 1734–1942* (Manchester: published by the author, 1977), pp. 15-21.

[57] Thomas W. Laqueur, *Religion and Respectability: Sunday Schools and Working Class Culture, 1780–1850* (New Haven, CT, and London: Yale University Press, 1976), p. 150.

[58] Lacquer, *Religion and Respectability*, p. 154.

[59] Watts, *Gender, Power and the Unitarians*, especially ch. 4; K. Gleadle, *The Early Feminists: Radical Unitarians and the Emergence of the Women's Rights Movement* (Basingstoke: Macmillan, 1995).

All laws of inferiority should be repealed. Compact supposes equality.'[60]
Sunday Schools indeed offered a significant educational role to women,
but this was hardly peculiar to Unitarians; it has been estimated that more
than half of all Sunday School teachers in England in the early
nineteenth century were female.[61] What mattered in this case was not so
much the numbers of female teachers engaged by Unitarian Sunday
Schools but the quality of their own education which they brought to
their labours. Many of them, especially the daughters of ministers or
prominent (and affluent) lay families had, as Ruth Watts has shown,
benefited from a domestic atmosphere which promoted something
approaching intellectual equality for women, of which the Aiken, Greg,
Martineau and Rathbone families were outstanding examples. Mary
Carpenter and her sister Anna were entered as pupils together with the
boys at their father's school at Bristol and received from him a strikingly
above-average education by the standards of the time.[62]

Unitarian preachers and Sunday Schools, however, possessed one
undoubted advantage. They did not incur the suspicion which fell upon
the popular, unlettered evangelical preachers who were the main targets of
Lord Sidmouth's bill of 1810. John Ross, from 1778 to 1792 Bishop of
Exeter, a diocese in which Methodism had attracted many converts, was
not referring to Rational Dissenters when he condemned Sunday Schools
as part of 'the unparochialising, the undomesticating, the puritanic
tendency of many new projects of education'.[63] When Bishop Tomline
used his visitational *Charge* of 1794 to exhort the clergy of the diocese of
Lincoln to promote Sunday Schools he did so in search of a corrective to
the popular evangelicalism which he later denounced so strongly in his
Refutation of Calvinism (1811).[64] Even Samuel Horsley, no friend to
Unitarians, made clear that his excoriation of Sunday Schools applied to
those which were opened in connection with what he called 'New
conventicles', where 'The pastor is often, in appearance at least, an
illiterate peasant or mechanic.' He believed that such schools amounted
to an evasion of the Seditious Meetings and Treasonable Practices Acts of
1795.[65] By contrast, Unitarians were among the best-educated sections of

---

[60] *The Works, theological, medical, political and miscellaneous, of John Jebb, with Memoirs of the Author by John Disney* (3 vols, London, 1787), II, p. 180.

[61] Snell and Ell, *Rival Jerusalems*, p. 282.

[62] Manton, *Mary Carpenter*, pp. 21-25.

[63] R. Polwhele, *Reminiscences, in Prose and Verse, consisting of the epistolary Correspondence of many distinguished Characters* (3 vols., London, 1836), I, p. 141.

[64] George Pretyman, *A Charge delivered to the Clergy of the Diocese of Lincoln... 1794* (London, 1794), p. 18.

[65] Quoted in F.C. Mather, *High Church Prophet: Bishop Samuel Horsley (1733–1806) and the Caroline Tradition in the Later Georgian Church* (Oxford: Clarendon Press, 1992), pp. 282-83.

the population and possessed a substantial material stake in the existing economic, if not the political and ecclesiastical, order. They regarded the semi-literate evangelicals demonized by Sidmouth with such disdain that some of their ministers, for example Thomas Belsham, actually approved of his unsuccessful bill.

There was, after all, no question but that Unitarians had every reason to wish for the maintenance of public order and to regard Sunday Schools as means of achieving that end. Lant Carpenter considered it a matter for self-congratulation and an important advertisement of respectability that none of his Sunday scholars or their parents had been involved in the Bristol reform riots of October 1831.[66] The question concerned the sort of order they hoped to bring about, and in whose interests it was to operate. While they had promoted Sunday School education to inculcate qualities which encouraged employability and thus reduced the burden of poor relief,[67] at least one motive for their so doing was a consciousness of the disproportionate burden of the Poor Law which fell upon those least able to bear it.[68] Alternatives were not confined to the antipodes of militant, even quasi-revolutionary, radicalism and uncritical acceptance of the *status quo*. A suspicion of the established constitution and an aspiration to reform it substantially were Unitarian characteristics. A legacy from late eighteenth-century Rational Dissent was the commitment to 'universal toleration', a value which informed much Unitarian Sunday School teaching. A Catholic priest was invited to preach at the anniversary sermon of Birmingham New Meeting Sunday School.[69] A sense of fellow-victimhood with Catholics meant that no Dissenting denomination gave stronger support to Catholic Emancipation in 1828–29 and the consequent overturning of the Protestant, as well as the Anglican, constitution than did Unitarians.[70]

In terms of educational methods, there was much that has a familiar appearance. The catechetical method of instruction was extensively used, a point of some importance when one bears in mind the increasing use of liturgical forms in Unitarian worship. At Birmingham New Meeting, Priestley had produced a catechism and its Sunday School used William Enfield's *Primer* and Mrs Barbauld's *Lessons*, both of which reflected the influence of the catechetical method. An early example of the books to be used may be found in the first plan in 1791 for a Sunday School to be

[66] *Christian Reformer* 1 (1834), p. 497.

[67] Turner, *Sunday Schools recommended*, pp. 26-27.

[68] See, especially, George Dyer, *The Complaints of the poor People of England* (London, 1793); and William Frend, *Peace and Union Recommended* (St Ives, 1793).

[69] Watts, 'Unitarian Contribution to Education', p. 317.

[70] See G.M. Ditchfield, '"Incompatible with the very Name of Christian": English Catholics and Unitarians in the Age of Milner', *Recusant History* 25.1 (May, 2000), pp. 52-73.

attached to the High Street Unitarian Chapel at Shrewsbury. Those to be provided for the scholars included Mrs Trimmer's *First Spelling Book for Boys*; her *First Spelling Book for Girls*; Mrs Trimmer's *Second Spelling Book*; the Psalter; Hannah More's *Historical Questions for the Use of Sunday Schools* and extracts from the *Cheap Repository Tracts*; and collections from Watts's *Hymns*.[71] This dependence upon books by authors outside their own tradition was characteristic of these early years; subsequently, Unitarians themselves wrote many of the works that were used, some of their adherents, such as John Holland of Bank Street Chapel Sunday School, Bolton, became prolific authors of Sunday School literature.[72]

Expectations of behaviour, too, had a conventional appearance. The rules for the Sunday School at the High Street Chapel, Shrewsbury, in 1791, included the following:

> That the Children shall be taught at the Chapel Vestry every Wednesday and Friday evenings from four o'clock till eight and shall assemble there every Sunday morning at nine o'clock and every Sunday afternoon at two o' clock to say their Catechisms and be instructed in Psalmody, after which they shall attend divine Service Morning and Afternoon at the Chapel.

> That the names of the Children shall be called over every time they assemble, and the names of the absentees and those who do not come at the hours appointed be wrote down or otherwise marked in a list to be prepared for that purpose, and delivered to the Committee, in order that such Children or their Parents be reproved; and, where the Committee think it necessary, the Children be expelled.

> That the Master see the Children come early, with their hands and faces clean, their hair combed, and their Apparel as decent as the parents can afford.

> That the Master's Instructions and Reproofs be given with mildness and patience.

> That such rewards be given to the Children, as their good conduct may deserve, and the Funds of the Institution will admit.[73]

The instance is typical of many.

A difference of emphasis, however, is immediately apparent in the attitudes taken by Unitarian Sunday Schools towards the encouragement of learning for secular ends. If one accepts P.B. Cliff's distinction between those Sunday Schools which saw themselves primarily as 'savers' and those which regarded themselves as 'educators',[74] Unitarians were

---

[71] Shropshire Archives: NO 4335/2/5.
[72] See Watts, 'Unitarian Contribution to Education', p. 321.
[73] Shropshire Archives, NO 4335/2/5.
[74] Cliff, *Sunday School Movement*, p. 43.

firmly in the latter camp. At Birmingham New Meeting, reading, writing and arithmetic were part of the curriculum from the 1780s and were not generally available in other Sunday Schools in the area. By the mid-nineteenth century, the Birmingham Old and New Meeting Sunday Schools established more advanced classes for older pupils who, it was hoped, might in due course become Sunday School teachers. The Old Meeting school taught geography, English history and physiology as well as the three 'R's, and the Sunday School Committee even expressed unease lest insufficient time be devoted to the more elementary subjects.[75] At Dukinfield, the Sunday School attached to the Unitarian chapel had a similar advanced class.[76] A liberal education for Sunday scholars was the ideal. As J. Byng, a teacher at the Derby Unitarian Sunday School, urged in 1831, 'Why confine them to reading the Scriptures merely, and perhaps to writing? Why not endeavour to give them a taste for reading and a love of learning, by giving them an insight of the treasures of intellect that lie before them?'[77] When John James Tayler addressed the anniversary meeting of the Sunday Schools Association in 1847 he advocated the study of the Bible as literature and exhorted Sunday School teachers to inculcate an appreciation of the beauty of poetry; his examples, significantly enough, were Mrs Barbauld, John Bowring and Emily Taylor.[78] The conflict over the appropriateness of the teaching of writing on the Sabbath was long and bitter; Unitarians were unambiguously on the side of teaching in their Sunday Schools writing and other skills which might be turned to secular advantage. While preaching respect for the Sabbath, Unitarians were not so exercised by the fear of its profanation as to confine teaching on that day to Bible classes. This, of course, also was not peculiar to Unitarians, but their approach contrasted with that of strict Sabbatarians, including many Methodists, as well as that of high-Calvinists such as William Nunn of Manchester, who insisted that writing should not be taught on Sundays.[79] The Unitarian emphasis leaned towards the fostering of aspiration rather than towards constraint.

It was no coincidence that some of the best-supported Unitarian Sunday Schools originated in towns and cities which also boasted a Literary and Philosophical Society, or that almost 80% of the Unitarian congregations which reported a Sunday School in 1832 also had a vestry

---

[75] Bushrod, 'Unitarianism in Birmingham', pp. 186-88.

[76] J.E. Hickey, *History of the Dukinfield Sunday School* (Dukinfield: G. Whittaker & Sons, 1928), pp. 25-26.

[77] *Monthly Repository* n.s. 5 (1831), p. 792.

[78] *Christian Reformer* n.s. 3 (1847), pp. 432-33.

[79] Ian J. Shaw, *High Calvinists in Action. Calvinism and the City: Manchester and London, 1810–1860* (Oxford: Oxford University Press, 2002), p. 89.

library.[80] Many Unitarians, were also 'men of science' and, in that respect as well as the theological one, could be said to belong to Arnold Thackray's category of 'marginal men'.[81] The central Unitarian objective was to use Sunday Schools and other forms of education to create a body of enlightened citizens—rather in their own self-image—with a broad religious tolerance, the intellect to exercise political and social responsibility and to possess rights. The emphasis upon mutual respect and courteous discussion no doubt bore the mark of the eighteenth-century culture of 'politeness', now much in academic fashion.[82] The method was one which gave a higher priority to intellectual conviction than to heart-warming. As Jeremiah Joyce put it in 1808, 'Unitarianism is not the doctrine that can make its way, in the same manner that methodism is gaining ground: the one can only appeal to the reason & understanding: the other by dealing out damnation to all around [and] terrify[ing] thousands to profess a faith in what they know not'.[83]

Thirdly, the role of Sunday Schools for Unitarians, as with other denominations, amounted to an essential branch of their philanthropic endeavour. I have suggested elsewhere that the depiction of Unitarians as, in J.E. Cookson's phrase, 'relatively indifferent to the hardships and degradations of the poor', requires qualification.[84] From the time of Catherine Cappe's attempt to form a female benefit club at Catterick in the 1760s and the remarkably effective Birmingham Brotherly Society, set up in 1796 by the Sunday School teachers of the Old and New Meetings, the work of Sunday Schools and philanthropy were closely connected. In Birmingham, the Brotherly Society, which soon came to add the word 'Unitarian' to its title, was a major reason for the popularity of the Sunday Schools managed by the Old and New Meetings and, later the Newhall Hill schools. Numerous pupils, and teachers, cited its benefits as a reason for their enrolment.[85] In return for carefully graded subscriptions, according to age, it offered sick pay, medical aid in cases of emergency, and funeral expenses. It subsequently was one of the contributing bodies to the Birmingham and Midland Mechanics'

---

[80] *Unitarian Chronicle* 8 (1832), pp. 146-47, 197-99, 324-25.

[81] See Arnold Thackray, 'Natural Knowledge in Cultural Context: The Manchester Model', *American Historical Review* 79.3 (June, 1974), 672-709, especially p. 678.

[82] See P. Langford, 'The Uses of Eighteenth-Century Politeness', *Transactions of the Royal Historical Society*, 6th series, 12 (2002), pp. 311-31.

[83] Dr Williams's Library, MS 12.58 (20): Jeremiah Joyce to Thomas Belsham, 2 December 1808.

[84] G.M. Ditchfield, 'Unitarianism and Philanthropy, 1760–1810', *Transactions of the Unitarian Historical Society* 21.4 (April, 1998), pp. 254-68; the quotation is from Cookson, *The Friends of Peace*, p. 28.

[85] Bushrod, 'Unitarianism in Birmingham', pp. 190-91.

Institute. At Lant Carpenter's Lewins Mead Meeting at Bristol, a form of medical insurance was also available. Particularly in the larger cities, Domestic Missions and Sunday Schools were closely associated in Unitarian congregations. The *Christian Reformer* in 1849, with some understatement, described the *Sunday School Penny Magazine* as 'A not unimportant ally of the Domestic Missionary.'[86] The influence of Joseph Tuckerman, the Unitarian minister at large to the poor in Boston, Massachusetts, has rightly been acknowledged in the development of these missions by British Unitarians, particularly in terms of the very limited place of charity, the emphasis upon self-help, and the importance of intellectual improvement. So, too, has the influence of Thomas Chalmers.[87] Tuckerman was present at the first yearly meeting of the Unitarian Sunday School Association in 1834 and his thoughts were published at length in the *Unitarian Chronicle*.[88] Unitarian Sunday School teachers in London were urged to work in close co-operation with Robert Philip, the city missionary.[89] In a retrospective glance at the previous half-century, the Rev. James L. Haigh of Liverpool explicitly linked the scriptural teaching offered by Unitarian Sunday Schools to social reform.

> People are only beginning to understand the Bible and look upon it with the right kind of reverence; not on account of its 'Divine origin' as it is called, but on account of its practical human interest and helpfulness. Its deep insight into human nature...makes the Bible of intense suggestiveness and value to poets, philosophers, and preachers, and all who delight in the *ideal*, down to statesmen, philanthropists, and social reformers, and all who delight in the *practical*.[90]

Much of this activity has, understandably, been described as status reinforcement and the imposition of the values of the middle classes. Yet a significant legacy to nineteenth-century Unitarianism from the more radical authors of Rational Dissent, notably George Dyer and William Frend in the 1790s, was that the poor had rights; that those rights included the right to education; and from education would follow

---

[86] *Christian Reformer* 17 (1849), p. 54. For important examples of Unitarian domestic missions, see David Steers, 'The Domestic Mission Movement: Liverpool and Manchester', *Transactions of the Unitarian Historical Society* 21.4 (April, 1996), pp. 79-103; and Alan Ruston, 'London's East End Domestic Mission', *Transactions of the Unitarian Historical Society* 21.4 (April, 1996), pp. 117-35.

[87] See David Turley, 'The Anglo-American Unitarian Connection and Urban Poverty', in H. Cunningham and J. Innes (eds), *Charity, Philanthropy and Reform: From the 1690s to 1850* (Basingstoke: Macmillan, 1998), pp. 228-42.

[88] *Christian Reformer* 1 (1834), pp. 495-98; *Unitarian Magazine and Chronicle* 2 (1835), pp. 614, 86-91.

[89] *Christian Reformer* 1 (1834), p. 497.

[90] James L. Haigh, 'Sunday School Ideals', *Liverpool Unitarian Annual* (1892), p. 44.

enfranchisement. Elements of this thinking may be detected in the relationship between Unitarian Sunday Schools and working-class culture. There is, admittedly, much to confirm the stereotype of Unitarianism as upper middle class, opulent and urban. There is no shortage of evidence of the adoption of patronizing attitudes towards their Sunday School pupils and their parents. As early as 1788 William Tayleur of Shrewsbury was writing of 'the lower class of good people', as the appropriate market for Unitarian propaganda.[91] In 1833 the annual report of the Unitarian Sunday School at Swinton claimed success for its efforts to inculcate what it called 'Habits of economy and forethought, too much neglected by the working man.' As a result, 'the penny which was once laid out in small confections &c. for immediate gratification and little good, is now in many instances resolutely saved, to augment a fund which is to provide useful things'.[92] There was much talk of the teaching of 'duty' in Sunday Schools—but of course 'duty' as defined by social superiors. It is well known that numerous Unitarian Sunday Schools were founded at the instigation, and at the expense, of local factory owners, such as John Fielden of Todmorden, while the research of K.D.M. Snell has identified a clear correlation between Sunday School enrolment generally and the prevalence of child labour.[93] Was this, then, yet another example of what has been called 'social control', preparing successive generations of children for a life of submission to factory discipline?

Undoubtedly, in the case of Unitarians, most children of chapel members had benefited from superior educational opportunities than those available to the children of the poor and, in most cases, did not need to be taught the three 'R's. In the earlier years of Unitarian Sunday Schools, it was for the children of the poor that their provision was primarily intended. Some eminent Unitarians, indeed, seem to have detected in the working classes an implicit threat to their own interests. Addressing the Unitarian Sunday School and Fellowship Fund at Greengate, Salford, in 1833, the Rev. Joseph Hutton spoke of his alarm at 'the spirit of hostility toward the rich displayed in the rules and resolutions of a trades' union at Leeds'. He feared that it was 'a hostility which...prevailed too generally in the minds of the poor'.[94] An essential part of the solution was to bring the different classes together in a spirit of co-operation within the Sunday School environment. The plan for the Sunday School of the High Street Unitarian Chapel, Shrewsbury, in 1791, exhorted members of the congregation to visit the school frequently, to

---

[91] JRULM: Letters of William Tayleur (unfoliated): Tayleur to Theophilus Lindsey, 18 September 1788.

[92] *Unitarian Chronicle* 2 (1833), p. 48.

[93] See Watts, 'Unitarian Contribution to Education', p. 325.

[94] *Unitarian Chronicle* 2 (1833), p. 311.

hear the children recite their catechism. They should also 'give them, in a plain, familiar and affectionate manner, such good advice and exhortation as is calculated to impress their young minds with serious and useful impressions'.[95] Joseph Tuckerman believed that the connection between 'the highest and humblest classes of society' constituted 'the excellence and glory of our Sunday-schools'.[96] The chapel was to become, in the words of P.B. Cliff, an 'educative community', a process reinforced by the extension of home visits, again advocated by Tuckerman and widely practised among most English denominations by the 1830s.[97] In 1832 an unsigned article in the *Monthly Repository*, perhaps reflecting a continuing Unitarian sense of exclusion, referred to the impact of working-class suffering upon 'the class just above them—that is, reader, you and me, and all who are dear to us'. The same article, in the spirit of 'educating our masters', emphasized the need for Sunday School education to provide for 'the youth of our labouring population' and described that population as 'once despised and all but powerless, but now strong and about to become mighty'.[98] In this enterprise, chapel members, their children, and the parents and children of the working classes all had important parts to play.

A Unitarian source in the early 1830s complained of a shortage of Sunday School teachers from the 'higher classes'; the schools, accordingly, were left 'to be conducted by persons just raised above those whom they teach, and with whom zeal must make up for scanty information'.[99] Of course, the presence of Sunday School teachers from working-class backgrounds, or not far removed therefrom, does not necessarily imply working-class management, or the inculcation of working-class values. Nonetheless, one is impressed by the amount of autonomy *vis-à-vis* managers and ministers that was available to Sunday School teachers. Moreover, there were areas where Unitarian Sunday Schools flourished within a genuinely working-class environment. They included the Methodist Unitarian schools in East Lancashire (with a few offshoots elsewhere, such as New Radford, Nottinghamshire).[100] Unlike many orthodox Methodists, Methodist Unitarians had no objection to secular education on the Sabbath, and their Sunday Schools taught history, geography and elementary mathematics, as well as reading and writing, as an autonomous and locally-generated means of upward

---

[95] Shropshire Archives, NO 4335/2/5.

[96] *Unitarian Magazine and Chronicle* 2 (1835), p. 89.

[97] Cliff, *Sunday School Movement*, p. 5.

[98] *Monthly Repository* n.s. 6 (1832), p. 161.

[99] *The Unitarian Magazine and Chronicle* 2 (1835), p. 89 n..

[100] H. McLachlan, *The Methodist Unitarian Movement* (Manchester: Manchester University Press, 1919), especially ch. 6; *Unitarian Chronicle* 8 (September 1832), pp. 234-5; Watts, 'Unitarian Contribution to Education', p. 29.

occupational and social mobility. Several of their teachers, such as John
Ashworth and Joseph Cooke, were genuine autodidacts. At the
Birmingham Unitarian Sunday Schools, middle-class sponsorship co-
existed for many years with control of the curriculum by teachers who
mostly came from working-class backgrounds. In 1834, however, a revolt
by the teachers against what they saw as unjustified interference from the
Sunday School committee provoked a secession from the New Meeting
Sunday School and the establishment of new schools and, subsequently,
the establishment of a new Unitarian chapel at Newhall Hill.[101] Ministerial
ideology and leadership were in many instances accompanied by a
surprising element of lay control and working-class influence in actual
weekly practice; ownership and control were not always synonymous.
The differences between the educational practices of high-Calvinists
within a relatively small area of Manchester led Ian Shaw to warn against
'the danger of generalization as to the motives and activities of the
leaders of early nineteenth-century Sunday School work'.[102] The warning
is an appropriate one and is all the more applicable to the much wider
regional variations between different types of Unitarian Sunday Schools.
'Social control' is too rigid a category to cover such a wide variety of
cases.

Finally, one must consider the role of Unitarian Sunday Schools in the
growth of a sharper sense of denominational identity in the early
nineteenth century. In the earliest days of Sunday Schools there was
much talk of a non-denominational approach; an irenical attitude can be
detected in the work of Joshua Toulmin of Taunton, and the first Sunday
Schools in Birmingham were intended to be non-sectarian.[103] The
catholicity of the Old Dissent pre-disposed Unitarians to reject any
imposition of credal tests or indoctrination. The Rev. Noah Jones invoked
the spirit of Philip Doddridge of Northampton as transcending 'the
peculiar errors of a sect or a party', while Charles Wellbeloved, the
Principal of Manchester College, York, many of whose students became
Sunday School teachers, famously claimed to teach what he called
'Christianism' rather than Unitarianism or Trinitarianism.[104] But a more
realistic prognosis was that of William Turner of Newcastle in 1786.

> But the principal advantage which I think the Newcastle Schools have over those in
> the South is, that they are each the offspring of religious societies, as such, and not
> of one general association of all parties; for, however liberal the idea of such an
> association may at first appear, it does not seem calculated to answer the primary

[101] Bushrod, 'Unitarianism in Birmingham', pp. 178-79.
[102] Shaw, *High Calvinists in Action*, p. 131.
[103] Toulmin, *Rise, Progress and Effects of Sunday Schools*, pp. 21-22.
[104] *Unitarian Chronicle* 2 (1833), p. 315; Wykes, 'Dissenting Academy or Unitarian
Seminary?', p. 104.

end of these Schools, viz. regularity and order in attendance on public worship. For when the direction of the Schools is committed to persons of different persuasions, disagreements are apt to arise about books they are to read, the places of worship they are to attend, and the ministers that are to instruct them; the visitors also neglect to observe their regularity, when they are sent to a variety of places, and when they are confined to one, the subscribers of a different communion complain; so that the conduct of such Schools is frequently very irregular. But where each religious community has a School under its own eye, one uniform plan is continually pursued in it; and each, from a principle of emulation (and there can be nothing but a laudable emulation in such a case as this) endeavours to make its own School most eminent for decency and order.[105]

This free-market suggestion renders more comprehensible the secession in 1787 from the inter-denominational Sunday School Association in Birmingham on the part of the Old and New Meetings. Their objection arose from what they claimed was a restriction upon the right of Dissenters to allow their Sunday School children to worship at their own meeting-houses rather than at the local Anglican churches.[106] The Unitarians were the first to secede and there ensued a debate as to the relationship between their schools and those of other religious groups. Where there was a small congregation with an energetic minister to undertake the teaching, the denominational thrust was often the more powerful. In February 1788 William Tayleur wrote of the new minister of the Shrewsbury High Street Chapel, 'Mr Rowe has begun to catechise with great success, & has more than 40 pupils. He is much favour'd by the Congregation & seems determin'd to use his utmost efforts to make the rising generation *real* Unitarians.'[107] In the case of larger congregations, many—perhaps most—of the teachers in Sunday Schools were not themselves Unitarians and there could hardly be an expectation that they would be. The Unitarian periodicals of the 1820s carried debates over the denominational or non-denominational ethos of their Sunday Schools. But in 1824 Mary Hughes, at the end of a life of commitment to Sunday School endeavour, articulated what was probably becoming a majority opinion:

We believe that our doctrines were those delivered by Christ and his apostles; and shall we not endeavour to give them pure and uncorrupted to the young minds whose tuition we undertake? If...they are merely to be taught to read, as in what now are called the 'British and Foreign Schools', without the inculcation of any particular

---

[105] Turner, *Sunday Schools Recommended*, pp. 55-56; Bushrod, 'Unitarianism in Birmingham', pp. 188-89.

[106] See John Money, *Experience and Identity: Birmingham and the West Midlands, 1760–1800* (Manchester: Manchester University Press, 1977), pp. 142-43.

[107] JRULM, Tayleur Letters (unfoliated), William Tayleur to Theophilus Lindsey, February 1788.

system of belief, it is nearly certain that ninety-nine out of a hundred will hold the same opinions with their parents and the world around them, opposite as these may be in many material points from what we esteem those of the New Testament... All other sects carefully implant in the minds of their young pupils what they believe to be Christian truth; and are they not most commendable for so doing?[108]

To some extent, of course, this was another dimension of the rivalry between Church and Dissent. The fear of the educational hegemony of the Established Church was a real one. But the distance between Unitarians and orthodox Dissenters was also widening. John Relly Beard was critical of all Trinitarian orthodoxy, not only that taught by the Church, when in 1833 he condemned non-Unitarian Sunday School teaching methods as excessively reliant on rote-learning and passivity. He complained that 'So much was taken upon the authority of the teacher that the pupil did not exercise the highest faculties of his mind; and partly on this account it was that orthodoxy gained so much amongst us.'[109]

In effect, Sunday Schools, though a significant symptom, rather than a direct cause, of denominationalism, helped to create a sense of common identity among the heirs of eighteenth-century Rational Dissent. The use of the expression 'Unitarian denomination' was common by the 1830s, and K.D.M. Snell has identified for Unitarians a relatively high correlation between their Sunday School enrolment and their overall denominational attendance.[110] The Unitarian withdrawal from the Protestant Dissenting Deputies and the General Body of Dissenting Ministers in the 1830s, together with the bitterness of the Wolverhampton and Lady Hewley cases, only enhanced this tendency and Unitarians hardly ever belonged to regional Sunday School unions. The denominational tendency among evangelical Dissenters—including the attempt of Wesleyan Methodists to bring Sunday Schools under their own denominational control—has been appreciated by historians and was emphasized in the Dr Williams's Library lecture of David Thompson.[111] The isolation of Unitarians from their fellow-Dissenters, as well as from the Established Church, was all the more emphatic. By the mid-nineteenth century, if not earlier, their Sunday Schools were more effective in the internal sense of consolidating the allegiance of the younger members of families who were already Unitarian than in proselytising or outreach. For all the similarities between many of their techniques and those of non-Unitarians, their Sunday School teaching possessed distinctive qualities,

---

[108] *Monthly Repository* 19 (1824), p. 391.

[109] *Unitarian Chronicle* 2 (1833), p. 309.

[110] Snell and Ell, *Rival Jerusalems*, p. 303.

[111] D.M. Thompson, *Denominationalism and Dissent, 1795–1835: A Question of Identity* (London: Dr Williams's Trust, 1985), pp. 16-26.

albeit sometimes in a rather nuanced manner, and those qualities played an important part in their denominational formation.

CHAPTER 3

The Baptist Contribution to the Sunday School Movement in the Nineteenth Century

John H.Y. Briggs

No aspect of Baptist life and work has been less well served by its historians than the story of its Sunday Schools. Yet during the nineteenth century they were foremost in the churches' outreach, consuming large capital and vast human resources. With the other young peoples' organizations (mutual improvement societies, brigades, guilds, Christian Endeavour, etc.) that they spawned, for many they became the public face of the church. The contribution of Baptist Sunday Schools, as measured by the 1851 Census, when some 155,400 scholars were recorded as enrolled, was, however, rather less than other denominations.[1] But as the century progressed that figure was to multiply by some 3.65 times, reaching a peak figure just short of 570,000 in 1906.

Sunday Schools were certainly an important part of the history of the nineteenth century. W.R. Ward is confident about his assessment: 'lay initiative…gave the Sunday School its primacy in the religious history of the period, for it was the only religious institution which the nineteenth-century public in the mass had any intention of using. The schools were the great triumph of municipal Christianity.'[2] Whilst many of the earliest town Sunday Schools were the fruit of cross-denominational initiatives, it was not long before denominational emphases emerged so that, in due course, Sundays Schools made their impact on ecclesiology. Professor

---

[1] T.W. Laqueur, *Religion and Respectability: Sunday Schools and Working Class Culture, 1780–1850,* (New Haven, CT, and London: Yale University Press, 1976), p. 48, where the following analysis of Sunday School enrolments is offered: C of E 42%; Methodists of all kinds 30%; Congregationalists 13.3%; Baptists 7.4%; RC 1.6%, with all other groups scoring less than 1.0%. The overall figures he provides are most impressive with total enrolments by 1851 in excess of two million or 56.5% of those aged 5–16 or 75.4% of the working class in that age range. By way of contrast the Church of England's 2004 strategy paper, *Mission Shaped Church*, ch. 3, offers the figures that whereas in 1900 55% of the nation's children attended Sunday School, the corresponding figure for 2000 was 4%.

[2] W.R. Ward, *Religion and Society in England, 1790–1850* (London: B.T. Batsford, 1972), p. 13

Ward once more: 'the Sunday School open to all rather than the covenanted meeting of baptized saints was the sign of the times. Evangelism rather than sanctification was the church's business, and the more the slogan of "the missionary church" caught on, the more the kingdom of God seemed delivered over to associational principles.'[3] This new activity caused a changed conception of church. But the impact was to be wider: a thoughtful focus on the educational task and the special needs of young people were also to question the shape of traditional Baptist theology.

Sunday Schools were the subject of numerous special sermons, often preached to raise funds, promotional lectures and pamphlets. Scrutinize the pages of the magazines and you will find there a constant stream of articles relating to their nurture and good running, reviews of a wide range of Sunday School publications, reports of their activities in this country and overseas, and of the societies formed to promote them. Thus, the first reference to Sunday Schools in the *Baptist Magazine*[4] is to be found in January 1811, at the beginning of its third year of publication. Note is made of the growth in the number of schools related to the newly established Sunday School Society, founded 1785, with some fifty-five added since April 1810. Since the foundation of the society almost 300,000 spelling books had been distributed alongside more than 63,500 New Testaments and just under 8,000 Bibles with upwards of 270,000 scholars enrolled in schools on the society's list.

Essentially a Baptist initiative, the society was the fruit of the fertile mind of William Fox, a wealthy draper and deacon at Abraham Booth's Prescot Street church whose intention was to universalize Raikes' useful experiment in Gloucester. The original group convoked to consider the new initiative met at the King's Head Tavern and was exclusively Baptist. When Henry Keene, a deacon at Maze Pond, articulated the assumption that the society be confined to members of the denomination, Fox replied 'I shall not be contented, Sir, until every person in the world is able to read the Bible, and therefore we must call upon all the world to help us.'[5] Accordingly, the new society sought to bridge the divide between Church and Dissent with a committee of equal numbers of churchmen and dissenters. At this stage the intention was that the work be Bible-based,

---

[3] W.R. Ward, 'The Baptists and the Transformation of the Church, 1780–1830', *Baptist Quarterly* 25.4 (October, 1973), p. 172.

[4] *The Baptist Magazine*, January 1811, pp. 39-40. An earlier issue supplied a review of Robert Hall's sermon which will receive separate attention. *The Baptist Magazine*, July 1810, pp. 394-96.

[5] J. Ivimey, *A History of the English Baptists* (4 vols; London, 1811–30), IV, pp. 83-84.

'excluding all catechisms'.[6] As in the north of England with the great
municipal endeavours, Sunday Schools early became one of the several
agencies that united evangelical Protestants together in common
enterprise, but the employment of paid teachers before it moved to
gratuitous volunteers limited the society's expansion in the early years.
The provision of Bibles and Testaments also increased its financial
burden.

The June issue of the following year contained an entry reporting the
first meeting of a second society, the Sunday School Union, strangely
nine years after its foundation.[7] 'The first meeting of this Institution was
held on Wednesday morning, May 13, 1812 at the New London Tavern,
Cheapside though it was established in 1803.' One of those foremost in
this initiative was a youthful W.B. Gurney, then aged only twenty-five.[8] A
member of the Parliamentary shorthand writers' family who held their
membership at Maze Pond Chapel, he was successively secretary, treasurer
and president of the society as well as serving as first editor of the union's
highly successful *Youth Magazine*. Among his many other philanthropic
activities, he served as Treasurer of Stepney College, of the Baptist
Missionary Society and of the Particular Baptist Fund.

If the Sunday School movement provided an early opportunity for co-
operation across denominational boundaries it also provided opportunity
for women to be involved in the church's mission. This happened at all
levels—locally as teachers, nationally in producing teaching materials,
(for example William Gurney's sister was early involved here) and also
by sitting on national committees. Very early on Miss Upton,
granddaughter of James Upton of Blackfriars, who had been involved in
Baptists' first attempt at a national union in 1812 and served as chairman
of the reconstituted union for its first two years in 1831–32, successfully
challenged their exclusion.

Robert Hall, minister successively in Cambridge, Leicester and Bristol,
sought throughout his ministry to help Baptist churches make an
adequate response to the double impact on denominational life of both
the Evangelical Revival and the fundamental social changes occasioned
by industrialization. Frequently consulted on Baptist polity and practice,
he saw the formation of schools dedicated to 'the education of youth in
the inferior walks of society', the working-class young, as one of the
'signs of the times' which indicated 'the advancement of our Saviour's
kingdom'. This, he set within the context of a prevailing social apartheid,
'the monstrous chasm' or 'unnatural separation' in 'whatever relates to

---

[6] The Sunday School Society was in fact the model for other cross-denominational
societies, see Stephen Orchard's discussion on p. 14 above.

[7] *The Baptist Magazine*, June 1812, p. 272.

[8] He was the most senior of the society's three initiators, Thomas Thompson and
James Nisbet both being eighteen.

the *mind'*, dividing ordinary working people from those higher in the community. Such differences could and should be eradicated: 'it is time to remember that our distinctions are exterior and evanescent, our resemblance real and permanent'. Benefiting himself from education in his father's manse, college in Bristol, and a degree course at the University of Edinburgh, he believed that education was crucial in liberating the permanent 'moral and spiritual' worth of the individual from the 'incrustations of poverty and ignorance'.[9]

It is not a surprise, therefore, to find Hall preaching in favour of Sunday Schools. This he did by arguing the importance of knowledge in general, and religious knowledge in particular. Whilst happy to argue his case in the context of a prevailing philosophy of 'utility', education was properly a religious task in so far as it equipped humankind to realize the stature of the personhood with which God created men and women as distinct from all other creatures. Unique to man was the ability to acquire and respond to a wide range of knowledge. The negative correlative of this was that to deprive someone of education was to deprive them of something essential to their divine creation, an indispensable mark of their humanity.

Rational recreation was a helpful antidote to that sensuous entertainment which inflicted so much damage on society. The development of mental resources exalted character. An appetite for reading provided ample opportunity for entertainment at home 'without being tempted to the public house for that purpose'. Furthermore, the reading man would almost certainly be moved to contemplate the future, not living for the present only, but making 'some provision for his approaching wants; whence will result an increased motive to industry, together with a care to husband his earnings, and to avoid unnecessary expense'. Thus 'when you have given the poor a habit of thinking, you have conferred on them a much greater favour than by the gift of a large sum of money, since you have put them in possession of the *principle* of all legitimate prosperity'. Conversely, ignorance parented disorder as could be seen in comparing the Scottish working classes, provided through free parish schools with the advantage of education, with their Irish cousins. Or again, Hall believed that revolution in France was a product of a want of education. Reflecting his doughty protestantism, he argued that, whilst the Church of Rome was 'a friend to ignorance', the churches of the Reformation had a vested interest in rationality and truth. This was now happily widely diffused through the printed page, which, at one and the same time, spread the Reformed faith, made for the

---

[9] R. Hall, 'The Signs of the Times', a sermon preached in Bristol, November 1820, in O. Gregory (ed.), *The Works of Robert Hall* (6 vols; London, 1866 edn), VI, pp. 186-87.

advancement of letters, and enabled men of science to share their findings.

The argument that to educate the poor was to lift them above their natural station in life and to destabilize society was swiftly dismissed. On the contrary, 'Nothing in reality renders legitimate governments so insecure as ignorance in the people.' Essentially loyalist in sentiment, Hall exhibited considerable confidence in existing patterns of government, in the Protestant North, at least. Whilst tyrannies exploited fear bred of ignorance, free governments depended on the cultivation of public opinion, born of a wide dissemination of knowledge, enabling citizens to deduce that government endeavours were for the welfare of the people, and thus to be seen as working for the public good.

Religious education was especially important because it both provided 'an authentic discovery of the way to salvation', and supplied 'an infallible rule of life'. Once readers had overcome the distortion of truth brought about by human sin, the scriptures, duly read, revealed the mind of God, often alluded to by Hall in the rather remote language of the 'Supreme Being', which underlines the consonance of his thinking with the rationality of the age. Nevertheless abstract learning on its own offered an insufficient goal, so Hall stressed the importance of Sunday School scholars understanding 'the necessity of the agency of the Spirit, to render the knowledge they acquire practical and experimental'. Thus the imperative for Sunday School teachers with regard to their scholars was, 'Lead them to the footstool of the Saviour; teach them to rely, as guilty creatures, on his merit alone, and to commit their eternal interests entirely into his hands. Let the salvation of these children be the object, to which every word of your instructions, every exertion of your authority, is directed.'

The context of a new century, surrounded by so many profound changes and potential crises, 'for which nothing can prepare us but the diffusion of knowledge, probity and the fear of the Lord', demanded dedicated service. 'These are not the times in which it is safe for a nation to repose on the lap of ignorance.' Thankfully the nation was witnessing many initiatives 'for the improvement of the lower classes, and especially the children of the poor, in moral and religious knowledge'. Hall, therefore, entertained high hopes that, 'Wisdom and knowledge shall be the stability of thy times, and strength of salvation.' That is to say, he saw no conflict of interests in Sunday Schools fulfilling at one and the same time both a civic and a religious purpose.[10]

---

[10] R. Hall, 'The Advantage of Knowledge to the Lower Classes, a Sermon preached at Hervey Lane, Leicester for the Benefit of a Sunday School', 1810, in Gregory (ed.), *Works*, Vol. II (1866 edn), pp. 149-64. In the Advertisement, Hall notes that his publication closely parallels a discourse on the same theme by his 'much esteemed friend' Francis Cox which he commends to his audience for their study.

Hall's comments and exposition may seem surprisingly condescending and time-serving to the existing interests of contemporary governments, especially from one often a radical critic. The religious mind, rather than distancing itself from the secular philosophy of the age—the pursuit of utility, the confidence in Reason, the social value of religion—sought to achieve its goals by working with and through such concepts. Hall's intentions were nothing if they were not firmly evangelical, but such evangelical concerns were not seen as in any way inimical to the rationalism of the age. The writer is clearly aware of class or difference of rank, but accepts this as part of the social order, confining his criticism to those who exploit it or push it to excess. With great confidence in the educational mission—knowledge was indeed power—Hall was convinced negatively, that where education was lacking, or defectively discharged, it led to a situation fraught with great social vulnerability. Hall was archetypal of what I would call evangelical rationalism, casting his arguments for Sunday Schools within a confident overall theology of the mind.

S.G. Green, perhaps the most prolific of Baptist apologists for Sunday School activity,[11] wrote in advocacy of their usefulness over a period of more than thirty years. Whilst suspicious of the over-exploitation of the emotions, his general approach is softer than the high rationalism of Hall, more ready to accommodate the different stages of child development. He was the author in 1857, the same year in which he became a tutor at the college in Bradford, of the Yorkshire Association Letter on *The Relation of Sabbath Schools to the Church*. This was written in response to Henry Dowson's letter the previous year on *The Remedies for the Present State of the Churches*, in which he indicated that 'the position which the Sabbath School occupies in connexion with the Church, needs review and reform'.

An example of what an unreformed Sunday School might look like comes from Stoney Street New Connexion School in Nottingham which provides this eye-witness account of a Sunday School treat to celebrate Queen Victoria's coronation in days before the widespread diffusion of the temperance conscience:

---

[11] Green was the son of another Samuel Green who was one of the very early graduates of Stepney College. Influenced by both Joseph Kinghorn and Andrew Fuller, he, like his more famous son, was a Sunday School enthusiast, reforming the school at Lion Street, Walworth, his most notable pastorate. For twenty-five years the father wrote lesson notes for the Sunday School Union. A life-like portrait of the younger Green is provided by his daughter, Lily Watson, in her novel, *The Vicar of Langthwaite* (London, new edn, 1897), where he appears as the gentle and scholarly Philip Hawthorne and his predecessor at Horton/Rawdon, James Ackworth, as Dr Yorke, 'massive in mind and body'.

A grand dinner was given to the Scholars. Two teachers beside myself fixed the tables in the graveyard by driving short posts into the ground over the graves over which we placed the boards. We had a liberal supply of beef and plumb [sic] pudding, and I am sorry to say a quantity of Ale was supplied to the children. The consequence was they became very demonstrative and we could not keep them in order as part of them were intoxicated. It was a sad sight to see such scenes with children of tender years feasting and drinking over the bodies of the dead along with those who ought to have known better.[12]

Later there was to be an almost total reversal of such practice with many a Sunday School spawning its own Band of Hope, as the temperance imperative became all consuming.

Green recognized both the importance of Sunday Schools to the church's mission and the difficulties encountered in successfully promoting them. If the church was 'the outward and visible embodiment of Christ's kingdom upon earth' then the Sunday School was 'one of the most effective means for the extension of that kingdom'.[13] Green was always anxious to stress that the family bore the prior responsibility—'parents have a responsibility which they can never delegate to strangers'. A weakness of the times was, in fact, the loosening of the family bond: 'Parents are careless—children independent and undutiful.' 'Even Christian parents too often neglect to maintain a godly discipline or confine it to the earlier years of childhood.' Accordingly, family responsibilities needed to be reinforced not lightened. Nevertheless, he believed that Christian parents would welcome assistance in discharging this sacred responsibility. Moreover, 'the condition of the thousands whose parents are incompetent or irreligious, creates a still more forcible appeal to Christian compassion'. In the ancient world 'the youth of Christian households' were the first to be admitted to the catechumenate, but other mainly young people 'who could be gathered for purposes of religious instruction, though not avowed believers' were early added to their number. The responsibility of the church, claiming ancient precedents, was for both the children of church members and for the children of the un-churched, living within its neighbourhood, with little sense at this date that these two tasks might conflict. In practice, the spanning of this divide was surely more difficult to achieve than Green's rhetoric would suggest.

---

[12] J.B Goodman (ed.), *Victorian Cabinet Maker: The Memoirs of James Hopkinson, 1819–1894* (London, Routledge and Kegan Paul, 1968), pp. 70-71.

[13] The following paragraphs are derived from his *The Relation of Sabbath Schools to the Church* [Yorkshire Baptists Association Letter] (Bradford: Yorkshire Association of Baptist Churches, 1857), pp. 1-20, from which all citations are taken unless otherwise stated.

Whilst the Puritans had laid emphasis on instructing the Christian young, their endeavours 'not only failed in reaching the great mass of the youthful population, but had fallen into all but universal disuse by the middle of the last century'. It was this neglect which provoked the compassion of Robert Raikes in Gloucester in 1780 in pioneering the Sunday School movement. Such individual action soon led on to church initiatives, so that by 1857, Green affirmed, 'without a school, none of us at least would consider a church to be complete'. It had to be admitted, however, that the Sunday School had been 'brought to the church from without, not originated from within'. This was the cause of some difficulties. 'The original separation in great measure remains, although a kind of oneness is professed.' Very often the only unity was that of place, with little common cause between congregation and school: indeed the latter was quite often the source of some annoyance because of noise, damage, etc. A once-a-year occasion for the congregation to provide funds for the school in the anniversary collection hardly constituted keen congregational interest. Rather there was little commitment to the work by the generality of the church members. 'The church supports the Sunday school, recognises it, perhaps is proud of it, but it cannot in any sense be said to be the church's charge or work.'

Sometimes the situation was worse: 'Positive alienation and mistrust are by no means uncommon. The church is jealous of the school, and the school suspicious of the church. The teachers form an entirely distinct body, with plans, discussions, resolutions of their own. Church meetings and teachers' meetings become rival assemblies.' Teachers' meetings become the fora 'for young and ardent spirits, self-willed in their independence, immature and often undecided in their religious character'. Sometimes the pastor was even barred from attending teachers' meetings. 'We often hear the school spoken of as the nursery of the church; but in such places the nursery has set up for an independent republic, and defies the rest of the family.' Such a situation was both 'disorderly and unbecoming'. The early promise of the Sunday School movement had in practice been blasted. Church and school had become separate, even competing, institutions.

All of this was most unsatisfactory. Reform was needed. The body overseeing the work of the school should derive its authority from the church and not exist independently of it. In addition to teachers, it should also include other senior members of the church, with the pastor *ex officio* serving as president. Whilst it was appropriate for this body, as the most knowledgeable about school affairs, to choose the superintendent, the appointment should always be dependent on ratification by the church. Next to the pastor there was no more important appointment than this—the appointment of one who would be 'a kind of pastor among the young'.[14]

The school to maximize its effectiveness needed to be properly housed, with separate classrooms for senior classes, and independent provision for the infants. 'Maps, class books, and a library will be liberally supplied, by a special subscription if necessary'—and certainly it should not be expected that the teachers themselves will provide these. Large investments were accordingly made into the erection of school premises. Even in village situations, the sanctuary was supplemented by a range of properly equipped rooms, initially for school activities, but which subsequently provided for a wide array of social activities. If there still had to be 'children's galleries' within the chapel these should be especially comfortable granted that the children who sat there would find it difficult to concentrate on the whole service, especially the sermon, therefore, they should be more comfortable, with better seating than provided for committed adults.

Teachers needed to be pedagogically qualified, but the primary qualification required was that they must themselves have experienced divine grace. The introduction of teachers to this sacred task should have about it 'something of the solemnity of an ordination to work in God's vineyard'. It was not a task for the youthful and immature, but rather for 'Christians of the largest intelligence, the widest culture, the most loving earnestness'—'the most highly qualified of its members'. That this was too high a requirement was not to be made an excuse for the appointment of 'incompetent teachers' or the acceptance of an 'inefficient school'. It was better to have fewer, larger classes than to use those who lacked qualification.

The pastor should be no stranger to the school room, but should rather develop some regular pattern of being seen there. A very useful function would be if the pastor were to conduct the weekly training class for teachers. Regular attendance at the Bible classes was also highly desirable, for 'the catechetical, conversational exposition of the Word of God among the young people of his charge', necessarily had a very high claim on his attention. Beyond that, there was a need for the whole church to be concerned about the welfare of the children growing up within its community.

Baptist churches had traditionally upheld 'the broad distinction between the regenerate and the unrenewed', trusting to 'the general

---

[14] The issue of the proper relationship between church and school remained an ongoing concern even at the end of the century. James Stuart, 'The Church's Responsibility in Relationship to the Young', whilst affirming the Sunday School as 'the most direct and practical form of the Church's ministry to the young' still found it necessary to underline that it was 'not a separate institution but a necessary branch of the Church's work'. See *The Baptist Magazine*, June 1899, p. 273.

doctrine of God's sovereign converting grace'. But these general truths, Green argued, needed particularizing to the conditions of the very young. Accordingly he posed the theological question as to how grace operated in their lives. The will of the child was 'subdued by a power, omnipotent always, but progressively manifested', 'leading, at last, to the grand declared decision...to serve the Lord'. In many cases the precise moment at which divine grace prevailed could not be determined, no more than it could be defined as to when precisely morning had chased away the night. 'Such cases will be more and more frequent, in proportion to the spread of a true religious training.' As Sunday Schools developed, churches should expect to find 'many a Timothy acquainted with the Scriptures from a child'. Christian leaders had to appreciate the subtle development of a child's consciousness of religious truth. Carelessness in such matters could all too easily lead to a youngster becoming, in the language of the fathers, 'gospel hardened'.

Green was suspicious of over-excited Sunday School events. He spoke of 'vain excitement' on Anniversary Sunday, even of competition between schools inculcated by some celebrations, which unhelpfully became simply occasions for the display of youthful talent. Sometimes the focus was all on musical elaboration, the attractions of the melody rather than the solemn content of what was being sung. Anything that gave exaggerated attention to individual children was highly dangerous, and was to be avoided, the strength of the warning being a clear indication that such practices were not uncommon. The announcement of the size of the collection before the service was concluded was not conducive to true Christian worship, though he did note in this respect that the situation had greatly improved 'of recent years'. In Green's judgment all these things were distractions from essential purposes. The excitement of the occasion became inimical to a young person using the occasion to make a decision for God; not surprisingly conversions in response to anniversary sermons were rarely recorded. Whilst the educational usefulness of Juvenile Missionary Associations, Bands of Hope and the like had to be admitted, there was danger when such organizations became ends in themselves and set up unhelpful bustle and rivalries. Sometimes such organizations set goals beyond realistic juvenile competence: 'It never was intended that children should be the reformers of society and the evangelists of the world.'

A wise church would make the Sunday School the focus of earnest prayer, especially for those who showed signs of responding to their teachers' labours. This should properly occur long before such youngsters formally indicated a desire to attend an enquirers' class, or made an inquiry concerning baptism, steps which should not be forced on children before they were ready for them. A monthly prayer meeting for the work of the school to which all church members, not just Sunday

School teachers, were invited, was highly desirable. Nothing, in fact, could better demonstrate a healthy relationship between church and school.

It was, argued Green, 'an unquestionable fact that Sunday School instruction has not, as yet, produced those effects upon the community which were once confidently predicted, and even now are sometimes fondly imagined. Comparatively speaking the number of conversions from the school is small.' There were two ways of considering Sunday School statistics—you could view them either from the perspective of church membership lists or the Sunday School Roll. Viewed from the former perspective, he was well aware that a high proportion of new members did count the Sunday School a formative instrument in their journey to Christian faith. But from the perspective of the Sunday School Roll, those who became church members were a small proportion of school enrolments—probably less than a tithe. Many enjoyed the secondary benefits of Sunday School—friendships, relaxation, stimulating activity, but they failed to respond positively to the schools' main purpose.

In particular, many schools failed to provide appropriate teaching for older scholars, undoing all the good work done with children of a younger age. The church was deficient in the attention it gave to those undergoing the vital transition from childhood to youth, failing to see that methods and skills, different from those successful with younger children, were needed, especially when worldly attractions became more enticing. Where special provision for this age group had been made, the response had been immediate.

Such failings were linked by Green in a significant passage to what he identifies as 'the general debate about "the general neglect of public worship in our crowded manufacturing districts!" The working classes, it is said, are alienated from religious institutions. With some exaggeration the assertion is true. Yet once we had these classes in their thousands—the men and women who now pass our places of worship with a sneer, to whom the Sabbath is only a secular holiday, and the Bible little more than the Koran. We had them in the days of their youthfulness, when they were sensitive, impressible, thoughtful; but we have lost them now and our town and city missionaries are plodding wearily, and all but hopelessly, among the scattered flocks of our Sunday Schools.'

Analysis of the Religious Census of 1851 led to the most disturbing deductions, namely that, with only rare exception, where Sunday School attendance was highest in proportion to the general population, there church and chapel attendance was lowest.[15] In counties like Lancashire

---

[15] Excluding London, England possessed forty-two towns and cities with a population in excess of 30,000. Of these nineteen had a Sunday School attendance above average, but of these all but four had a church/chapel attendance below the average. In five towns

and Yorkshire, he asserted, 'Where Sunday Schools are largest, the sanctuary is most neglected.' Of course there were explanations: the manufacturing districts had grown very rapidly, and in such areas the populations were biased to the younger age range. In these circumstances Sunday Schools had been more quickly formed that churches, which arose from the more time-consuming process of collecting a viable congregation. Indeed, without the preliminary work undertaken by Sunday Schools it was highly likely that the deficiency on church/chapel attendance would have been even higher. But when all the explanations had been put in place it could not be denied that the schools had not raised up a community of regular churchgoers. Thus the limited achievements of Sunday Schools in the first half of the nineteenth century was readily and realistically admitted. There was, therefore, a need for renewed effort in making Sunday Schools effective, to 'raise up not only Christians, but intelligent Christians'. This was the crucial need of the times, for 'The secret of half the infidelity of our day is superficial acquaintance with the Book of God.' Green moved quite easily from statistical analysis to pietistic exhortation: 'Without prayer, we can never hope for a blessing; but prayer without wise and strenuous effort, is but a mockery. Let these be combined in our Sunday School labours, and the promises of God assure us that the largest success will follow.'

A quarter of a century later Green was still arguing in favour of Sunday Schools and the best ways to run them. His most extended consideration of the topic is to be found in a series of lectures given at Regent's Park College funded by the Errington Riley Trust, established 'to render assistance to students for the Christian ministry in view of their future work for the spiritual work of the young people in their congregations...in what is perhaps the most important, as it is certainly the most hopeful, department of work for Christ'.[16]

At pains to establish his evangelical credentials, Green affirmed his commitment to the forgiveness of sins through Christ's blood and justification by faith alone. But the way in which these doctrines were to be applied to children led him to develop new softer lines of apologetic than those traditionally adopted. Against the assumption of preachers that a pattern of moral failure needed to be identified, 'before the good can triumph', Green argued that, whilst this was often the case, it was neither 'natural nor inevitable'. 'Neither in Scripture nor in reason is there

---

the number of scholars on the books of the Sunday Schools actually exceeded the number present at worship at any one time on Census Sunday.

[16] Errington Riley of Hexham was for many years Secretary of the Sunday School Union for the North of England. Green's lectures, published under the title, *Christian Ministry to the Young: a Book for Parents, Pastors and Teachers* (London: Religious Tract Society, 1883), at the request of the Principal and students of Regent's Park College, were also delivered at Cheshunt College.

warrant for the belief that in dealing with the soul the Spirit of God must postpone His efficacious workings until the full development of the moral nature.' 'The growth of reason, thought, affection, is gradual, and at first unconscious.' There was no necessary sequence of events from sin to salvation: indeed, a child could appreciate the compelling attraction of the love of God long before the moral senses had developed a refined sense of good and evil. This pattern of gradual development corresponded to the testimony of many dedicated Christians unable to discern any moment of crisis or sudden change in their lives. Indeed, to press for such a testimony might well cause unnecessary anxiety in say the candidate for church membership or communion. Richard Baxter, troubled by just this issue, discovered at length that 'education is as properly a means of grace as preaching', that is to say he grew into faith without a sense of crisis. This was also the experience of the Moravians, who 'make their churches schools of holy nurture to childhood', and accordingly their followers advanced into membership without any sense of convicting crisis.[17]

With such exemplification in mind, Green pleaded for a recognition of the patient work of the Holy Spirit amongst the church's young people within homes and churches. This led on to the question as to when youngsters should be admitted to church membership. Whilst Green was aware of cases where this had happened at the age of 12/13, wisdom suggested that this should occur at 'an age when the habits are fixed, and the profession can be accepted as a deliberate and binding vow for life'. This corresponds to Baptist usage of the concept of 'the age of discretion', an Enlightenment-based concept if ever there was one, but very central to Baptist staging of human development as derived from their particular concept of baptism. If this timing of human development was correct, then the catechumenate became an important stage in progress towards maturity. It had to be conceived of as a time for appropriate instruction, which should not then be cast in terms of earnest exhortation to conversion but of assurance that the youngster was already secure within the love of God. On this basis Green was quite clear that too much introspective interrogation was inappropriate as provoking unnecessary anxiety and concern. Children should not be made to suffer from an exaggerated impression of conscience, nor be frightened by graphic pictures of future punishment—the graphic depiction of everlasting turmoil which was most injudiciously included in many children's books. This was not to argue that 'the sterner aspects of the Gospel' should be hidden from the young, who certainly needed to become aware of the evil of sin. But it was best that experience and the consequences of moral failure spoke to the young, not some great doctrine built upon dread. Alternatively, too much questioning of the

---

[17] Green, *Christian Ministry*, pp. 14-15, 17-18, 19, and 20.

spiritual development of the young could lead to the equally dangerous parrot-like recitation of what in effect were other people's experiences. Thus, without intention on their part, the young were led into a 'kind of experiential duplicity', producing the responses, not of their own self-conviction, but those they thought their teachers wanted to hear. The young believer was best advised to think less of his own soul and more of the Saviour, and be encouraged to trust in God and develop bonds of affection with the Redeemer, which would lead into an understanding of the great doctrines of the faith such as the atonement. Thus Green affirms, 'Many a spirit, brought into fellowship with God, begins with a trust and ends with a doctrine.'[18]

How often, one is left pondering, does this commentator use his juvenile audience to look for changes or to suggest theological understandings which he desires for other reasons? As Principal of Rawdon he provoked suspicion amongst the churches of Yorkshire and Lancashire where his theology attracted the description 'latitudinarian'.[19] He believed that 'A child's theology...will be very simple. Simple, and yet within its limits it must be intelligent to be effectual.' The love of God made demands upon the mind as well as the heart and the will. To speak about the need for the study of biblical and dogmatic theology and of Christian ethics sounded ponderous—but 'the elements of these studies ought to form part of the mental furniture of our young disciples'. Too much appeal to the emotions at the expense of real teaching, represented a serious criticism of what was happening in many schools, for 'it is only when knowledge, reason and conscience sustain the quickened emotions that these have a permanent effect on the character and the life'. Emotions should not be undervalued but emotional encounters needed to be secured by other aspects of experience. Thus the danger of seeking to harvest too early—take an early crop and thereby damaging the principal harvest—becomes apparent.[20]

Debate on the desirability of separate services for children or how the regular worship of the congregation might be made more attractive for them rumbled on. Reference was made to the social divide that used to exist in the old fashioned pattern of the family pew 'screened by the tall sides, for soothing the younger members of the household' as over against 'the children's gallery for the Sunday School often well out of the way of the congregation', 'with guardians and sentinels told off to check misbehaviour and to promote attention'. Very often then the experience of worship was of something not understood but which had to

---

[18] Green, *Christian Ministry*, pp. 21, 22, 30-31, 24, and 25-26.

[19] A.C. Underwood, *A History of the English Baptists* (London, Kingsgate Press, 1947), p. 209.

[20] S.G. Green *The Pastor in the Sunday School* (London: Alexander and Shepheard/Bradford: Thomas Brear, 1884), pp. 1-12, 27, 28, and 29.

be endured. This was the source of the idea of separate services which became fashionable in the mid-1860s. The concept was good: 'Children's galleries were to be abolished; the little ones were to be delivered from their thraldom in the family pew.' Instead, simultaneous services adapted to the separate needs of children and adults—that for children to embrace 'cheerful singing, simple prayers, lively and interesting addresses'—were introduced, but there were practical difficulties in finding sufficient able leaders in a period prior to school teaching becoming a widespread profession in society at large. More importantly there were objections from the point of view of principle: 'The separation between the Christian household in its collective capacity and the Christian congregation is to be deprecated... It seems, on any showing, a false or an exaggerated individualism which would send us to the house of prayer as isolated units, each one for himself.' By contrast Green believed it important that a child's earliest memories be of the worship of God in the company of the family, rather than of the schoolroom and teachers.[21]

Ministers should be the children's pastors from the first, with children from their earliest years experiencing their influence. So children of church members should sit in public worship with their parents not their teachers, and this of itself might induce more parents to be present for worship. But there would still be some for whom the teachers must supply the parents' lack, but this should be within the body of the congregation and not separate from it. The great need was to secure their attention rather than to discipline their boredom by compulsory methods. Were this to be done it would help to stem the loss of Sunday School scholars on reaching maturity.

Attempts to make the services of the whole congregation child-friendly should not be too extreme because there must necessarily remain elements which children could not grasp. On the other hand, children often understood more than they were given credit for. Beyond that, 'It is part of the fitting discipline of childhood to have placed before them, in a thousand ways, facts, thoughts, truths which they cannot as yet understand.' In the same way they should be encouraged to read scripture though this contained deep truths which as yet they do not see. So it would be a real loss if their experience of worship was confined to that of a children's service, for 'there is a useful discipline also in the habits of self-restraint and seriousness that are cultivated by attention at public worship'.[22]

However, there were benefits for all in making services more attractive, not by employing ritual which was wholly repudiated, bur rather through

---

[21] Green, *The Pastor*, pp. 41, 43, and 44.
[22] Green, *The Pastor*, pp. 47, 48, and 49.

greater participation in employing modest liturgical forms. If such actions were thought too formal, he questioned, 'may there not be as much formalism in tedious prayer and dolorous psalmody as in a more varied and animated strain?' Where free prayer was used, those leading worship should have the needs of the young very much in their minds, so that the young could recognize in the words spoken 'the voice of their own hearts'. The sermon itself had to display 'the old, old, lessons of simplicity and earnestness'. Language had to be straightforward and arguments well focused, for the sake of the whole congregation, but especially for the young, whose only chance of finding any clue to a speaker's or a writer's meaning is often 'lost in a cloud of words'. Further, children had an infallible ability to nose out the insincere, and showed little capacity to be persuaded by the merely conventional. The impact of the whole could be enhanced by greater economy of expression with the old forty-five minutes reduced to twenty-five to thirty minutes, not simply for the sake of children but to the advantage of all.[23]

The year after Green published his *Christian Ministry to the Young* he was asked to address the autumn assembly of the Baptist Union on *The Pastor in the Sunday School* (8 October 1884). By this date it was necessary to relate the activities of the Sunday School to what was happening in the day school. Accordingly, Green confessed that 'the form and outline of Scripture truth are often better taught in the day school'. It was not for the church 'to add to the "over-pressure" by which young brains...are already sufficiently taxed'. Rather it was the task of the Sunday School teacher to exploit the significance of what had already been taught. Questions were now being raised as to the compatibility of the Sunday School's two functions—a missionary agency among the un-churched, and an instrument for developing the children of church members in the faith. Green was anxious that Baptist ministers initiate special pastoral classes—including not only Sunday School children, but the young people of the congregation. 'For we would, as far as is possible, unite all.' Seeds of distinction were clearly evident even though he sought to overcome such potential divisions, based not only on the parents' standing within the church, but also on social class. The Sunday School existed to gather together 'the children of all classes in the congregation, and so to supplement, without superseding, the influence of many a Christian household'. 'The "Sunday scholars" are not to be looked upon as of inferior grade to the rest of the young people; but the school, according to its true intent, is the ground where all can meet. It is the younger portion of the great Christian family: not the charitable provision for the otherwise ignorant and destitute, but like the Christian congregation itself, the gathering of

---

[23] Green, *The Pastor*, pp. 51, 54, and 58.

those who, on one day of the week, at least, can forget the distinctions and separations of social life, to find in the truth of God, and the love of Jesus, the attractiveness and joyfulness of a common home.'[24]

Baptists were obliged by the restrictions they placed on Christian baptism—'the rejection of baptism as the initiatory ordinance of childhood'—to develop a special praxis with regard to the children in their community. Children already enjoyed a provisional place within the Christian community, congregation and family, a connection with Christ's church, but this had to be sealed personally by profession in baptism. But this should not come as a sudden and unexpected event, but rather as the culmination of a process, growth in grace progressing 'hand in hand and side by side with all other growth'. In another publication Green had spelt out this particular Baptist understanding of the place of children within the divine economy. 'The child-disciple, although remaining for a while without the pale of church membership, has yet a very real and vital connection with the Church. He is not as a heathen, but is [as *sic*] already a candidate for fellowship, or to adopt (in another sense) a word from the early Church—a *catechumen*... The child will be encouraged to pray; not told that he must be converted before his prayer is acceptable to God. He will hear of God continually as a Father, and of Christ as the Saviour who certainly loves him. Instead of the well-meaning earnestness with which bewildered young souls are often urged "to give their hearts to God," not well understanding what this may mean, the glad tidings will constantly be told that God in Christ is reconciled, and gives us help to be good and pure.' Told by a friend that this was a marvellous argument for infant baptism, he begged to disagree, arguing that in the New Testament baptism did not initiate a child into a process of instruction, but rather represented 'the seal of a conscious and deliberate discipleship, a personal and responsible putting on of Christ'. Because Baptists did not see baptism as the sacrament of dedicated childhood that did not mean they valued the careful nurture of young people in the life of the church the less. The best way to reply to their sacramental critics, though the language of sacrament was one he put on one side, was to engage the more earnestly in this sacred task.[25]

S.R. Pattison, for many years the Baptist Union's legal advisor and also for thirteen years its treasurer,[26] addressed the Autumn Assembly of the

---

[24] Clifford was of like opinion: *General Baptist Magazine*, April 1875, p. 126: 'Caste will be totally excluded. Divisions will not be known. Cliques will shrivel into nothingness.'

[25] Green, *The Pastor*, pp.1-12; and *Christian Ministry*, p. 12.

[26] Pattison was born in Stroud in Gloucestershire and brought up in the Church of England. Being un-persuaded by an essay he himself wrote in defence of infant baptism, and under the influence of Baptist Noel, he became convinced of Baptist views and was baptized by Samuel Nicholson of Plymouth. Trained as a solicitor in Launceston in

Baptist Union in October 1869, *On the Relation of the Sunday School to the Congregation and the Church.* In arguments reminiscent of Robert Hall's evangelical rationalism, reinforced by his profound interest in science, he exhibited a general confidence in truth and knowledge as the arena in which God spoke to his creatures 'by appeals to the understanding'. Since man had been created with 'a free rational soul', he had a responsibility to use this gift, an obligation unaffected by the Fall. Whilst there were indications of God's purposes scattered across nature and imbedded in human intuition, the greatest was contained only in the supernatural gift of divine revelation. But the scattered elements existed without proper order, making it incumbent on humankind to organize them: 'The knowledge concerning God whether intuitive, natural or revealed, must in some way be made a science by each person for himself.' This highly cerebral approach to the transmission of Christian understanding and insight, and indeed the whole task of ordering human experience, was made a compelling argument for Sunday School instruction. 'Religious truth', argued Pattison, to be effectively received 'must be offered to us in a manner adapted to secure the end. This requires agency, the agency is called teaching.' The Holy Spirit's clear role in this did not negate human obligation. Certainly it was the Spirit's work to 'augment the impressive power of certain truths concerning the Saviour, but does not even in this supersede or displace the natural action of the mind.' God's act of creation placed a high premium on human intelligence, such as was not lightly to be put on one side.

Teaching thus became an inescapable part of Christian mission in which all were obliged to participate. The task was defined as the obligation 'to bring our own knowledge of the supernatural into vital relation with the natural knowledge' already possessed by those being taught. Bible truths had to be related to the natural experience of those to be influenced. This was not a responsibility to be off-loaded on to the specialist or indeed the church itself: 'the believer is the teacher not the church; the Bible is the book not of the church but of the wide world'. Pattison intriguingly argued that suspicion of creeds had led Nonconformists to become careless about the communication of Christian doctrine and as a result their concern for knowledge deteriorated. The function of Sunday Schools, seen as struggling 'from philanthropy into religion', and here termed 'the lost engine', was

Cornwall after undergraduate studies at University College, in default of a Baptist church he joined the Independents, and became their Sunday School superintendent. When in 1853 he moved to London, he joined William Brock's new Bloomsbury Chapel. Alongside his legal and church work, he was a keen geologist, twice serving on the Geological Society Council, one of many pious field scientists who saw their geological hammer as a tool for revealing the awesome nature of the created order.

justified not so much by social need as through intellectual perception of the nature of human responsibility within the created order. By implication this appears to address the old issue of Sunday Schools which were almost independent of the church in terms of their governance and function. By contrast, Pattison asserts, 'The school, the class is church business. The church has the right and the duty of appointing teachers and of requiring an account. The Superintendent should report progress and ask consent and aid at every church meeting.' Beneficiaries should not be confined to the young or the poor, but should be more universal. Too often the children of parents 'of higher social position' were denied Sunday School instruction. 'Miscellaneous notions, picked up from formal attendance on the public worship, supplemented by a few promiscuous remarks heard in the home circle and coloured by the superficial wash of fictitious literature' was no substitute for the consecutive teaching given in Sunday Schools. It was potentially disastrous if intelligent, gifted youngsters moved, uninstructed, into leadership positions, for all stood in need of education. Instructed in the faith they became obligated to share it with others. Thus he argued, 'there is a college of religion wherever there is a church of the living God, a professor wherever there is a living Christian'.

Social divisions within the church could have very dangerous outcomes; responsible for a lamentable lack of interest amongst the middle and upper classes in doctrinal issues, they left such persons vulnerable to ritualism and infidelity. Lack of solid instruction allowed erroneous views of scripture to infiltrate the public intelligence: 'The tendency of modern thought, is not to throw away Scripture but to dilute it.' Another aspect of the same phenomenon was the low regard that divinity was accorded as an academic discipline, with the supposition that it was 'no true science', not 'a province for research, but one crammed with foregone conclusions to be learnt by rote'. Though the modern reader may doubt the role accorded to Sunday Schools, Pattison believed they were capable of changing public consciousness, thus alleviating the anti-religious mind-set of the age.[27]

Turning to my last major commentator, Fabian pamphleteer and leader of radical Baptist thinking, I thought we might in John Clifford encounter a more fundamental critique of the Sunday School movement—but hardly so. Criticism there was, but largely of approaches which smacked too much of the institutional, with a championing of the importance of personal relationships. The church to its shame 'substitutes interest in an institution for sympathy with a soul, gifts to a machine, for loving, yearning effort to redeem the lost'. 'The world cannot be saved by

---

[27] S.R. Pattison, *On the Relation of the Sunday School to the Congregation and the Church* (London: Yates and Alexander/Leicester: Winks & Son, 1869), pp. 1-11.

machines, it must have men', prayerful men of spiritual gifts utterly dedicated to the task. So immediately Clifford focused on the spiritual quality of the teachers.[28] Sunday Schools' highest priority must be effective evangelism. His *The Surest Way of Bringing the Young to Christ: a word to Teachers and Parents*, was first presented to the third annual conference of the Children's Special Service Mission, the forerunners of the Scripture Union, in 1875. To bring the young to Christ was one of the church's most important tasks: 'For this our schools exist; our teachers think and speak, and pray, and our evangelistic band conducts its special services. Sure that the chief need of the child is Christ, that there is no other foundation on which to begin building the character of the youngest.' All else was subsidiary. What Clifford termed 'collateral results'—'apprehension of ideas about Christ...the meaning of His mission, firm intellectual grip of a creed referring to Him, and even well-regulated behaviour'—were no more than that, useful but not essential. The church would have failed in its task 'if the young are not brought into living trust in the Lord Jesus as an actual Saviour, and a personal and loving friend'.[29]

The emphasis was essentially existential. The question was posed, 'What does the phrase bringing a child to Christ mean. Substantially what Andrew did for Simon and Philip for Nathanael—to manage to bring them face to face with Jesus of Nazareth', so the task today was 'to get an interview between the child's spirit and Christ' and then to get them enrolled as learners in the school of discipleship. Do not, he warned, expect finished discipleship in a moment, rather, 'we want a sense of need, a willingness to learn, a distinct choice of Christ as Saviour and Teacher, a ready trust, and a hearty, open, face-to-face talk with him and that is enough. They are brought to Christ.' The task was about establishing interpersonal relations, bringing 'a heart to a heart'. The emphasis was emphatically on *'personal influence through directly personal action.'* 'Why', he asked, 'is the school so much more successful than the pulpit in attaching souls to Christ, but for this reason, that the teacher can deal personally and immediately with each child in his class?' Clifford bore his own testimony: 'I have taught Bible Classes of adults, of young men, and of young women. I have conducted children's service for two years. I have been observant of Sunday schools for a quarter of a century; and I am not more sure of anything than I am of the fact that success in bringing souls to Christ depends, instrumentally

---

[28] J. Clifford, 'The Home, the School and the Church; or Increased Union in Sunday School Work', a paper read to the Second London Convention of Sunday School Teachers at the King's Weigh House Chapel, 10 February 1874, *General Baptist Magazine*, April 1875, pp. 122 and 124-25.

[29] J. Clifford, *The Surest Way of Bringing the Young to Christ: a word to Teachers and Parents* (London: Marlborough?Leicester: Winks & Son, 1875), pp. 3-4.

speaking, more on personal efforts to speak wisely, naturally, directly, and from a full heart, with children and with adults than anything else whatsoever.' Abandoning vague abstractions, agents of the kingdom, engaged with the immediate, the practical, the actual, the conversation individualized to the needs of a particular individual. The teacher was one of Christ's living epistles and therefore they must uphold the highest standards for, 'They [the children] read us.' There was urgent need for teachers to take the initiative and speak to individuals: 'Speak with reality in your tone, with naturalness, with genuine love for souls. Speak as Christ Jesus Himself would, tenderly and lovingly, and you shall not speak in vain.'[30]

Clifford witnessed to the continued widespread expectation that the school would function as the 'stock-ground' or 'nursery' of the church, and to that end much good work was done. 'But the church does not carry the young in its heart'; it exhibited a passion for preaching, a passion for overseas missions, but there was a lack of an 'on-pressing passion' for child evangelism. But lack of unity between church and school, as also between teachers and parents, imperilled the work. Too many parents were indifferent and others 'more effectively counterworking our purposes than the seductions of the streets, and the delusive falsehoods of pernicious literature'. Some parents used Sunday Schools to 'file down to an imperceptible tenuity their sense of responsibility for the religious culture of their children'. Others, meaning well, are so ignorant of what is involved that they 'hinder where they seek to help'. All this underlined the need to educate parents to their responsibilities. The roots of these difficulties were identified as 'false theories as to child piety, a wanting to pluck mature fruit whilst there is not and ought not to be anything but beautiful and delicate blossoms, theological misconceptions of the spirit and range of the gospel of the Lord Jesus'. Beyond this the work was put in jeopardy by a love of luxury, 'the engrossing demands of trade', worship of fashion, though there were perceptible signs of improvement in these matters, with much more co-operation between all involved in recent years.[31]

'We can make able chemists, clever mathematicians, and successful engineers', Clifford challenged, 'but of the art of growing children into Christly men, of educating them in piety, binding them to God...of this we have nearly all to learn.' The method of effective communication for such a task was too little understood. The engagement of parents in the task would hopefully inculcate more confidence in what the school was seeking to achieve. But this would be to no avail unless the church

---

[30] Clifford, *The Surest Way*, pp. 5-7, 8-9, 11-12.

[31] Clifford, 'Home, School and Church', pp. 122-23. The lack of parental co-operation, should be compared with 'atheist and godless parents' who want their children to have 'the guidance of our schools', p. 123.

community itself, under proper pastoral leadership, underwent fundamental change. 'The church must be suited for the reception and nurture of child piety, and should so act as to encourage godly children to expect a place in the church family, and to pass into it by a transition as easy and natural as that by which the fragile bud becomes the expanded flower.' Reform of Sunday Schools necessarily involved reform of church. Because every good church should have a surplus of labour it ought to be able to staff local Ragged and Mission Schools. Taking this strategy further, Clifford advocated combined endeavours to deploy surplus labour by ecumenically sponsoring new Sunday Schools in Board School or other premises. Such undenominational effort was much to be desired because of the demands of the field.[32]

In some senses, then, the story comes full-circle with a renewed appeal for ecumenical action. In between we have observed the inter-relationship of concern for Sunday Schools both as social agents, and their more specialized function in nurturing the church's own young, caring and nurturing a catechumenate. That was to become increasingly problematic, however much denominational leaders sought to play it down. Sunday Schools sought to serve both the church and society, but transfer from school to church for ever showed wastage figures that could not but provoke endless questioning. Whereas at the beginning of the century many Sunday Schools had enjoyed a semi-autonomous existence, all but separate from their sponsoring chapels, that had largely been overcome by the century's end. Alongside the social imperative, the century had started with an equally strong enthusiasm based upon a theology of mind, which often came close to a delight in reason for its own sake, though always arising out of strong convictions as to the implications of the doctrines of creation and incarnation. As the century progressed, commentators became more convinced of the need to feed into their school work concepts of child development which had the impact not of denying but of softening inherited doctrines and the teaching and preaching which arose from it. For Baptists at least, whatever else Sunday Schools might achieve they were expected to be a converting agency and because of that a high premium was put on the development of personal relationships as modelling what the exercise was all about. Whilst the impact of Sunday Schools on secular society has been questioned, there is no denying that they had a profound impact on the nature of the church and its discharge of its basic duties of preaching and teaching.

---

[32] Clifford, 'Home, School and Church', pp. 124, 125-26.

CHAPTER 4

Sunday Schools—A Family Passion

Faith Bowers

We have to record the death of Mr Augustus Benham of Chandos-street and Bromley, Kent, which took place at his residence, Amberley-house, Bromley, on Saturday after only a short attack of pleurisy. Mr Benham was well known in religious and philanthropic circles. His chief interest lay in the promotion of Sunday school work in this country and in continental Europe. For 27 years he was an honorary secretary of the Sunday School Union, to which he rendered signal service by his far-seeing judgement and wise administration, as well as by his personal service in the superintendence of schools. He died in the 58th year of his age, and leaves a widow and seven children.[1]

This announcement makes no mention of Augustus Benham's business (although his firm still functioned at the Chandos-street address)[2]—just his passion for Sunday School work. It was an interest shared with other members of his family, his church and his business partner. Being a good Baptist, I shall begin at the local church and then move to wider Sunday School Union (SSU) circles.

Bloomsbury Chapel and its Sunday Schools[3]

In December 1848 a large new chapel opened in Central London. It was a pious speculation of the railway contractor and MP, Morton Peto. William Brock, a minister of evangelical Calvinist persuasion, who favoured an open communion table, was to preach with a view to gathering a church. The chapel 'was filled from the first'[4] and seven months later a church was formed which would only practise believer's baptism but would welcome into membership professing Christians from other traditions.

---

[1] *The Times*, Tuesday 8 January 1884, pp. 9-10.

[2] The Science Museum has an advertisement for a portable vapour bath manufactured by Benham & Froud about 1890.

[3] For more on the chapel and its schools, see Faith Bowers, *A Bold Experiment: The Story of Bloomsbury Chapel and Bloomsbury Central Baptist Church, 1848–1999* (London: Bloomsbury Central Baptist Church, 1999).

[4] Bloomsbury Chapel Foundation Statement, 25 July 1849.

Of the sixty-two founder members, seven were Benhams. Four brothers, James, Frederic, Augustus and John,[5] and their sisters, Emily and Jane, transferred from the Congregational church at Paddington Chapel. Eliza, James' wife, came from the Baptist church in Prescot Street, Stepney. A third sister, Harriot, was baptized later that year. Subsequently thirteen more Benhams joined the church, and a further three contributed to the church's agencies, including the father, John Lee Benham, who founded the family firm of manufacturing ironmongers.[6]

Being a member of this Bloomsbury church has never been a 'spectator sport' (I speak from nearly fifty years experience), and no time was lost in establishing a range of benevolent, educational and missionary agencies at the chapel and at a mission hall in the dreadful slums nearby. The Benhams spread their interests across these activities, but all took a lively interest in work with the young.

The chapel had a large basement schoolroom for both Day and Sunday Schools. Both took boys and girls. The Sunday School was set up by John Francis,[7] previously superintendent of the New Park Street[8] Sunday School in Southwark and secretary of the South London Auxiliary of the SSU. He set about canvassing the Bloomsbury neighbourhood, recruiting teachers and scholars. The Sunday School opened on 25 March 1849 with twelve boys and seven girls. By October there were 115 boys and seventy-three girls on the books, with an average weekly attendance of 118. They had seventeen teachers, but reported that more 'could be usefully employed'.[9] Classes were small—six to eleven children per teacher (compared with forty-five to sixty-five in the Day School). In May 1850 visitors were recruited to call at absentees' homes and canvass for more scholars, being careful not to draw children away from other local Sunday Schools.[10] The Sunday School was entirely and gladly financed by the church.

---

[5] Another brother, Edward, a printer, had already experienced Brock's ministry in Norwich, and may have encouraged his siblings to try the new chapel.

[6] John Lee Benham & Sons, Ironmongers, Bath Makers, Stove, Grate and Kitchen Range Manufacturers, and Hot Water Engineers, of Wigmore Street (f.1817).

[7] John Francis was the Athenaeum's in-house publisher. He took a leading part in the campaign against 'taxes on knowledge'—stamp duty on newspapers.

[8] The Baptist church with a distinguished past which was soon to call C.H. Spurgeon to London.

[9] Information about the schools comes from the manuscript minutes of the Schools Committee, covering both Day and Sunday Schools for the first four years, and from the annual reports of the Sunday Schools published in the *Bloomsbury Chapel Year Books* 1850–1905, when the church was reconstituted.

[10] Brock recorded, 'We deemed it incumbent on us to avoid all interference with neighbouring Sunday Schools. It was our determination to receive no children who were obtaining religious instruction elsewhere. We communicated our determination to the several superintendents, and assured them that our object was not sectarian competition

Francis himself began the Bible class for older boys but was keen to
devote his energies to the domestic mission, so he soon handed over the
superintendency to Frederic Benham, while Joseph Meen, the Day School
master, took on the Bible class for 'older youths and young men'
(apprenticed by fourteen, they were 'men' early in those days). James
Benham was secretary to the committee which managed both schools for
the first two years. Thereafter half the Sunday School Committee was
chosen by the church and half by the teachers.

Bibles and hymnbooks were sold to scholars, and SSU magazines given
as rewards. The children's charitable offerings, between £50 and £100 per
annum went to missionary work. Teachers held monthly prayer meetings,
while senior classes formed their own prayer circles. A Sunday afternoon
training class for teachers is mentioned in 1868, but may have been long-
standing. In early years the Bloomsbury School arranged internal
examinations quarterly, but later scholars took SSU Scripture
Examinations. The clear link with the SSU is in contrast to the Day
School which held firmly aloof from the British and Foreign Schools
Society (because it accepted government money).

The Bloomsbury Sunday School met at 9.15 a.m. and 2.30 p.m., with
a separate children's service following morning school. At first older
children went to the main service but Brock's preaching was beyond
them, so from 1854 separate children's services were held at the mission
hall, a change remembered as 'very welcome to us scholars' by a former
scholar,[11] who recalled how 'Every Sunday morning the long procession
of scholars left Bloomsbury Chapel doors at about half-past ten... The
scholars walking two by two, and the teachers with their classes passed up
the old Moor Street, with its shops for the sale of birds, second-hand
clothes, and general stores all open. The good order and the generally
attractive appearance of the scholars...helped to fill the school.'

Branch Sunday Schools were established through the domestic
mission. In 1856 the chapel and the mission Sunday Schools each drew
about 400 scholars. Two further schools were opened nearby and
numbers remained high in them all.[12] In 1879 they recorded a total of
1,358 scholar attendances, with ninety already church members. They
were served by 110 teachers. By 1891, when the densely-packed slums

---

but generous co-operation. The rector [of St George's, Bloomsbury] heard of this from his
superintendent, and on the same Sunday evening I received from him a letter expressive of
his warmest sympathy...' C.M. Birrell, *The Life of William Brock D.D.* (London: James
Nisbet, 1878), pp. 181-82.

[11] Frederic Todd, 'Recollections of an old SS Scholar', *Bloomsbury Magazine*,
February 1893.

[12] In 1879 the chapel had 155 scholars in the morning and 400 in the afternoon, the
Moor Street Mission Hall 119 and 443, while a third school in Denmark Street drew 241
in the evening.

had been replaced with 'model' flats, the schools still had 880 scholars, of whom 220 were over fifteen.

The chapel Sunday School probably catered, like the Day School, for children of the 'respectable poor or of small tradespeople', the mission schools would have drawn the poorest children. District visitors helping destitute children often provided basic clothing to make them fit for the local Ragged Schools. The mission Sunday School offered midweek evening classes in the 3Rs (reading, writing and arithmetic), followed by singing. At the chapel singing lessons provided 'innocent recreation', and from 1873 a Wednesday evening meeting for former scholars, with lectures, readings and recitations, provided some ongoing education for youths who went straight to work from elementary education.

The Sunday Schools had their own sick fund, clothing fund and a savings bank where weekly deposits earned 5% interest. There were Christmas parties, summer excursions, and parents' teas. They each had their own lending libraries, with wholesome literature, both religious and of general interest. Attentive children borrowed books as a reward. In 1862 the chapel Sunday School library had 600 books, with half normally out on loan. The teachers had a separate library. (They probably drew on SSU resources for these libraries, but I found no specific reference to this.)

In 1891 the Sunday School introduced a 'further inducement to wholesome reading' in the form of a monthly magazine. Bloomsbury news and local advertisements were bound into the *Silver Link* for two years and then into the *Home Messenger*, which had wider appeal. Readers liked this substantial monthly, full of factual articles and moral stories, and in 1898 it was adopted as the church's first magazine.

A Sunday School festival, inaugurated in October 1877, moved in 1894 to March, 'the proper anniversary time', becoming the 'Ash Wednesday Meeting'. The Sunday School had indeed opened in March. 'Ash Wednesday' became a great reunion day and was taken over for the church anniversary—although the chapel opened in December and the church was formed in July! It is only since 1999 that the church has celebrated its own anniversary date. Both magazine and anniversary indicate how central the school was to the life of the church.

The Benham Family's Contribution

James Benham, the eldest brother, was one of the original five deacons, the first church treasurer, and an infants teacher in the Sunday School. A keen supporter of the Baptist Missionary Society, he helped found the Young Men's Missionary Association and worked for it all his life, and was also an officer of the Baptist Building Fund (1861–85). Meanwhile the family business flourished under his leadership.

Frederic, James' business partner and the Sunday School superintendent, was also secretary of the West London SSU Auxiliary. Emily was secretary of a Ladies' Bible Class. The youngest brother, John, served the Bloomsbury Sunday School for fifty years, as teacher (from 1849), superintendent (1862–70), and then treasurer for twenty years (1879–99).

Augustus taught older boys, and was remembered by Frederic Todd[13] as a painstaking teacher who used SSU lessons and maps and other visual aids, and offered his class occasional prizes for essays. Todd won one for 104 foolscap pages on the 'Life of Christ'. Augustus was first secretary of the Bloomsbury Discussion Class for Young Men, a midweek meeting which grew into the Bloomsbury Young Men's Association with 250 members by 1865. He also served on the committees of the chapel's Domestic Mission and Sick-Poor Relief Society, and was a deacon for two years (1862–64), resigning because he was away too much, but Sunday School work claimed his special attention.

The family firm could not provide for all John Lee Benham's descendants, so Augustus went into a separate business, Benham & Froud, Coppersmiths. The firm was not a great success, although a quick search on the web in 2004 shows that the products—candlesticks, kettles, etc—still appear in antique shops and auctions (e.g., a jelly mould priced at £235).

Bloomsbury and the SSU

The Bloomsbury Sunday Schools belonged to the West London Auxiliary of the SSU. SSU records[14] are patchy for the relevant period, but by 1851 (two years into the life of the Bloomsbury school) both Frederic and Augustus Benham were West London representatives on the SSU General Committee. Augustus was then aged twenty-five. By 1854 they were joined by fellow church member, the Day School master, Joseph Austen Meen, as an elected member of the General Committee. It is hardly surprising that, when the SSU arranged a mass canvass of London in 1856, 118 Bloomsbury people were involved. That year the West London auxiliary acquired a new finance secretary, the young William Brock, elder son of the Bloomsbury minister.

The General Committee was large—apart from the chairman, treasurer, and four joint secretaries, there were twenty appointed members, plus four from each of the four London regions. So up to forty-two men met monthly, with occasional extra meetings. A minimum of six attendances

---

[13] 'Recollections of an old SS Scholar', *Bloomsbury Magazine*, February 1893.

[14] The surviving minutes and annual reports are in the University of Birmingham Library Special Collections. My thanks are due to the archivist, Philippa Basset, and her staff for access to these.

in the year was required of members, and five constituted a sufficient quorum, but attendance was generally high. Among other business the General Committee was required to pass all bills before payment.

Originally the SSU served schools within five miles of the General Post Office, organized into four London regions. By 1854 there were seventy-two country unions across England and Scotland, and work was spreading across continental Europe and through the British Empire. Personal subscribers that year included Morton Peto and Frederic Benham from Bloomsbury, and three other Benhams—Mrs and Miss Benham (perhaps aunts), and D. Benham Esq of Burton Crescent.[15] This must be Daniel Benham, probably the elder brother of John Lee and uncle of Augustus. He appears to be the family's first SSU enthusiast. He presumably inherited his father's tin-plating and ironmongery business in the City, and was a man of some means, who could subscribe £100 (by 1860) when ten guineas was the 'going rate' for a life subscription and £100 equalled Mr Meen's annual pay as Bloomsbury day-school master. The SSU had published in 1839 a 104-page book by Daniel, listed in 1854 as 'Benham's Hints on Self-Education', price 3d.

The West London Auxiliary drew up petitions in 1854 against the proposed opening of the Crystal Palace on Sundays and asked Morton Peto to present these in the House of Commons. Four years later the SSU report noted that this peril had been averted—for the present. Another issue of Sunday observance prompted SSU protest in 1874—against the Sunday opening of museums. Both proposals were likely to tempt away young scholars.

In 1855 Augustus was unanimously voted on to the General Committee, serving until his death twenty-seven years later. Judging from the minutes, extant from 15 May 1874 to 26 April 1878, Augustus was assiduous in attendance. In 1874–75 he was at all twelve monthly meetings, though not at two extra meetings, probably arranged at short notice. In 1875–76 he attended all twelve, as did four more of the twenty-five committee members. In 1876–77 he managed fourteen General Committee meetings, and in 1877–78 eleven, plus one extra meeting.

In 1855 the committee chose the design for their new Jubilee Building at the Old Bailey. The winning architect was Charles Gray Searle, who transferred with his wife Kate from the King's Weigh House to Bloomsbury in 1857. Mr Searle ran a successful Young Men's Bible Class: in 1863 forty-five regularly squeezed into the north vestry, a room measuring only 5.4 x 3.2 metres. The next year Searle reported that sixteen of these young men had become church members, eight had left to teach in the Sunday Schools, and two to become district visitors; the

---

[15] Efforts to find additional confirmation for the suppositions which follow have been unsuccessful.

rest took turns to distribute tracts. Vacated places were quickly filled. The
class also met on Friday evenings for prayer and mutual instruction, and
had its own library. In 1865 they left the vestry for a larger room in Red
Lion Square, growing to 128 in 1866, of whom sixty were church
members. Meanwhile Mrs Searle ran a class for young women in their
home. The SSU's chosen architect was clearly attuned to Christian
education. The 1857 annual report is missing, but by 1858 Augustus was
one of the four SSU honorary secretaries. Life subscribers now included
Frederic (£20), Augustus (£25), and their father, John Lee Benham (£21),
while the youngest of the brothers, John, was making an annual
subscription (£1-1s-0d).

Joseph Meen lectured for the SSU and was on the teacher-training
team. In 1860 the SSU published Meen's illustrated *Historical and
Descriptive Geography of Palestine* at 2s clothbound. This was to prove a
'bestseller'. Joseph Meen was an innovative schoolmaster at a time when
the Normal Schools were beginning to develop teacher training. While
still working with monitors and training pupil teachers in the Bloomsbury
Day School, he sent some, including his daughter, to train at the Borough
Normal School. I was fascinated to find him as a respected colleague of
the Benhams in the SSU context: at Bloomsbury he was by then at odds
with the Day School's management committee and his premature death
came there as something of a relief. While James Benham was secretary of
the school committee, relationships with Meen were good—the forward-
thinking Benhams were probably more sympathetic to the teacher
ambitious for his pupils than some other Bloomsbury laymen. Later
committee members suspected that Meen was giving these 'respectable
poor' children ideas beyond their station. Bones of contention were
teaching girls *fine* needlework (*plain* was sufficient for their station in
life) and teaching chemistry to older boys. Science education was very
new at that time. In fact, Meen's syllabus in the 1850s compares
favourably with the 1890 requirements for Standard IV, the top level of
elementary education. In 1855 the committee minutes complained that

> The higher branches of Education were pushed too far, whilst too little attention
> was given to needlework, and domestic matters in general. But, it was thought, so
> long as the Evangelical Principles were so well taught as they had been, and Mr
> Meen continued Master, no change could well be made.

The SSU seems to have been more appreciative of his enthusiasm for
education. As well as the *Geography of Palestine*, soon available for 1s 6d
clothbound or gilt-edged at two shillings, Meen edited the *Bible Treasury*,
with a circulation of 7,000 per month. The 1863 SSU report mentions
another of his works, *Power and Privilege*, surprisingly described as 'a
New Yorker's address to the Parents of Sunday Scholars'. That year, at
special youth meetings on Tuesday, 16 April, Meen, ever interested in

science, 'much interested the young people by experiments on the air-pump and voltaic battery, with explanatory observations'. Two days later he was taken ill and died the following Wednesday. The SSU records this with genuine sorrow.

In 1860 the SSU made constitutional changes. Five miles from the General Post Office no longer covered the growing capital, so the Union would accept all schools associated with the metropolitan auxiliaries, which could now send to the General Committee one representative for every 500 teachers: both West and East qualified for five, North three, and South four.

At a West London teachers' conference on 7 February 1860 Joseph W. Froud gave a paper 'On the use of illustration in Sunday School teaching'. This was Augustus' business partner.[16] The next year Froud joined Frederic and Augustus Benham on the West London Committee, which now covered 115 Sunday Schools, with fifteen district and branch secretaries and fourteen visitors (but, alas, no figures for teachers or scholars). Frederic came off the General Committee in 1863, but remained active on the local committees. In 1870 Joseph Froud joined the General Committee.

By 1871 another Bloomsbury member had been roped in to train Sunday School teachers. Benjamin Pask gave a preparatory class that year on 'The Unforgiving Servant' as part of the training class programme. In 1874 he gave a demonstration infants' lesson, and the next year ran summer classes for teachers on Sunday mornings at the Jubilee Building on constructing lessons and methods of training. By 1877 Pask represented West London on the General Committee and the next year was president of the SSU Normal Class. New publications included, among the 'Tracts for Teachers', his *Christian Bands; or Young Christian Associations, their Object and Work*, price 2d. In spite of Pask's advocacy, Bloomsbury did not form a Christian Band until 1885, when it was described as a link between Sunday School and church, to encourage those 'seeking the Saviour but not yet wholly yielded'. (One of the commitments undertaken by this Bloomsbury Christian Band was the

---

[16] *Post Office London Street Directory*, 1861, commercial section, has entry 'Froud, Joseph William, coppersmith: see Benhams & Froud'. The entry for Benhams & Froud lists them at 40-42 Chandos Street, Charing Cross. This confirms that this was Augustus' business partner. At this date it was Benhams in the plural because the youngest brother, John, was also involved in this business, but later he joined his elder brothers in the flourishing Benham & Sons. Benhams & Froud are described as 'copper & platina smiths, braziers, brass manufacturers, zinc workers, bath & jelly mould makers, copper & zinc casement, lantern, skylight & sash makers, copper & zinc roof layers & weather vane makers'. Entries for other years are similar.

provision of flowers for the communion table on Sundays, 'a beautiful innovation'.[17])

The West London Auxiliary report for 1877–78 shows Pask and James Benham on the regional committee, while Walter Benham, James' younger son, was the honorary secretary for minutes and one of two Central Branch secretaries. Pask was an examiner for the regional Senior Scholars' Scripture Examination, and Walter Benham for the Middle Division. Frederic Benham, now in Bloomsbury's sister church at Regent's Park Chapel, had left the committee but was a trustee of the Jubilee Fund. West London now had 149 schools, with 3,021 teachers and 35,064 scholars. Of these, 25% were infants, and 15% over fifteen, while nearly 1,500 scholars were already church members. The West London Committee had set up a new mission school on undenominational lines in Tower Street, Seven Dials—virtually on Bloomsbury's 'patch' but presumably with the chapel's approval, for James and Walter Benham both subscribed to it and Walter Benham and Benjamin Pask were on the managing committee. By 1877 Daniel Benham had died, but there is a new name among the North London representatives on the SSU General Committee, Mr T. Benham of Blackfriars. He may have been Daniel's son—perhaps a cousin of Augustus.

Benjamin Pask died on 8 February 1878. Although only on the General Committee for three years, he had long been active for the SSU, had served on the Publications and Visitation Committees and been president of successive Normal Classes. The SSU paid his widow £60 for the stock and copyright of his book, and issued photographs of him at 6d, presumably as a fundraiser.

The Joint Secretaries and SSU Activities

The 1870 annual report shows how the four honorary SSU secretaries divided the work between them. William Groser, who was also the editor of the *Baptist Magazine* and secretary of the Baptist Irish Society, was responsible for minutes and correspondence. Fountain J. Hartley kept the statistics. John E. Tresidder looked after visitation. Augustus Benham took care of trade and finance. All four were among the SSU trustees. They evidently had a paid secretary, for in October 1874 Mr Gilbert's salary was raised to £150 and he was allowed ten shillings a week for a boy to assist in the secretaries' department.

The four worked hard. In 1872, for example, there were eighteen General Committee meetings, and 544 sub-committee meetings. Each secretary looked after several sub-committees. The minutes for 15 May 1874 list twelve of these: Continental, Exhibition, Library, Local

---

[17] *Bloomsbury Magazine*, February 1899.

Examinations, Publications, Extension, Finance, House, Lectures, Trade, Training Class, and Visitation. More were added during the year: Sunday Vigilance, Building, Senior Entertainments. The next year they even set up a Daily Prayer Sub-Committee. The chairman and four secretaries were *ex officio* members of them all. Other committee members could evidently choose their interests, for sub-committee numbers range from four for the House Sub-Committee to seventeen for Publications.

According to the SSU obituary note, Augustus served on the Business, Centenary Celebration and Continental Mission committees. He must also have been involved with those on Publications, Trade, Building and probably House. One is left wondering how he found any time to run his own business. If Froud was also giving considerable time to SSU committees, it is not surprising if their firm failed to flourish!

The General Committee minutes for 1874–78, including reports from the sub-committees, show the range of activities, including those for which Augustus Benham took responsibility. An idea of the size of operation is given by the need for 1,500 copies of the 1874 annual report.[18] Although the officers and committee members were among 'the great unpaid',[19] the SSU employed at least thirty-eight people, listed in the minutes of 18 May 1878 (and including neither the secretaries' department nor housekeeping staff). Most of those listed related to areas for which Augustus was responsible. Publications required a superintendent, two assistants, a messenger, and a man in charge of woodcuts. The trade manager, who was paid £350, supervised thirty-two staff[20] in the counting house, front shop, saloon, and departments dealing with the *Chronicle*, wholesale and export trade, the country unions, the warehouse, packing and advertising.

The SSU's fourth object was 'to supply the books and stationery suited for Sunday schools at reduced prices'. The Trade Sub-Committee oversaw the production and sale of books, magazines, leaflets, etc, involving approval of books, negotiating with authors, copyright matters, purchase of paper, printing, sales, and keeping accounts. There was a considerable turnover, largely on small, low-priced items. In 1872, for example, sixty new publications were issued and the year's sales amounted to almost £31,000 (£30,984-5s-11d).

In June 1874 the Trade report included plans for a double-sized Christmas issue of *Kind Words* to be sold at 6d, efforts to increase trade

---

[18] 1,350 for the country unions, auxiliaries and subscribers, and 150 to bind with the auxiliary reports of the four London auxiliaries.

[19] Committee Minutes for 21 August 1874.

[20] Counting house: cashier (£200), ledger clerk (£130), + 3; front shop and saloon: head of department (£150), 3 salesmen, 2 assistants; wholesale and *Chronicle* department: 3 staff; export 2; country department: 6; warehouse and packing: 8; advertisements: 2.

with America, tenders for paper, an increase of fire insurance on stock to £2,000, and the purchase (£10) of the plates and copyright of *The Youth's Key to the Bible* by the Revd Thomas Timpson. Other business that year included dealing with Sankey over an alleged breach of copyright, printing tenders, negotiating an author's contract, approving books and the *Sunday Portfolio*—twelve large coloured prints and 'explanatory letterpress' for 7s 6d. They received from Switzerland 500 sets of eighteen coloured prints of Scripture subjects, to be sold in packets of six for one shilling. They had had printed 20,000 copies of the SSU *Pronouncing Dictionary of Scripture Proper Names*, 10,000 for direct sale, while 5,000 were bound with a Bible, references and index, map and six pictures for six shillings. Recent prize essays had been printed for sale. In May 1874 alone new SSU publications included elementary lesson papers, infant class texts, pictorial lesson papers, pocket lesson books, magazines, and one book (not named).

On 23 October 1874 they launched the *Sunday School Chronicle*, superseding the older monthly circulars. The new, sixteen-page monthly had a print run of 100,000, and was supplied in bulk orders at a halfpence per copy. The editor, Benjamin Clarke, needed an assistant (30s per week), and the shop an extra sales assistant. In January 1875 a grim note reports a hiccup in delivery of the *Chronicle* because a boy's arm had been drawn in and had broken the machine (there is no comment on the poor boy's condition). In February they decided the annual convention issue should be offered in bulk at half price to local unions for free distribution. They produced a cover at two shillings, presumably to bind successive issues together. In April they arranged to post bills advertising the paper at Metropolitan railway stations.

The Trade Sub-Committee arranged in 1874 for an SSU display at the Sanitary and Educational Exhibition in Glasgow, but decided the next year to forgo the Industrial Exhibition at Leighton Buzzard. Trade also negotiated the contract for an extension to the Old Bailey building, and purchased furniture for this and arranged gas fittings, shelving, safes, etc. A nightwatchman was employed until the building was secure. The new building opened on 3 March 1875. Meanwhile the Finance Committee sold the remaining lease of the Paternoster Row premises to the Religious Tract Society for £4,145, arranged a building loan, and chased up subscriptions. In November 1874 they decided to urge associated churches to take an annual congregational collection for the SSU, sending a circular about this, with a 'moderate-sized' catalogue of publications.[21] Some churches proved willing; others said they already had too many collections. Finance also decided to supply a copy of all

---

[21] The catalogue decision was added in January 1875.

publications to committee members with a view to promotion: so had to buy pigeonholes for all the committee members.

The 1875 minutes include details of the annual accounts Augustus Benham presented to the General Committee. A total income of £5,268 was comfortably over the expenditure of £4,060. The income included £2,350 trade profit, plus overseas sales, subscriptions and donations. The high proportion of sales income made the Union less reliant on voluntary giving than many other church organizations. Expenditure included £600 spent on providing libraries and £700 in grants to European partners.[22]

The SSU library, in the headquarters building, primarily served London. In November 1874 there were 1,251 subscribers (comprising 664 male teachers, 278 female teachers, 234 boy scholars, and seventy-five girls). The librarian's salary was raised by £10 to £85 p.a. on completion of a year's service (September 1874). There were separate reading rooms for the sexes, and in 1875 they decided to allow senior scholars (fifteen plus) to use these. Teachers from provincial unions might use the Reading Room at 2s 6d for five years. There was a lending library—and overdue fines contributed to the funds. A museum contained objects to help teachers, like the model of the Tabernacle which they decided to renovate (November 1874). The Library Sub-Committee vetted all new books. After stocktaking during the summer closure they decided which books to replace or rebind.

The SSU also provided subsidized libraries for local Sunday Schools. The data is incomplete but each library appears to have cost between £4 and £5. In 1874 they provided 471 libraries for scholars, plus 233 for teachers. Schools evidently paid about three-quarters of the cost, since the year's outlay was only £604. These libraries, especially for the teachers, must have included SSU publications, but the size of the business also enabled the Union to make favourable deals with other publishers: for example, in February 1875 they agreed to sell Cassell's *Child's Bible*.

Continental work, for which donations were expressly received, appears to have related chiefly to publications. In 1874 work is mentioned in

---

[22] 30 April 1875 at a special committee meeting before the annual members' meeting. Receipts included: trade profit to 31 March of £2,347-10-2; annual collection, Exeter Hall, subs and donations—£1,149-17-5; rent of rooms £15; Continental/America &c £2,251-3-4; Gadsby's collection £4. Total income £5,767-10-11, which was reduced by £500 transferred to capital in the published accounts. Balance in hand £1,207-18-1. Payments: expenses—visitation, senior scholars' meetings, training class, introductory class, annual and other meetings, printing reports, circulars, advertising, postage, stationery, repairs, gas, coals, insurance, salaries (£199-13-0); cost of lending libraries (471 + 233 teachers' libraries) less the payments towards them (£603-17-8); reading room expenses less subs and fines (£115); publications, book grants, school extension (24—£185); cash grants to France, Belgium and Spain, Germany, Italy, Switzerland, Holland, Sweden and Hungary (£690-10-3). Total £4,059-12-10.

France, Switzerland, Italy and Belgium. All these appear the next year, and also Spain, Germany, Holland, Sweden and Hungary. Visitation appears to have been a form of inspection. In 1873–74 this sub-committee reported on five schools visited, in Ipswich, Great Marlow, Rochester, Bromsgrove and the Isle of Wight. Yet the following October they reported on fourteen more—probably these were in or near London. The Visitation Sub-Committee also made arrangements for the annual May conference and other meetings—in 1874 a public meeting against the 'sale of intoxicating liquor on Sundays', and the Universal Day of Prayer for Sunday Schools (25-26 October). They recommended a three-day convention of teachers (6-8 February 1875 at the Weigh House Chapel), and organized the General Committee's annual excursion—that year by water from Hampton Court to Weybridge. The Extension Sub-Committee made grants to help extend Sunday School buildings. Thus in May 1874 four grants were made of £7 or £10, and a further three in June.

Local examinations covered both the scholars' and teachers' examinations. Teachers were examined on Scripture, history and doctrine; on evidences of Christianity; and on the principles and art of teaching. In 1874 an extra examination was offered on 'The Content and Interpretation of Scripture', for which the textbook was S.G. Green's *Written Word*.[23] Ministers were paid five to ten guineas as examiners. In 1875 the committee reported that 900 teachers had entered these examinations. Pass rates on the various sections were around 85%, with about 20% getting distinctions.[24]

Considerable effort went into teacher training. The full range of classes is not clear, but a third introductory class was introduced in June 1874, and presumably there were more advanced classes. A Tonic Solfa Class was mentioned when a teacher left and a replacement was needed. Although the committee members were all men, there were plenty of women teachers, and women wrote texts and gave demonstration lessons. Model lessons at this period drew 80-100—'even in the rain'. In 1874 a

---

[23] See J.H.Y. Briggs, 'The Baptist Contribution to the Sunday School Movement in the Nineteenth Century', pp. 47-49 above.

[24] Thus in 1874 the Scholars Advanced Examination in October was on 'The Life and Ministry of Christ, as recorded in Gospel of St Mark', examined by the Revd Edward Medley, BA, tutor of Regent's Park College, and W.G. Lemon, LLB. For the Teachers' Local Examinations in March 1875 the subject for Scripture, history and doctrine was 'The Books of Joshua and Judges', with 'Murby's Manual' as textbook, and a map. For evidences of Christianity they studied Archdeacon Paley's 'Christian Evidences'. For principles and art of teaching, Groser's 'Our Work' and 'Ready for Work', and Cooper's 'Principles and Art of Teaching'. The Extra subject was examined by the Revd Dr Henry Allon, of Union Chapel, Islington. I have been unable to find out more about W.G. Lemon.

conference 'On Morning Schools' was attended by 140 superintendents and secretaries of local Sunday Schools.

In addition to the central activities, lecturers went out to churches, sometimes with a *panorama* to illustrate their talk. The latter were popular—there were 125 panorama bookings in 1875. The SSU offered at least two—one on Ireland and a new one on America. An older panorama, 'Up the Rhine to Italy', had evidently done the rounds and was sold to the Auckland SSU in New Zealand.

Through the winter months the SSU ran a series of senior scholars' entertainments for over-fifteens. These were always packed out. Concerts and musical evenings with lectures alternated with lectures, and with readings and impromptu speeches. Some lectures were illustrated, for example, one with 'dissolving views' of Egypt; some involved scientific demonstrations. Thus Mr Pask gave a demonstration lecture on 'Spectrum Analysis', which was then being developed into practical use. Readings were evidently chosen by scholars—the sub-committee decided they must have good notice of these to check their suitability.

Other committee activities included repeated but vain attempts to obtain the use of Board Schools on Sundays, and equally vain attempts to get Moody and Sankey to address a great meeting of Sunday School teachers. An annual subscription (five guineas) to the Palestine Exploration Fund indicates the Union's interest in new knowledge relevant to the Scriptures. Correspondents in August 1874 included 'Mr Thos. Cook, the Excursionist'—but no details were given.[25]

As with other Free Church bodies, the May meetings at Exeter Hall were a highlight of the year. In 1875, the SSU's took place on 5-6 May, when well over 7,000 were expected to attend, including 100 ministers. 5,050 tickets for the sermon were issued to senior scholars. Three conference sessions considered 'How to reach the Young Men and Women who have left our Sunday Schools', 'How may Country Unions be made more efficient and useful?' and 'The present Religious Awakening and its lessons to Sunday School Teachers'. There were specimen lessons—'To an Infant Class', 'To a Scripture Class' and a 'Blackboard Review'—sessions for prayer and praise, and one on 'Hymns and Tunes for Sunday Schools'. During these meetings 500-600 meals were provided at the SSU house.

Moving forward a few years, *The Times* for Wednesday, 21 January 1880, records that 'an influential deputation' from the SSU and the Church of England Sunday School Institute and other kindred bodies had waited on the Lord Mayor, seeking the use of the Egyptian Hall of

---

[25] Thomas Cook, a General Baptist from Leicester, started his career as a travel agent by organizing a temperance excursion. See *ODNB*.

Mansion House on 28 June next for their centenary celebrations.[26] This was granted, and they were offered the Guildhall too. A week later a letter[27] in *The Times* from Augustus Benham set out the arrangements for the week 27 June–4 July 1880. Various activities across the United Kingdom and the colonies included a service in Westminster Abbey and the Mansion House meeting.

Augustus died after a short illness in 1884. The SSU annual report carried a lengthy appreciation, part of which reads:

> During this long period...his clearness of judgment, his wisdom in Council, and his energy in action, have only been equalled by the genial loving spirit which he has uniformly displayed and which has endeared him to all with whom he has been brought into contact... The universal respect in which Mr Benham was held was testified by the kindly references made to his decease in the daily journals and the religious press, and this respect was abundantly manifested by the large numbers who attended the funeral...

His three brothers and nephew continued to support the SSU to which Augustus had been so devoted.

Appendix

The Sunday School Union

The Sunday School Union was founded in London in 1803. The objects were

> 1. To stimulate and encourage Sunday School teachers, at home and abroad, to greater exertions in the promotion of religious education.
> 2. By mutual communication, to improve the methods of instruction.
> 3. To ascertain those situations where Sunday Schools are most wanted, and promote their establishment.
> 4. To supply the books and stationery suited for Sunday Schools at reduced prices.
> In carrying these objects into effect, this Society shall not in any way interfere with the private concerns of Sunday Schools.

The Union was to consist of the ministers and teachers of Sunday Schools 'within a circle of five miles from the General Post Office' who have subscribed during the previous year not less than 4s per annum to either of the four auxiliary unions or their branches, together with subscribers of 10s 6d to the Union. Subscribers could have books at a reduced rate. £10-10s would secure a life subscription. The annual meeting in May

---

[26] *The Times*, Wednesday, 21 January 1880, p. 8a.
[27] *The Times*, 28 January 1880, pp. 10-11.

would elect the committee and officers. The General Committee had to pass all bills for payment. No-one supplying trade articles to the Union could serve on the committee. A further regulation decreed that all committee meetings would open and close with prayer.

Although this was a London Society they envisaged from the outset that country SSUs might also subscribe and report annually and would then qualify for Union books at the cheap rate. In 1824 a resolution was passed only to accept auxiliary and country unions if conducted by people 'of orderly character...who hold the doctrines of the Deity and atonement of Jesus Christ, the Divine influences of the Holy Spirit', and that 'all Scripture is given by inspiration of God'. By 1854 there were seventy-two country unions across England and Scotland, and the work was spreading on continental Europe and across the British Empire.

CHAPTER 5

The Significance of Baby Babble:
P.T. Forsyth's *Pulpit Parables* and their Context[1]

Clyde Binfield

I

What might baby babble have to say about the development of a great theologian? And what might that theologian's use of baby babble suggest about the children (of all ages) to whom he ministered? When that theologian is P.T. Forsyth there is some point to such questions. For historians much of Forsyth's fascination is a matter of context. To earth the man is to understand him more and to appreciate his continuing significance more fully. This paper earths him at the point at which his first book appeared. Children are at the heart of it.

That book, or rather the half that he wrote, since a fellow minister wrote the rest, offers as unlikely an insight to the Forsyth of posterity as it offers a representative insight of Forsyth the Victorian minister. Forsyth's standing for us is as a twentieth-century theologian who has retained his excitement for twenty-first century readers. Although he became a man to mark in the 1890s, the books by which his reputation lives were written in the last twenty years of his life; but to package him as a twentieth-century theologian will hardly do. It is too restrictive. Forsyth's theology was distilled in two-sevenths of his life-span. The preceding five-sevenths were passed in the preceding century. This twentieth-century theologian was a nineteenth-century man. His intellectual prime was Edwardian; his cultural and political formation was Victorian.

There are other contrasts, indeed contradictions. This theologian, whose work proved foundational for readers formed in the century of total war, wrote some of his least satisfactory work under the pressure of war. He wrote it, moreover, in a college principal's study. His theology is

---

[1] The genesis of this paper lay in what was delivered as the Shergold Lecture (primarily for Lay Preachers within the Congregational Federation), at Narborough Congregational Church, Leicstershire, 10 June 2000. I am indebted to Dr Williams's Library, which holds a collection of Forsyth-related material, largely deposited by his daughter, Mrs. Jessie Forsyth Andrews.

in that sense academic. Yet rigorous and profound though this academic's mind was, his published work remains curiously undisciplined. He hides nothing but he is not a man for precise references or copious footnotes. His books began as lectures. Theirs is the stimulus of the spoken word, nuanced by paradox and artful ambiguity. They convey the lecture room's privileged immediacy, minds gathered unevenly to pursue a common quest, fireworks in a fog for some, light at the day's end for others.

Perhaps they are closer to sermons and here we are closer to earthing their author. This college principal had been in pastoral charge of five distinctive churches for twenty-five years before he became responsible for training the ministers of such churches. I have used the word 'church' rather than 'congregation' because Forsyth's churchmanship was Congregationalist. The congregations over which he ministered and for which he then trained ministers were duly constituted churches. This was the context for his own developing sense of the Church.

Here the ambiguities compound the contradictions. Congregationalists stood in the orthodox, Reformed, Protestant tradition. They were trinitarian and evangelical. They were also widely and increasingly regarded as having placed themselves at the liberal-most edge of evangelicalism. Forsyth's first two churches were at that edge and Forsyth looked over it with them. He had left college in circumstances which could not easily be squared with sound order.[2] For ten years he figured in no official denominational handbook. His ordination was not recorded in the national *Congregational Year Book* although the service was fully reported in the local press and his college principal, a nationally known London minister, and the minister of the largest and oldest neighbouring church, all took prominent parts.[3] Neither Forsyth nor his first church was affiliated to the Yorkshire Congregational Union and neither he nor his second church was affiliated to the London Congregational Union until he joined that Union and the London Congregational Board in 1884, a year before leaving London for Manchester. This young minister was apparently a loose denominationalist and that sort of looseness frequently

---

[2] Forsyth Papers, Dr Williams's Library London (hereafter FPDWL): 'New College London: Extract from 386 Council Meeting at the College, October 1st 1874'.

[3] FPDWL: Leaflet about the Public Reception of P.T. Forsyth at Shipley Congregational Church, 19 and 23 November 1876. Ordination statement, *Shipley and Saltaire Times*, 25 November 1876; note confirms participation by Revds J. Baldwin Brown, J. Robertson Campbell, and Samuel Newth in envelope marked firmly in ink, 'Ordination' (although they use the word 'recognition'), and dated 23 November 1876. Arguably the ordination/recognition occurred too late for insertion in the 1877 *Congregational Year Book*; even so Forsyth's first *Year Book* mention is 1885, and his Shipley church is steadily returned as vacant.

signified extreme views. In the 1870s and 1880s extreme views among Congregationalists were more likely to be liberal than conservative.

Yet we know the end of this particular story. Forsyth's continuing influence is a conservative influence. It is strongest among evangelical Protestants; but it is arguably so because this pronounced liberal altered direction, not to return to some original evangelicalism so much as to retune the evangelical motor of an historic and therefore catholic faith whose defining tones were bound for him to be both Protestant and Congregational. He did not renounce his past. He subsumed it. Indeed, it was not so much past as formation. This paper, therefore, has three strands. One is Forsyth's evangelicalism, and therefore by implication his liberalism. A second is the role of youth in his life as pastor, principal, and man. A third is the light shed by his first book, which was a volume of children's addresses.

II

It has been conventionally assumed that Forsyth's evangelicalism became clear (the word 'conversion' is often used) during his fifth, Cambridge, pastorate 1894–1901. That was the point at which Forsyth was marked out for higher things and, insofar as it was possible for a Congregational minister, was being groomed for them. It was the point at which his change of direction was publicly avowed on a national denominational stage.[4] His previous churches in Shipley, Hackney, Manchester, and Leicester, could all be regarded as theologically liberal. The ministers called by those churches, or invited by them to preach with a view, suggest that. So does what is known of their network of leading members.[5] Yet there is persuasive evidence that Forsyth's 'conversion', to use the convenient shorthand, developed during three of those pastorates. Leslie McCurdy, most investigative of current Forsythians, places it

---

[4] For two comprehensive studies of Forsyth see W.L. Bradley, *P.T. Forsyth: The Man and His Work* (London: Independent Press, 1952); T. Hart (ed.), *Justice the True and Only Mercy: Essays on the Life and Theology of Peter Taylor Forsyth* (Edinburgh: T&T Clark, 1995) (this contains an invaluable bibliography). For Forsyth as pastor see C. Binfield, 'P.T. Forsyth as Congregational Minister', in Hart (ed.), *Justice*, pp. 168-96; for Forsyth as principal see C. Binfield, 'Peter Taylor Forsyth: Pastor as Principal', in A.P.F. Sell (ed.), *P.T. Forsyth: Theologian for a New Millennium* (London: The United Reformed Church, 2000), pp. 7-40.

[5] See Binfield, 'P.T. Forsyth as Congregational Minister'. See also C. Binfield 'An East Midland Call: Its Context and Some Consequences: The Genesis of Clarendon Park Congregational Church', *Transactions, The Leicestershire Archaeological and Historical Society* 79 (2005), pp. 108-27..

between 1884 and 1891.[6] Those dates are denominationally significant. In 1884 Forsyth joined the London Congregational Union and Board and in 1891 he became Chairman of the Leicestershire Congregational Union, publishing his chairman's address under the suggestive and integrative title, *The Old Faith and the New.*[7] What was crystallized in Leicester began in Hackney. This suggests a cumulative process which might encourage the historian to feel that when considering Forsyth's reinterpreted evangelicalism due emphasis should be placed on the continuing liberal components of that reinterpretation. Those components are more cultural than theological but in the context of a vigorous, sensitive, authoritative, pastoral ministry (contrasting qualities which deserve equal weight) they become important.

It is here that youth and Forsyth came to the fore. Forsyth's first two books were published in these crucible years and they could not have been more 'cultural'. The more important of the two, speaks for itself: *Religion in Recent Art: Being Expository Lectures on Rossetti, Burne Jones, Watts, Holman Hunt and Wagner* (Manchester and London, 1889). It was published while he was minister at Clarendon Park, Leicester, but it was primarily the product of his ministry at Cheetham Hill, Manchester. The other book, however, has its own significance although its title does not speak quite so plainly: *Pulpit Parables for Young Hearers* (Manchester and London, undated but 1886). It was published, therefore, while Forsyth was at Cheetham Hill but it was primarily the product of his ministry at St Thomas's Square, Hackney. This is the book on which this paper will concentrate, but first there has to be some more earthing.

No Congregational minister and certainly none of Forsyth's contemporaries would have dared ignore his 'Young Hearers'. Forsyth did not. One of his first published pieces, *'Maid, Arise': A Sermon to School Girls*, was preached in Shipley Congregational Church, Sunday 18 July 1878, and one of his last addresses as a minister in pastoral charge was a contribution late in 1900 to a 'Symposium on the Alleged Decline in Sunday School Attendance'.[8] In 1887, while still at Cheetham Hill, he contributed to the *Christian World Pulpit* on 'Sunday Schools and

---

[6] L. McCurdy, *Attributes and Atonement: The Holy Love of God in the Theology of P.T. Forsyth*, (Carlisle: Paternoster Press, 1999), especially pp. 26-38.

[7] Bradley, *Forsyth*, pp. 36, 43; McCurdy, *Attributes*, pp. 14-15, 31-3; *Congregational Year Book*, 1885, p. 247; 1892, p. 307, which lists him as *Deputy* Chairman of the Leicestershire Union.

[8] P.T. Forsyth, *'Maid, Arise': A Sermon to School Girls, Preached in Shipley Congregational Church, Sunday 28 July 1878* (Bradford: T. Brear, n.d. [1878]); P.T. Forsyth, 'As to the Causes of Decline', in 'The School at the End of the Century: A Symposium on the Alleged Decline in Sunday School Attendance: Some Opinions and Suggestions', *Sunday School Chronicle*, 13 December 1900, p. 850.

Modern Theology', and in May 1913 he wrote to the *British Weekly* about 'The Church and the Children'.[9] A year later, in June 1914, he was at Stockwell College, where teachers were trained by the British and Foreign School Society, for its valedictory day. He had come, as the meeting's chairman put it, 'to say words to those girls who were going out of the College'. Such things were expected of ministers and the problems which Forsyth's words addressed were perennial: faltering attendances at Sunday School; facts preferred to interpretation, the letter preferred to the spirit, at Sunday School. Even then teachers were underpaid and over-inspected. Few of Forsyth's words, however, were ever quite as their hearers expected and perhaps never quite as they remembered. Even so, each word told. Here was a principal who remained a pastor, who retained a keen sense of the place of children and young people in their own right in the Christian commonwealth. Here, moreover, was a principal who was always careful to distinguish between boys and girls, young men and young women. That may be no more surprising than the fact that his careful differentiation can come too close to stereotype for the comfort of later sensitivities, but in its day it was judiciously subversive and in June 1914, on the eve of the Great War, Forsyth enlisted Stockwell's women teachers-in-embryo into the Christian commonwealth, 'the growing up of each individual member of society into a holy temple of the Lord; an ideal society, a true brotherhood of mankind, the kingdom of the new humanity, which is the Kingdom of God'.[10] Is there anything in those words which might not be dismissed as rank utopian liberalism, even socialism, rather than true congregationalism? Yet how else might he have incorporated and interpreted young men and women?

III

This is the point to explore two youthful elements in Forsyth's earthing: the college and the Sunday school. As a college principal for twenty years Forsyth was a formative influence among young men. That needs qualification. Gravitas told; for twenty years Forsyth aged while his pupils stayed young. For five of those years war exercised its distorting influence and for a further two years illness took over where war left off. Nonetheless, a modern generation accustomed to ministers who at their youngest are middle-aged needs to remember that in Forsyth's day they were in their twenties. Even if the rhythm of their schooling meant that

---

[9] P.T. Forsyth, 'Sunday Schools and Modern Theology', *Christian World Pulpit*, 23 February 1887, pp. 123-27; 'The Church and the Children', *British Weekly*, 15 May 1913, p. 169.

[10] *Educational Record: Proceedings of the British and Foreign School Society*, October 1914, pp. 106-12.

many were already experienced in trade or commerce, and sometimes in manual work, Forsyth's students were still on the young side.

The second element focuses on the Sunday school rather than the college. Whatever the changes in Sunday school culture the Sunday school remained a key fact in any minister's pastoral experience. It loomed large and often powerful, affording a strategic link with social worlds far removed from normal chapel life. Sunday school earthed the culture and politics of evangelical Dissent in the complexities of contemporary industrial society. It was a radical acculturation.

An oblique yet relevant illustration might be drawn from outside this paper's period and beyond its immediate denominational range. It comes from Liverpool's Wesleyan Methodism c.1821. A young man who in modern jargon would be a teenager has just become a teacher in the Leeds Street Chapel Sunday School. On weekdays he can be found, as yet tentatively, at the interface between the construction industry and the architectural profession. His background is financially rickety because his father is a Micawber of purest essence. He meets his future wife at the Leeds Street School. Her father is clambering out of the Micawber classes and he opposes his daughter's marriage. The young couple disobey him and never look back. Ahead lies prosperity and, for our Leeds Street teacher, a seat on the council, a knighthood, and an assured place as a shaper of Liverpool's town and streetscape. Politically he shapes as a Gladstonian and culturally he becomes a Ruskinian. Religiously he is something of a vagabond (and not wholly unlike Ruskin and Gladstone in that regard either). He has the combativeness of the obstinate moderate and in turbulent times for Methodists this takes him out of Wesleyanism into the Wesleyan Methodist Association and on to Congregationalism. That spiritual journey has a spatial aspect because it takes him from the town centre to the suburbs until he sinks at the last into a generalized Anglicanism. Like too many of his sort, this natural Nonconformist is entirely innocent of ecclesiology although his professional career as an architect has bred in him an instinctive appreciation of order.

All this lies in the future, with some relevance for the themes of this paper. The prime relevance, however, lies in the formative importance of the Leeds Street Sunday School.

> The Sunday School was to me a new world of activity and energy: the republican form of government; its teachers' meetings; its library; the connexions and friendships to which it led; and the constant current of healthy excitement which it generated, in addition to the usefulness of the main objects at which it aimed, were, to me, sources of the keenest enjoyment and, I think, of improvement.[11]

---

[11] J. Allanson Picton, *Sir James A. Picton: A Biography* (London: Isbister, 1891), especially pp. 67-68.

That is a key quotation. Note its components: excitement, enjoyment, usefulness, improvement. All these the Sunday school developed at a careful remove from chapel proper. Wise ministers took note; here were young souls urgent for salvation. The wisest ministers, however, knew that soul salvation and the fullest education of the whole boy and the whole girl went hand in hand. A culture was in the making as well as the Church.

IV

That illustration has not been taken entirely at random. It comes from *Sir James A. Picton: A Biography* (London and Liverpool, 1891). The biographer is Picton's son, J. Allanson Picton. The name and the date should be noted. In 1891 Allanson Picton was Radical MP for Leicester where Forsyth was in the midst of a growing and municipally influential ministry. In that year Forsyth was inducted to the chair of the county Congregational Union. Allanson Picton's politics are best conveyed by the titles of his three most recent books: *Oliver Cromwell: The Man and His Mission* (1882), *Lessons From the English Commonwealth* (1884), and *The Conflict of Oligarchy and Democracy* (1885). He was the sort of man to whom Forsyth warmed. Indeed Picton's younger brother married into one of the most prominent families in Forsyth's Leicester congregation and Picton's first wife came from a correspondingly active Manchester family of Congregationalists, several of whom were prominent in Forsyth's previous church.[12]

There were yet more suggestive links between the two men, for Picton had himself been a Congregational minister. For twenty-three pastorally successful if denominationally choppy years Picton had ministered to three churches before leaving pulpit and pastorate for politics and Parliament. That was in 1879. His ministry had been energetic. He turned each of his churches into a hotbed of mutual improvement and adult education. He cultivated a reputation as Congregationalism's *enfant terrible*, excitingly unorthodox. He was an advanced liberal in politics and religion, fatally compromised in conservative eyes by his role in the Leicester Conference of 1877, an admirable, quixotic, inspired, inevitable yet irresponsible attempt by a group of younger Congregational ministers, timed to coincide with the Congregational Union's autumnal assembly at Leicester, to broaden the terms of communion among Christians.[13] They aimed at that occupational hazard for

---

[12] For James Allanson Picton (1832–1910) see *DNB* and *ODNB*. His first wife was Margaret Beaumont, of Cheetham Hill and Wilmslow; his sister-in-law Mrs William Henry Picton, was Mary Helen Stafford, of Leicester.

[13] For the Leicester Conference see M.D. Johnson, *The Dissolution of Dissent, 1850–1918* (New York: Garland Publishing, 1987), pp. 63-114.

Congregationalists, an ecclesiological minimalism. Generations and styles and theologies clashed. It was a denominational watershed; or it was for those who were aware of it. Some of its protagonists moved out of Congregationalism. Picton was one of these. Others stopped at the brink. Forsyth, newly ordained but as yet officially unrecognized, was one of these.

It is easy to dismiss those who fail to stay the course. Orthodox historiography has duly dismissed Picton. We should be less ready. Take for example his pastorates. There were three of them between 1856 and 1879. The first was at Cheetham Hill, Manchester. Picton was its second minister; Forsyth, who followed twenty-two years later, was its fifth. Then came Gallowtree Gate, Leicester, a cluster of whose members were to be found twenty-one years later as core members of Forsyth's church at Clarendon Park. Picton's third church was St Thomas's Square, Hackney, where Forsyth was his immediate successor, settling in the long wash of the Leicester Conference. So it must have been natural for Congregationalism's liberals to see Forsyth as Picton's successor in more than the pulpit of St Thomas's Square, that church for the London version of the Picton classes.

Forsyth's London ministry, like Picton's and like the Manchester and Leicester ministries which were to follow, was active in civic and cultural matters. Picton's Sunday afternoon lectures to working people on secular topics, which Frederick Rogers regarded as a forerunner of Pleasant Sunday Afternoons, and his three terms on the London School Board (whose School Management Committee he chaired), were the counterparts of Forsyth's service as a school manager or of Forsyth's book-borrowing from Dr Williams's Library, or his weeknight lectures on contemporary or literary topics, Browning for example, and Tennyson.[14] Forsyth took his share of social and political work: for the Charity Organisation Society, or platforms shared with Henry Fawcett, Liberalism's blind doctrinaire, or with Picton himself.[15]

St Thomas's Square was, in fact, the confirming point of Forsyth's Congregational ministry. He came from a newly formed cause in the Bradford hinterland, which never quite found its way, to a historic if now notorious and therefore marginalized church in a long-established London suburb. The church was seventeenth-century; its building was late eighteenth-century (a fragment still survives); he was heir, therefore, to a local tradition which stretched past Henry Forster Burder, its pulpit prince in the earlier nineteenth century, to Matthew Henry and the

[14] (F. Rogers) 'Picton', *DNB*; *Inquirer*, 19 November 1921.
[15] 'Lorna' (Jane T. Stoddart), 'Dr P.T. Forsyth of Cambridge: A Special Biography', *British Weekly*, 7 March 1901.

Ejected.[16] But in 1879 St Thomas's Square was a sticky pulpit to fill. It was no longer affiliated to either the London or national Congregational Unions. Its minister, particularly if he were Picton's successor, was bound to be a marked man. As a *British Weekly* correspondent recalled forty years later, 'it had seemed probable that the young minister might follow his predecessor along lines that led the latter ultimately to sever his connections with the churches and to devote his noble powers rather to the exposition of Spinoza than of any faith distinctly Christian'.[17]

Yet, even though the church's days were numbered, that was not how it turned out for its new minister. St Thomas's Square remained resolutely excluded from the denominational lists and Forsyth remained personally attached to Picton. 'It was a memorable event to hear Mr Picton pray', he recalled years later, when Picton had left public life for North Wales, 'The severe intellectual veracity of the man appealed to me... He was a fine combination of spiritual passion and intellectual power.'[18] But the direction had changed. As has been seen, Forsyth—though not his church—was admitted to denominational lists in 1884. His warm recollection of Picton's power was carefully phrased. In that *British Weekly* correspondent's words

> It was after he succeeded (the then Rev.) James Allanson Picton as minister of St Thomas's Square Church, Hackney, that Dr Forsyth had that great spiritual experience to which allusion is made in determining the trend of his life and ministry... From Mr Picton himself I had at the time the story of Dr Forsyth's conversion.[19]

That was written in 1921 and the writer was inevitably affected by knowing how Forsyth's life had turned out, but Leslie McCurdy's examination of how the tone of Forsyth's theological writing changed progressively between 1884 and 1891 is persuasive and the general account of the older memories, however telescoped their detail, rings true.[20]

A few days after the *British Weekly* printed the recollection of Picton and Forsyth another correspondent, 'F.R.C.S.', wrote in with his memories of student life in London thirty-seven years previously.[21] That would place them in 1884. FRCS, then 'a medical student, unsettled in

---

[16] St Thomas's Square is encapsulated in A. Mearns, *London Congregational Directory and Church Guide, 1889* (London: Alexander & Shepheard, 1889), p. 85.

[17] C.E. Larter, letter, St Mary Church, 18 November 1921, in *British Weekly*, 24 November 1921.

[18] 'Lorna', *British Weekly*, 7 March 1901.

[19] C.E. Larter, *British Weekly*, 24 November, 1921.

[20] McCurdy, *Attributes*, pp. 26-38.

[21] 'A Medical Man's Tribute to Dr Forsyth', *British Weekly*, 1 December 1921.

matters of belief by the scientific teaching of the materialistic school', was attracted to St Thomas's Square by a course of lectures which Forsyth offered 'on the origin of the Gospels'. FRCS was hooked. He liked their content, and he retained the notes which he had taken, this sentence among them: 'The Word of God was not the Bible; it was left for us to get as low as that. The Bible contains the Word of God—Jesus Christ.' He liked the speaker's style: a summary chalked beforehand on the blackboard; questions and discussion afterwards; and always a collect to preface the lecture itself: 'Prevent us, O Lord, in all our doings...' (words 'always ever since...associated with my memory of him'). He liked them sufficiently to continue at St Thomas's Square. He found Forsyth's literary lectures 'a great treat' and if on Sundays congregations 'were comparatively scanty' yet 'to students like myself, unsettled in their religious thinking by the current materialism of the day, it was a godsend to find a preacher of outstanding intellectual power, who had fairly faced our modern difficulties for himself, and yet preached Christ with all the fire and earnestness of a prophet'. He remembered especially a phrase in one of Forsyth's prayers 'thanking God for the "dark dis-peace" which besets us when we stray from Him'. He also remembered what was clearly a clincher of a sermon: Forsyth's farewell to St Thomas's Square, a 'dramatic denunciation of the men who had applauded him for preaching a more liberal religion because it seemed to them to permit the moral laxity which they preferred to a higher life. Looking up from his manuscript, he peered round the congregation. "I hope I have offended such men" he said. "I think I see some of them here tonight"'.

That has the ring of Forsyth at any stage of his ministry but it has a special resonance for 1885, nine years on from his ordination. It is, however, also important to note what follows immediately in FRCS's account: 'His sermons to children were delightful, and were enjoyed by the adults in his congregation as much as any.' Some of those sermons are surely to be found in *Pulpit Parables for Young Hearers*.

V

Pulpit Parables appeared in 1886. It is a deceptively small volume, prettily bound with a deft design of wayside flowers and foliage, their orange, yellow, green, and russet merging and now faded. There are twenty-four 'parables' each prefaced by a biblical text, their general tone sufficiently indicated by their titles. These range from 'Sleeping Beauties' to 'The Voyage Down the Time-River'.[22] That, however, is not by Forsyth but by his collaborator, J.A. Hamilton, who contributed half

---

[22] P.T. Forsyth and J.A. Hamilton, *Pulpit Parables for Young Hearers* (Manchester: Brook and Chrystal, n.d. [1886]).

of the parables. The volume is nonetheless a unity although its contents can be distinguished from each other by more than their authors' initials. Hamilton's parables tend to be longer and more artful than Forsyth's. They are more roundedly satisfying, better for reading at bed-time: 'The Land of Enchantments; or, The Might of Little Things', 'The Man in Grey; or Conscience Defiled'.[23] Forsyth's are more uneven in length, content, and storyline, although the structure of each is carefully massed. Through Forsyth's parables one engages more directly with the personality of their author. There are unexpected gleams, a quirkiness. He is a man to know, a tease who can be teased in return.

Together the authors celebrate, indeed exploit, the Victorian discovery of childhood. That was not a new discovery for Puritans. Forsyth and Hamilton were treading not just in the steps of Ann and Jane Taylor 'of Ongar' (and 'Twinkle, Twinkle, Little Star') but of Watts, Doddridge, and Bunyan too, though their present path was more immediately flagged by George MacDonald, Andrew Lang, Charles Kingsley, with firm direction from Robert Browning, the whole of it set by Ruskin. Their mission was to foster the growth of the soul in Christian stature. They had a problem of proportion, for they were not children although they had to respect their hearers and readers as children. They sought, therefore, 'to avoid thrusting upon their young readers thoughts which are not adapted to healthy childhood and its "natural piety"'. This had two important consequences. First, given the 'danger of confusing the minds and consciences of children by trying to give them conceptions and experiences which properly belong to adult minds only', it followed that 'some themes which are usually regarded as essential have been...deliberately omitted. And certain positions are not to be considered denied because they are reserved.' In other words there is likely to be a delicate doctrinal pivot. Secondly, given that the 'monstrosity of juvenile Pharisaism' must at all costs be avoided lest 'the whole subsequent growth of the soul' be warped, there was an emphasis on the imagination, an 'early enlisting' of that 'king-faculty...in the service of faith'. But if the imagination is to be enlisted, much must be left to the imagination. Much must be left unexplained; and yet all must make immediate contact with the circumstances and aspirations of their hearers (or readers).[24]

That might seem to be a prime recipe for theological liberalism striking at the most suggestive and vulnerable sections of the Church. It is certainly a recipe for that sentimentality which the later Forsyth so disliked. And so *Pulpit Parables* might seem at first reading. On examination, however, it might strike differently, coming across as a

---

[23] Forsyth, *Pulpit Parables*, pp. 95-105, 116-125.

[24] Forsyth, *Pulpit Parables*, pp. v-vi.

delightfully presented collection carefully suggestive of the faith once delivered yet still ready for fresh hearers poised to grow into it as their experience matures. It provides a rare insight into the technique and culture of a Christian communicator and into the way in which a living faith endures.

At this point some attention should be paid to Forsyth's collaborator. John Arthur Hamilton (1845–1925) was two-and-a-half years older than Forsyth and he lived for three-and-a-half years longer. He was born in the Potteries, trained at Rotherham, and he held three pastorates in fifty-four years: Crowle (Lincolnshire), Saltaire (Yorkshire), and Penzance (Cornwall). He died three days after his last church appointed him its Pastor Emeritus.[25]

Hamilton and Forsyth briefly overlapped in 1878–79 when they were near neighbours. Hamilton was newly arrived in Saltaire and Forsyth, recently married and soon to become a father, was shortly to leave Shipley. Saltaire was a much stronger cause than Shipley. It had a magnificent church, then barely twenty years old, an awe-inspiringly purpose-built Sunday school, a good manse, and a strategically mixed congregation. It basked in the excitingly compromising glow of England's best-publicized example of contemporary industrial paternalism. Saltaire was a community in which education and mutual improvement positively hummed.[26] Hamilton's pulpit parables, therefore, were delivered there, perhaps at Crowle, rather as Forsyth's were delivered in Hackney with perhaps some in Shipley, even—publishers' schedules permitting—in Manchester. Their small volume thus uncovers a considerable geographical spread.

Hamilton's share of it was extended in three more volumes, described in his obituary as nature study sermons for children. That obituary summarized him thus: 'One of the old Independents, he was a fearless seeker after truth, and a man of wide culture.'[27] Perhaps that should be taken at face value, for Hamilton also wrote *John Milton, Englishman* and he helped Forsyth prepare *Religion and Recent Art* for publication, but perhaps it is coded language for an inveterate liberalism. Hamilton, Forsyth's collaborator, twenty years later also helped R.J. Campbell, Forsyth's erstwhile friend, prepare *The New Theology* for publication.[28]

[25] For John Arthur Hamilton (1845–1924), see *Congregational Year Book*, 1925, p. 147.

[26] For Saltaire, the creation of Sir Titus Salt (1803–76), see Barlo and David Shaw, *Balgarnie's Salt with Commentary and Additions* (Saltaire: Nemine Juvante (Saltaire) Publication, 2003); J. Reynolds, *The Great Paternalist: Titus Salt and the Growth of Nineteenth-Century Bradford* (London: Maurice Temple Smith, 1983).

[27] *Congregational Year Book*, 1925, p. 147.

[28] R.J. Campbell, *The New Theology* (London: Chapman & Hall, 1907), p. vii.

Views change, perspectives are transformed, but relationships are not always terminated in their wake or backs uncompromisingly turned.

VI

Perhaps a children's sermon reveals more of its preacher than the main sermon. Forsyth's *Pulpit Parables* are engagingly revealing of their author. For a start, we find that he is a Scotsman, seaside-up: 'I was born by the sea. I was brought up by the sea. A mile or two inland, in the dead of night, when all else was quiet, I used to hear the sea singing a lullaby to the fisher children on the shore beneath the moon and all her family of stars.'[29] But he had become a London Scot, reduced to snatched visits, to 'living a few weeks ago up among my own Scottish hills', even if more often such scenes 'rose before my mind as I passed a shop window in an ugly London street the other day'.[30] London was now perforce his rule and measure, as when he described a mountain, 'only as far away as from Hyde Park to the Bank'.[31] But at least a London Scot could take his Young Hearers to the zoo, where they might see a tiger or an eagle, or he could take them into his own tree-encircled garden, with its central plot surrounded by a path, a month off from being ablaze with rhododendrons.[32] That, presumably, was at 266 Richmond Road, en route from London Fields to Dalston.[33]

He also has a daughter, 'a little candle of the Lord...but I won't say any more about her light, lest you might be jealous and she might be proud'. And he likes animals: 'Everybody who is fond of animals (and I think Jesus was, from the way He spoke of sheep and birds for example) speaks of them as he and she.' He is observant of his friends: 'A friend of mine has a picture of the head of [a donkey] as large as life in his dining room, and I always covet it. I break the tenth commandment and covet my neighbour's ass.'[34]

---

[29] 'A Seaside Sermon', Forsyth, *Pulpit Parables*, p. 86. Forsyth sounded Scottish; a dozen years later a sermon-taster commented, '"Church" and "world" are safe tests, and Dr Forsyth emerges from them an unmistakable Scotsman. A certain hardness of tone is a minor indication of origin, though it is softened in quiet passages.' A Country Cousin, 'First Impressions of Dr P.T. Forsyth at Cambridge', *The Christian World*, 15 December 1898.

[30] 'Jesus and the Playing Children', Forsyth, *Pulpit Parables*, pp. 213, 214.

[31] 'The Snow-Maiden', Forsyth, *Pulpit Parables*, p. 32.

[32] 'Prison Lights', Forsyth, *Pulpit Parables*, p. 50.

[33] *Congregational Year Book*, 1885, p. 297. The house is still there.

[34] His daughter Jessie was born in 1879 and in later years he had a cat called Clootie. In his Shipley days he had noticed a picture, 'In the dining room of one of my tasteful friends', of a flaxen-haired girl, paddling; 'Prison Lights', pp. 50-51; 'The Child, The Angel, And The Father', Forsyth, *Pulpit Parables*, pp. 169, 168; Forsyth, '*Maid Arise*'.

That quip might serve to introduce some radical quirks. Thus he is offended by the ugliness of mourning: 'When our friends die we put on ugly black clothes... And before very long it will not be good manners to put these black clothes on. I always tell people who I think won't be offended, that it is not a nice thing to do when their friends go to a better and happier world. And I think it will before long cease to be the fashion.' Then there is music, another focus of life in London: 'within the last week I have heard some great and wonderful music performed in London, representing the movement and magic of the deep and sounding sea'.[35]

Above all he likes to travel—to Scotland, of course; to Lancaster, early one March, looking across the silver stretch of Morecambe Bay to the snow covered hills of Lakeland, Black Combe, Coniston Old Man, Helvellyn, 'and far to the right is Ingleborough'. Best of all, however, was 'the sight of mightier snows in foreign lands'—Switzerland, for example, in the shadow of the Jungfrau. Foreign lands have more to them than mighty snows. In Germany there is 'one of the greatest and grandest churches in the world', Cologne Cathedral, 'which has the highest spires in the world and one of the strangest histories...in which I stood a few weeks ago, as I have often stood before'.[36]

And already from learning about the man we learn something about his hearers. If this is St Thomas's Square, they may be relatively few but they will nonetheless be the relatively prosperous and relatively educated children of church members and seatholders. They were middle-class young people, taught to be considerate to servants and to make the most of their gendered roles. This is how he starts 'Mirror Hunting':

What would you say if you found that the new servant stopped for a minute at every mirror she came to about the house?

If at this one she fixed her cap, with a long glance out of the tail of her eye as she moved away; if at that one she smoothed down her hair and patted it, as if she were petting it for its good behaviour; if at that other she smiled on her teeth for their whiteness, and pouted her lip for its redness; and if at that other she was so lost in the study of her own face, and so full of design for the sweetest bonnet, that she started with a little scream when a ring at the bell recalled her to her duty; I say, if she went on like that, what should you think?[37]

Can servants really be like that? Just like their mistresses? Or like little girls anywhere? Now add this exposition of Cinderella. The text is from

---

[35] 'Sleeping Beauties', Forsyth, *Pulpit Parables*, p. 1; 'A Seaside Sermon', Forsyth, *Pulpit Parables*, p. 85.

[36] 'Prison Lights', Forsyth, *Pulpit Parables*, p. 51; 'The Christ Child And His Bearer', Forsyth, *Pulpit Parables*, p. 126.

[37] 'Mirror Hunting', Forsyth, *Pulpit Parables*, p. 66.

Isaiah 61.3, 'Beauty for ashes', so the transition from Isaiah to Cinderella has a certain logic:

> ...I don't think Cinderella was a sluttish girl. I think, as she was a lady to begin and to end with, she was a lady in her kitchen too. She was a lady in so far as this—she must have been neat and tidy.
>
> Nobody need set up for a lady who can't begin with tidiness and cleanliness. I daresay her sisters may have been people who dressed loud and went out to parties, where they talked a great deal and displayed their cleverness, and played on the piano, and showed their fingers to be as fast and noisy as their tongues. But very possibly at home they were lazy lie-a-beds, who, if they hadn't had servants to keep things straight, would have been as dirty and untidy as any woman with a drinking husband and half-a-dozen children. But I can't think Cinderella was like that. I think she was a modest and retiring girl, who didn't push herself upon people, but being, as I say, a real born lady (I mean a lady in her heart), she had the instinct of cleanliness and tidiness, the lovely lady's instinct of giving beauty for ashes, turning disorder into order, and litter into neatness. So I think it likely she kept her kitchen tidy, and her dishes clean, and her covers shining clear, and her little bedroom sweet and airy, with a flower in the window, which she coaxed from the gardener.[38]

What are we to make of that? Superficially it is as good an illustration of class, gender, and role stereotyping as one could hope to find. Yet, apply it to the Hackney of the early 1880s and its values begin to seem more subversive than appearances might suggest.

So much for girls. How good is Forsyth at holding a boy's attention? This is how he begins 'Prison Lights' (Acts 12.7: 'A light shined in the cell'): 'I have heard of people who describe this life of ours altogether as a prison. That is not your opinion, I hope. Nobody who enjoys a game of cricket is very likely to think of life as a prison house.'[39] And here is a glimpse of 'A Christmas Sermon'. Forsyth has been describing a Christmas tree which is being decorated behind locked doors while the children of the house peep at it through the keyhole

> And then you want another peep. And your brother happens to want one at the same time. And your heads meet at the keyhole with a crack that makes your eyes brighter, because wetter, than ever. Then, as you must not cry before your sisters' little friends, who, you are sure, think you a hero, you choke it down, and it goes off in a queer laugh, and next moment...the door is flung open.[40]

Now compare that uncomplicated picture of Victorian suburban family life with three vignettes from 'Helpers and Hinderers'. This is a jolly,

---

[38] 'Sleeping Beauties', Forsyth, *Pulpit Parables*, pp. 3-4.
[39] 'Prison Lights', Forsyth, *Pulpit Parables*, p. 48.
[40] 'A Christmas Sermon', Forsyth, *Pulpit Parables*, pp. 112-13.

sentimental, clever piece playing on words because Forsyth is determined to introduce us to the Great H family: 'The letter H, you are aware, is a letter that plays a great part in the language, but it is one that does not always meet with the respect due to a family of such aspirations.' A lot of aspirate fun follows with dropped and assumed Hs. Then we meet two brothers, H. Elper and H. Inderer. Of the former we learn that 'Dogs and horses took to him in an extraordinary way...and when he grew big himself, he became a fine, quiet soldier, and finally a distinguished officer, who feared nothing, failed in nothing, spared himself in nothing, and said little or nothing.' Oh, stiff upper-lipped young Hackney man, how different you are from your brother who as a boy 'was thin and sly; but as he grew up to be a prosperous man he became stout, and instead of calling him sly, people only said he was a smart man of business... He made a large fortune by always managing with his great cleverness to pop in before other people... His wife was sadly afraid of him, and his children used to become very silent and timid whenever he was known to be about.'[41] More stereotyping? Or more shrewd subversion of a type of Hackney man, in the manner of Forsyth's farewell?

Perfect Hackney man was an educated man. He was artistic, literary, musical, and independent. And perfect Hackney man had his mirror image in perfect Hackney woman; she was all that, and clever. Forsyth loved clever women. There was a pulpit parable for each such ideal. The ideal Hackney artist was a Pre-Raphaelite: a man or a woman with an eye for a moral, storied landscape, such as stretches before us in 'Baby Babble'.

> And the mother's face hung over her child like a happy moon, and her black hair was like high heaven's dark blue, and her eyes were like stars in a twilight night. Then he went out of doors. And when he lifted up his gaze, lo, there was not a cloud to be seen, and it seemed as if it was neither dark nor light. It was like daylight without the sun, or like midnight without the dark. For above him was the great, round moon, and a family of little stars such as no man could number were shining upon the blue floor of heaven which no man can measure. And away upon the fields that ran to the distant hills, were scattered the dwellings of other men, with mothers and children, and the stalls of cattle, and the folds of sheep. And there flowed the river, with the sleeping fish beneath the stones, and far, far away was the sea with the great rocking ships and plunging whales. And the heart of this man was filled and lifted up. The moonlight, flooding the sky, and gilding the fields, and white as the silent river, was like the glory of God which covers all things, and gives them peace. And he was so full of solemn joy, of beasts and babes, of men and their mothers, of heaven and its God, that he could not be silent, so he broke out into this eighth Psalm, which is a hymn of praise.

---

[41] 'Helpers and Hinderers', Forsyth, *Pulpit Parables*, pp. 149-53.

That is why people praise God, who do it best.[42]

That is painterly writing. It is Holman Hunt in words. It is suggestive yet precise: colour, composition, creation—the story of humanity caught and ordered in a moral landscape as in a Pre-Raphaelite painting or, better yet, a medieval masterpiece. It is word-painting for children who have illustrated books to hand or art-galleries which might be reached by omnibus or tram. It is all that and a deft illustration of what a psalm is, for it expounds the text, Psalm 8.2: 'Out of the mouths of babes and sucklings hast thou ordained strength...' It is the wordscape of 'Baby Babble', those 'words not to be written by any pen in the world'.[43] We will return to that.

Our Hackney word artist is also a word musician. The rhythms of Forsyth's prose are too Browningesque ever to make for easy reading, but he has a powerful sense of sound. How he must have enjoyed preparing and delivering 'A Seaside Sermon'. The text is Revelation 1.15: 'His voice was as the sound of many waters.' Music is on his mind: 'Do you know that there is a music in the sea—not noise merely, but noise with God in it—music?' And there follows a painting and a tone-poem, a recreation of the sounds of the sea, the accompaniment to children splashing and bathers shouting, calling to each other above the 'sound of every wave that tumbles on the shingle or the sand':

> ...the rush of it as it runs along the beach...the hiss of it as it draws back...the rattle of the pebbles one upon another which it carries back with it...the thump, thump of the steamer...the creaking of the oars in that rowboat...the ship...with all her sail set is hissing through the water, while her cordage creaks, and her mate shouts to the wheel, and the cabin boy is squabbling with the captain's dog. And the winds are piping in many keys, and the sea birds are shrieking with wild swift joy. And all these things are many sounds, which...make up the one mysterious voice and music of the sea... We speak of the silent sea, but there is little silence for those who have ears to hear.[44]

There we have Charles Kingsley and John Ruskin in bold conjunction. What a pity that Forsyth died far too soon for the age of Aldeburgh and *Peter Grimes*, but for a man who had been to Bayreuth there was always the *Flying Dutchman*. This is an oratorio of a tone poem. It is moral seascape as 'Baby Babble' is moral landscape and we are sailing through it in quest of the text with a master at the helm.

Two themes (or are they tides?) emerge through Forsyth's musicianship. One is the sea: 'My mind is full of the sea. The grass by the coast is often salt with the spray carried in by the breezes... Now my

---

[42] 'Baby Babble', Forsyth, *Pulpit Parables*, pp. 186-87.

[43] Forsyth, *Pulpit Parables*, p. 186.

[44] 'A Seaside Sermon', Forsyth, *Pulpit Parables,* pp. 85, 87-88.

mind is saturated and salted with the savour of the sea and the sight and the sound of it are with me night and day.' Sea myth and fairy tale are lightly handled: 'nobody ever really saw a siren or a mermaid. It was one way of representing beautifully the charm of water and the music of the sea.' So the music mounts until, as yet quite briefly, the second theme can be introduced. It is God in Jesus: 'And so, if you sat at the right hand of God, who has all the world at His feet, what unspeakable music would rise to your ears from the manifold and awful concert of the mighty sea!'[45]

Surely the association is inescapable; as yet we are all seascape but an answer begins to suggest itself to that perennial question, 'how can I know that God hears my prayer?' That question is not asked but its answer is part of this Seaside Sermon's music and Forsyth develops it. God sends us men who have 'such ears in their soul that they can perceive some of the meaning of the world's great sea-voice, and they are able to translate for us some of the music and magic of the sea-soul of the earth. These men are poets, or painters, or musicians… Now, mankind is a great, great sea, and the souls of men and women are like the waves which cover the face of the great deep.'[46] It is time to break into another tone-poem or perhaps to go on stage, to join the chorus at the climax of grand opera: the *Mastersingers* this time?

> Babies are crying and crowing, boys are shouting, while the girls whisper, and the birds sing; women are smiling and rippling with gladness and moving among men like a quiet tune; again they are full of fierce jealousies, hatreds, and bitter words, or they are crushed with grief for the little ones to whom they used to sing. Men are lustily moving about their noisy business, shouting in public conflict, preaching quiet or jubilant truth, or, again, cursing God and each other, or groaning beneath blows and losses from which they never rise.[47]

It is time to marry land and sea, nature and humanity, to transmute such universal babble, such babel, into prayers which have been understood and thus answered: 'God has sent us…a soul in whom there sounds the echo of those many waters, which I have described as the stir, and passion, and glow, and pain of the great human soul. He has sent us Jesus Christ.' That is not quite the end of this Seaside Sermon, for there is an undertow, a coda that makes sense of what we have been hearing. It is this: 'When we *understand* Jesus, we get such a knowledge of the human soul as from poets or musicians' we get of the music of the sea. And 'His voice is as the sound of many waters.'[48]

[45] Forsyth, *Pulpit Parables*, pp. 85, 86, 89.

[46] Forsyth, *Pulpit Parables*, pp. 89-90.

[47] Forsyth, *Pulpit Parables*, p. 91.

[48] Forsyth, *Pulpit Parables*, pp. 92, 93.

It is a masterly composition. As for the manner, and leaving the theology to one side, one man's sentiment is another man's sentimentality, and the tone is certainly romantic. It is also intelligent: 'When we understand Jesus...'. We should focus on that intelligence.

Forsyth, the local school manager, is very consciously the educationist. The faith of his Young Hearers may not have been deepened by his pulpit parables but their education would certainly have been enlarged. He aims to make them at ease with contemporary literature, fairy stories (his age made an art form of the fairy tale), the classics, and European culture and tradition, weaving them naturally into his purpose. If FRCS had found Forsyth's literary lectures on Tennyson's 'The Two Voices' or Browning's 'A Death in the Desert' a treat, so Forsyth's Young Hearers were in their turn duly exposed to Browning. In explaining God's need for them he tells a parable: 'I found it in what they call a poem, that is, a story with the beauty uppermost.' It is Browning's 'The Boy and the Angel'.

Browning was London Congregationalism's own poet; he had been brought up as one of them. With Ruskin he was the man who had done most to make Italy safe for English Protestants. Through Browning Forsyth (who expounded 'Pippa Passes' in 'Baby Babble') can bring Italy to Hackney. 'The Boy and the Angel' finds its climax in St Peter's Rome. Forsyth transposes that great alien church home to St Thomas's Square.

> Being an archangel Gabriel knew most things... He flew to Rome. It was Easter day and he descended upon the great church of St Peter's.

> On Easter Day the pope joins in a splendid service of praise to God in this great church, and Gabriel found him in his robing room putting on his grand attire to take part in the gorgeous worship. It was a new pope, who had slowly risen from poverty by his piety to be the very head of the Church. He had been a labouring man, who, after a great sickness, became a priest, and at last, after many years, the pope... He was now on the eve of doing what he had longed as a boy to do—praising God in the pope's great way from St Peter's Church at Rome.[49]

There is no disparagement of Rome there, unless it is in the words 'grand' and 'gorgeous'; there is considerable understanding.

St Peter's was not the only Roman Catholic cathedral transported to St Thomas's Square. Cologne, as has already been seen, was another, with its 'splendid coloured windows...full of figures and faces looking down at you from the midst of golden glory or heavenly blue. And there are many fine pictures and great statues there, and a multitude of interesting things, which men in large caps and long red cloaks take you to see.

---

[49] 'The Child, The Angel, And The Father', Forsyth, *Pulpit Parables,* pp. 172, 174.

Under one of the coloured windows there is a huge column...and sometimes, when the sun shines through the window, the column is tinted with all the hues of the rainbow, and made to look as if it were a part of the wall in the New Jerusalem, which was garnished with all manner of precious stones.' And fastened to the column 'is a gigantic figure, in carved wood, of a man with a huge staff in his hand, who seems to be trudging along with a beautiful child seated upon his shoulders'. Thus we are launched on the story of St Christopher or, rather, 'the story they tell about him...a very beautiful story, whether it be true in every part or not'.[50]

That is an important touch. Forsyth is confident when he handles stories of saints in his pulpit because he lightly but tellingly displays the critic's touch. To explain a mermaid does not destroy the power of the mermaid idea any more than the distinction between story and history need destroy truth. That is the realism which allows Forsyth to draw Cinderella and the Babes in the Wood to the attention of his young Hackney hearers. Here, for example, is Forsyth's version of Sleeping Beauty.

> I have heard of another princess who did what Cinderella very nearly did when she was dozing and dreaming by the kitchen fire. This other princess actually did fall asleep, and everybody about her fell asleep. The king, her father, slept, his chancellor slept, his chamberlain slept, his guests slept, his butler slept, and the very wine in his bottles; his horses slept, the cats and dogs slept, the mice and rats in the walls slept, the very cocks slept, and one went off in the middle of a long crow which was, thereby, turned to a headless yawn; the trees slept, and the grass, and the sunshine slept upon all. And how long they all slept you know, and what a Sleepy Hollow the palace became, and how the signs of neglect and decay settled down over all. And the hedge, which grew slowly in their sleep, thickened round about the palace and it became more and more difficult for anybody to get in. And the dust settled upon the windows so that even the sun could not enter, wide-awake as he is. And there they were, none in bed, but all asleep.
>
> Isn't that like the way careless and untidy habits grow up upon you?[51]

In just the same imaginatively common-sense way Forsyth takes them into the world of classical myth: 'Are you tired of my preaching? Well, I will preach by a parable and tell you an old, old story... Long, long ago...in the glorious land of shining Greece...' The story is of Echo and Narcissus. Here is its ending, reminding us of how much vintage Forsyth there is in this early Forsyth

---

[50] 'The Christ Child And His Bearer', Forsyth, *Pulpit Parables*, pp. 127-28.

[51] 'Sleeping Beauties', Forsyth, *Pulpit Parables,* p. 6.

...and at last he dwindled into the long thin flower which now bears his name, with a face still lovely, and a sweet eye craving admiration still, but with a slender stem of a body and no strength of manliness in it at all.[52]

If these pulpit parables open up a catholic, classical education, bringing young Hackney into its cultural heritage, they are also purveyors of puritan education. Here is the climax of 'Prison Insights': 'You remember the Wars of the Roses, the Red Rose, the House of Lancaster, and John of Gaunt. Well, I went to see Lancaster not long ago, and the great old castle, now a jail, where John lived.'[53] He climbs to the top of the castle keep and is astounded by the view which, of course, he describes.

Then I thought how dreadful is the beauty of nature, like the beauty of the tiger's skin [always the unexpected gleam, yet not quite unexpected because he has just been talking of the tiger caged in the zoo]. Here I am standing to gaze upon it on the summit of deep, old misery, among the relics of cruelty and wrong... How could I help remembering that I should not have been so free to enjoy the sight but for the struggles and captivities of such men as some of those who lived and died beneath my feet? I had the light of liberty which is more than the glory of a thousand hills.[54]

He follows his guide down to the dungeons and hears the guide say,

'This is where George Fox was confined'. All of a sudden I felt a kind of fear. I felt I was on holy ground...somebody had been here far greater and grander than he... If George Fox lay here in the dark it was not dark for him. Jesus had been here... We are freer to-day because of George's prisons, and his prisons were more bright and open to him than most men's liberty, because of the visitation of Jesus to his soul.

I tell you in that dungeon I felt it was a solemn place, and there was something about it like what you feel on entering a room from which a lady has just gone out, only much higher than that. When I returned to the light of day, it seemed almost common; and I looked again at the hills, and I was more sure than ever that the light of the Lord which shines in the heart and soul is fairer than the sun, and clearer than the moon, and more terrible to the foes of freedom than an army with banners.[55]

That is a history lesson in the heritage of what a few years later was to be nicknamed the 'Nonconformist Conscience'. In it George Fox is super-imposed on time-honoured Lancaster, with a whiff of Cromwell's Ironsides. And should a younger hearer seek to know more of George

---

[52] 'Mirror Hunting', Forsyth, *Pulpit Parables,* pp. 69, 70-71.
[53] 'Prison Lights', Forsyth, *Pulpit Parables,* p. 51.
[54] Forsyth, *Pulpit Parables,* pp. 51-52.
[55] Forsyth, *Pulpit Parables,* pp. 52-53.

Fox, after this object lesson on light and liberty, then Forsyth has already implanted the Quaker insight of the inner light.

Forsyth's pulpit parables certainly laid the foundations for a liberal education, arguably for such a liberalism as might affront orthodox adult hearers alarmed at what he seemed to leave to the young imagination. Art, literature, nature—was there not a sentimentalist's tendency to pantheism, sufficient at least to tempt the unwary listener? There can be little doubt that Forsyth likes to trail his coat. Several times he verges on catastrophe but he always draws back. That drawing back is a much more powerful witness to evangelical truth than it is a temptation for the unwary. It is what attracted FRCS to St Thomas's Square. This can be illustrated from two of Forsyth's parables.

'The Child, The Angel, And The Father' illustrates God's need of us. Perhaps for Forsythians it also illustrates the Forsyth who famously described his younger self as a lover of love rather than an object of grace:

> ...the kind of need that God has for us all is a heart need, a love need... He needs for love and not simply for use. For God is love and all the needs of love are heart-needs. It is not His purpose only but His heart that needs the cats, and dogs, and sheep, and donkeys, and children, that He scatters so plentifully on the earth.[56]

The unexpected order of that last sentence stops Forsyth short of sentimentality. He is, after all, speaking to children and his text (Luke 19.31: 'The Lord hath need of him') sprang from the donkey which carried Jesus on Palm Sunday. The order—donkeys and children—allows Forsyth, who has been talking happily about donkeys, to consider children as people.

> Well, young folks that are always thinking a great deal of themselves are people I for one don't like. But I don't like that you should always be made to feel as if you were of no consequence, and always snubbed, and always afraid to open your mouth lest you should make a mess of it. So I want to teach you this, that even if you are a donkey, or if people call you so, still the Lord has need of you.[57]

That is where Browning's 'The Boy and the Angel' comes in, its story leading to Forsyth's punchline: 'And I am sure the Lord has need of you, dear children. Because for one thing, if He hadn't children first what would He do for men and women afterwards...'[58]

If love is a motif of 'The Child, the Angel, and the Father', it is equally so of 'The Christ Child and His Bearer', Forsyth's appropriation for Christmas of the Christopher story. 'Jesus is a King, but He is the King of

---

[56] 'The Child, The Angel, And The Father', Forsyth, *Pulpit Parables*, p. 170.

[57] Forsyth, *Pulpit Parables*, pp. 170-71.

[58] Forsyth, *Pulpit Parables*, p. 176.

Love', is how he almost ends it, 'and the way of love is the way of doing things for people.' But then he adds a 'last word for the older children'. It is a foretaste of the older, later, Forsyth.

> Some people think it is such a nice, sweet, easy thing to have to do with Jesus. They read pretty stories about the child Jesus, and the Christmas time...and they feel that it must be a very happy thing...to carry this sweet image about the world... But a day comes when it is hard to carry Christ...the burden...calls all your most earnest manhood and womanhood into play. The simplicity of Christ taxes all the depths of your soul and all the muscles of your conscience and will.

> You took up the simple, gentle Christ, and you have found before long that you had pressing on you the burden, the sins of the world. How could you come through it all if He did not carry you far more really than you Him... And so we who lightly, though sincerely, take, in our sentimental youth, the name and yoke of Christ, shall find, as life becomes more earnest and strained, the load of the Saviour on us grow and grow, and His demand tax us in the torrents of the world, till we bend and almost break; and when we come, saved but hardly saved, to the other side, we shall discover that we carried our Christ in the strength of a Christ that first chose us and bore us and carried us in the days of old.[59]

'Saved but hardly saved': the whole passage, but especially that textually ambiguous yet triumphant phrase, has the ring of the man under whom young FRCS sat, the man who in January 1884 preached on 'Pessimism' to St Thomas's Square and in 1891 recapped his evolving faith in 'The Old Faith and the New' for the benefit of Leicestershire's representative Congregationalists. It has the autobiographical stamp that Leslie McCurdy has discerned in those two sermons.[60] Was Forsyth confiding more to his Young Hearers than to their elders? Had Cologne something to do with it?

The dark side of life shadows several of these Pulpit Parables. 'For we died because God needs our death' startles as an apparent afterthought, slipped into 'The Child, The Angel, And The Father', though it should not be unexpected when the text is 'The Lord hath need of him' and one might infer (though it is nowhere stated) that the parable was delivered on Palm Sunday.[61] Its insertion is careful, indeed artful. 'Mirror Hunting' introduces a manic dimension. Forsyth must have had his Young Hearers squirming with fascinated delight, sharpened into horror, and he must have known that he would have had their parents quite simply squirming. He leads them into it with the lightest of touches.

---

[59] 'The Christ Child And His Bearer', Forsyth, *Pulpit Parables*, pp. 133, 135-36.
[60] McCurdy, *Attributes*, pp. 27-36.
[61] 'The Child, The Angel, And The Father', Forsyth, *Pulpit Parables*, p. 169.

A witty clergyman once went into an empty room hung round with mirrors, and he said he thought it was a meeting of the clergy, and was delighted.

Now is this the happy life?...

If I wanted to drive anybody in my power into misery and madness, I think I know the way in which it could be done. I would suggest that they should be put into a room which was covered all over the walls and ceiling with mirrors; and I would let nobody see them, and I should never let them out; they should speak to nobody; they should be left in solitary confinement, only not in the dark. No, I would give them plenty of light—that would be part of my plan. And there would be no windows to look out at, the light should all come from above. And it should come through frosted glass panes, so that the blue sky could never be seen. But the only thing they should see would be themselves over and over and over again in these mirrors. And every time they moved a limb a hundred limbs would move around them, and every wink would be answered by a shower of winks, and every time they lifted their eyes hundreds of eyes would stare at them from all sides, and if they got up in a rage a hundred men would rage and dance to keep them company, and if they raised their faces to the sky there would be no sky but scores of their own terrified faces looking down upon them day after day. They would have no companions round them, only images of themselves mocking every movement; and they would have no face of God over them, only reflections of their own face and their own passion. Can you conceive how horrible this would grow to be?... Now just as a man would go mad if he had no society but his own image, so those who move about in pure self-seeking are what we might call morally mad...a derangement, not of the wits, but of the conscience.[62]

Is Christ in any of these parables? The question has to be asked. 'Sleeping Beauties' skims as close to the verge of liberal catastrophe as might seem possible: 'Don't you remember how the prince came at last to the sleeping beauty and woke her with a kiss, and set everything going again...?' 'One day, a prince who loves your sleeping soul will come, and will force his way through to release it. Christ will wake you up, one day, to beauty and life again.'[63] Has the Christ of 'Sleeping Beauties' been subsumed happily ever after in the fairy-tale, Disneyworld-before-its-time, 'One day my prince will come'? Is the Forsythian realism which immediately follows—'But when you have been waked up, then your pain and sorrow will begin'—no more than a touch of Grimm, like the hall of mirrors?[64] Some readers will leave that as an open question; their

---

[62] Was that witty clergyman Sydney Smith? 'Mirror Hunting', Forsyth, *Pulpit Parables,* pp. 67-69.

[63] 'Sleeping Beauties', Forsyth, *Pulpit Parables,* pp. 7, 8. Even here there is the common-sense note: 'But, don't you also remember what a very difficult task he found it to be; what a business it was to get through that hedge, how many fears and fevers he had to encounter on the way? You remember that?'

[64] Forsyth, *Pulpit Parables,* p. 8.

jury will still be out. Others will remember that these are parables for Young Hearers. Their Christian imaginations are to be enlarged, not signed, sealed, and delivered; and Forsyth is a consummate artist in such enlargement, not least in his suggestion of the naturalness of Christian story (as indeed of fairy story). This can be illustrated in three of his parables: 'Baby Babble', 'A Christmas Sermon', and 'The Snow-Maiden'.

'Baby Babble' has an engaging, characteristically unexpected yet wholly convincing passage about why people praise God; but it is more than that, for it is an exposition of the text, uniting Psalm and Gospel in young hearers' minds:

> ...their hearts are so full that they run over. The baby's joy is so full that it soon overflows its teacup of a heart with shouting, and crowing, and that nonsense which is such music to women and to God. And this man's joy was so full that he overflowed too with a song of gladness in words of praise...[and as this man looks]... The tongue of nature was unloosed, and the very sky seemed to speak and sing like angels at a Christmastime. Like Christmas angels the world seemed to sing, for it sang round the little child in the manger of this man's heart... And so, because he felt the great power and majesty of God, this man felt the mighty power that lies in a little child... These great thoughts about God made him think great thoughts about everything else—about babies too. So he says to God, 'Out of the mouths of babes and sucklings Thou hast founded strength.'[65]

'Baby Babble' is not explicitly described as a Christmas sermon. One that is such a sermon explores the proverb, 'The understanding of man is the candle of the Lord' (Proverbs 20.27). It is crafted for growing intelligences in a world where houses were now gas-lit but where candles still lit one to bed. So Forsyth turns at once to his text.

> Your Bible says the spirit of man but it is better to say the understanding. You don't know exactly what your spirit is, but you do know what your understanding is. If I asked you, you would say you learned things with your understanding. You do sums with it. When you say six and four are ten, and eight are eighteen, and two are twenty—you do that by your understanding... And whenever you see the reason of anything, you see it by the light of your understanding. Your understanding is like a candle set up in the dark inside of your head, so that you can see your way about among all the things that come pouring in at the doors—at your eyes, ears, nose, and so on. Your mind is your candle.

> But what does my text say? It says your mind, or your understanding, is the candle 'of the Lord'. Isn't that strange?[66]

---

[65] 'Baby Babble', Forsyth, *Pulpit Parables*, pp. 187-88.

[66] 'A Christmas Sermon', Forsyth, *Pulpit Parables*, pp. 106-107.

What follows is an exposition of the candle, 'a common sort of candle possibly—not even coloured perhaps, nor carved as some pretty candles are, but just an ordinary white candle, which might even be tallow. And it has a common sort of candlestick—perhaps a tin one, or a plain china one. Both...quite good enough for you to go to bed by, and better indeed than you need to see to sleep by.'[67] After the exposition comes some gentle application, its tone a perfect example of the temper of Victorian Congregationalism, and at the end there is a clinching illustration of candle care. The whole is an essay in perspective. First, the application,

> ...as you grow wiser and wiser at school, and read harder and harder books, and converse with clever men and women, all that is light rising and shining within you. And it comes from God... And the growing understanding of man is not his own light, but the candle of the Lord.

> If you would remember this, it would keep you from being conceited when you thought yourself clever... Whatever brains you each have are a gift and portion of the wisdom of God. All you have to do is to make the best of them.[68]

As for the illustration of candle care, it is a deft reminder that young tempers fray easily at Christmas, tinged by Forsyth's instinctive pessimism which he tweaks into realism.

> But mind, you little candles, no guttering and no grumbling... It is always a bad and short-lived candle that flares. No smouldering...and giving off an evil smell... And when the Father and Master of this radiant world, going round to watch His candles snuffs you or sets you straight, see that you shine the brighter and cheerier for it than before... If He snuff you, and seem almost to extinguish you; if He disappoint you, and seem to crush you, you will know now what it is for! They snuff the candles because they were burning badly, to make them shine with a perfect gleam, and smile with a free unflickering and untroubled smile.[69]

That 'Christmas Sermon' was delivered in the decade when electric light began to appear in rich and up-to-date households, extinguishing candles as gaslight had not quite done. Our view of candles is neither Forsyth's nor his hearers', which is no doubt one of the reasons why 'Jesus bids us shine' is no longer sung.

The Snow-Maiden' (text, 'I saw a great white throne', Revelation 20.11) tells of a weekend spent in an enclosed Swiss valley: 'We were very tired and glad to rest on Sunday, for during the week we had travelled many hundred miles.' But there was the Jungfrau. 'It was more than two miles high. If we had been in a boat on the sea it would have

---

[67] Forsyth, *Pulpit Parables*, p. 107.

[68] Forsyth, *Pulpit Parables*, pp. 108-109.

[69] Forsyth, *Pulpit Parables*, pp. 114-15.

been close upon three miles straight up to the top... I never saw such a mountain before, *so high, and yet so near!*' Forsyth was transfixed by its colour, and the intensity of its whiteness. 'Do you remember that story in the New Testament about the transfiguration of Christ?' How Peter and the others were heavy with sleep, 'just like my friend and me, who were sleeping with heavy heads while the morning sun was shining white outside our window upon the transfigured hill?' How many children's addresses now allude to the Feast of the Transfiguration? Then Forsyth brings together the whiteness and the sounds, indeed the whole process of a great mountain. This one 'they call...The Maiden, because it is a white thing of exceeding purity, and radiance, and dignity, and peace'; this one surely has the mountain sounds of the Mount of Transfiguration ('And they heard strange voices up there like the silver blowing of unseen winds upon holy horns'); this one makes him think of Mary, Mother of Jesus, 'carrying her shining boy upon her shoulder, and beaming herself upon the whole world in radiant joy'; this one comes as *Revelation*, for it is a great white throne, a place of terror and mystery ('The sound of the avalanche is like the voice of God'), to which extraordinarily the locals are quite inured. Or is that so extraordinary? '...is it not the same with ourselves? The presence of God stands over us every day.'[70] The whole makes for a conclusion which is a perfect encapsulation of Forsythian sentiment.

> As this great severe mountain can sometimes look so sweet and gentle, so the most high God has the richest kindness in His face. Where do we see the kindness in the face of God? In the face of the Lord Jesus Christ. God is not altogether a dreadful judge—a white-throned king. He is the same who kissed the children and was kind to poor women, and made simple folks love Him. Yea, and they were ready to die for Him; and they would not have done that if He had frightened them, and nothing more. Would they?[71]

That question is not quite rhetorical. It reminds us of the sense of proportion which makes each of Forsyth's pulpit parables and which informs another of his questions: 'if He hadn't children first what would He do for men and women afterwards?' Such a sense illuminates his commands, 'Jesus, you see, didn't always find children nice, but He always found them interesting.'[72] So, one feels, children always found Forsyth, more so perhaps than many adults.

---

[70] 'The Snow-Maiden', Forsyth, *Pulpit Parables,* pp. 32, 33, 34-35, 36.
[71] Forsyth, *Pulpit Parables,* p. 38.
[72] 'Jesus and the Playing Children', Forsyth, *Pulpit Parables*, p. 212.

VII

There is room for three last words. In May 1948 Hugh Stafford, a retired Quaker schoolmaster from Hitchin, wrote about his memories of Forsyth:

> He was my minister for nine years, six while I was a schoolboy in Leicester, and three at Cambridge. Later I often stayed at Hackney College where he was Principal. I do not suppose that in those early years I ever fully understood his sermons. It was no easy discipline to listen. He seldom preached for less than 40 minutes, and one's mind was kept at full strength all the time. Nevertheless it was profoundly impressive. Every sentence, one felt, came white-hot from the furnace of his spirit... One emerged, rather battered perhaps, but humbled, strengthened, and above all filled with the sense of the tremendous import of religion... That sense has never left me since.[73]

Although that recollection is too late to be of St Thomas's Square and sounds more like Emmanuel Church, Cambridge, than Clarendon Park Leicester, it ties several ends. Forsyth kept his pastoral friendships in good repair. The Staffords were a prominent Clarendon Park family. Eight of them were founder members and one of these was still in membership when her nephew wrote from his retirement in Hitchin. John Stafford, twice Mayor of Leicester, thirty-two years a councillor, thirty-one years a JP, twenty years an alderman, seventeen years Chairman of the Borough Lunatic Asylum Committee, was a provision merchant and cigar manufacturer.[74] Percy Stafford, his youngest son and partner, tennis player and golfer, superintended Clarendon Park's Sunday School, 450 strong.[75] Hugh Stafford, John's grandson and Percy's nephew, became a schoolmaster. He taught at Caterham, the boarding school for sons of Congregational ministers, from 1899 to 1937, becoming the second master and on occasion its acting headmaster, and notable in the 1930s for his school sermons. Generations of pupils recognized him as a formative influence, among them the formidable New Genevan, J.S. Whale.[76] It is tempting to see a mediation of Forsyth's influence. It is also tempting to see the mediation of other, but entwined, influences. Stafford became a Quaker, which suggests theological liberalism as well as pacifism; and a Leicester aunt of Stafford's married Allanson Picton's brother. Family coincidence need have no bearing of any kind on religious mentality but the spiritual and mental air of *Pulpit Parables*

---

[73] FPDWL: *Baptist Times*, May 1948.

[74] For John Stafford (1822–1910), see W. Scarff and W.J. Pike, *Leicestershire and Rutland at the Opening of the Twentieth Century* (Brighton: W.T. Pike, 1902), p. 184.

[75] For Percy Evans Stafford (b. 1860), see Scarff and Pike, *Leicestershire*, p. 185.

[76] For John Hugh Stafford (d. 1951), see E. de C. Blomfield, *A Century at Caterham* ([Caterham: Caterham School], 1983), p. 71. This school history is dedicated to Hugh Stafford, who had written its predecessor.

blows from Hackney to Cheetham Hill to Clarendon Park invigorating those who lived in it.

Who listens to a children's address and what do they most recall? Three years after Hugh Stafford wrote down his boyhood recollections and in the year of his death, I went with my parents to a morning service at Union Church, Mill Hill. I recall a crowded congregation in what seemed to a ten-year-old to be a spaciously modern red-brick church. I also recall the children's address. Its theme was 'Stirring up Mud' and the illustration that led to the message was of a mug of drinking chocolate on to which was poured hot water, though the chocolate stayed like a thick mud at the bottom until it was stirred. That was how you drank hot chocolate back in 1951. We had all done it, just as we had all stirred up mud in our lives. I remember nothing more of that service but 'Stirring up Mud' came to mind when reading *Pulpit Parables*; even an illustration in a children's address can be Forsythian. That is not too far-fetched a thing to say if one reflects that the minister at Mill Hill Union in 1951 was Maurice Watts, and he was very conscious of having been one of P.T. Forsyth's students at Hackney College.[77]

The last word comes from the Whitley Lecture for 1999–2000; it is, therefore, a Baptist word:

> Children come with a spiritual health warning. They are dangerous for us because they embody the values of the Kingdom of God. Yet we do not see children and what they represent. Children are dangerous because by being small and vulnerable, they enable us to exploit and abuse, ignore and dominate them in ways which oppose the values of God's Kingdom. We do not hear children, or the voice of God in them. Jesus taught that mature discipleship consists in protecting and welcoming, emulating and learning from children. But children are still oppressed, marginalized or overlooked in church and society today, as throughout much of history, even Christian history.[78]

That lecture's rhetoric is of its age, turn of the twentieth and twenty-first centuries. P.T. Forsyth, at least implicitly, had got there more than a century before.

---

[77] For Maurice Watts (1892–1979), see *United Reformed Church Year Book*, 1980, p. 259. His regular quoting of Forsyth in sermons at Mill Hill is recalled by T.J. Wright (T.J. Wright to C. Binfield, 25 February 2004).

[78] Anne Dunkley, 'Seen and Heard: Reflections on children and the Baptist tradition', *Baptist Historical Society*, Newsletter, April 2000.

CHAPTER 6

Sport and the English Sunday School, 1869–1939

Hugh McLeod

Philip Cliff's thesis on the history of English Sunday Schools begins with an idyllic depiction of chapel life in his native Yorkshire in the 1920s and '30s:

> I count myself fortunate to have been born into a home which had been nourished by at least three generations of Sunday School workers. Through my parents I was fortunate to know the richness of church, Sunday School, and a congregation live with organisations for children and young people. The Choir came to sing after church on a Sunday evening, and Saturdays were either at home or away with the Cricket and Football groups. I could look round the church and see my parents, aunts and uncles, family friends and my grandparents. It was in this community that I discovered the richness of worship and grasped the meaning of the sacraments which age has not withered.[1]

It is significant that Cliff mentions sport as a memorable part of his own Sunday School experience—and significant too that sport never gets more than the briefest passing reference in the rest of his thesis. Cliff's memories cover the latter part of the golden age of Sunday School sport which I take to be from the 1890s to the 1930s, and indeed the inter-war years probably mark its peak, though it is hard to be certain about this because of the paucity of sources. And there may be significant regional and local variations. The Sunday School press is most helpful in the 1880s and '90s when the introduction of a sporting programme was still controversial. By the 1920s and '30s it was largely taken for granted, and for the most part neither historians of sport nor historians of religion have seen Sunday School sport as a matter of any great interest. In Mike Huggins' valuable new history of Victorian sport Sunday Schools rate just two mentions. Huggins also exaggerates the extent to which

[1] Philip B. Cliff, 'The Rise and Development of the Sunday School Movement in England 1789–1980' (PhD thesis, University of Birmingham, 1982), Acknowledgements.

Nonconformists, and especially Methodists, were still opposed to sport in the 1890s.[2]

The major exception to this neglect is Jack Williams' work on cricket in Bolton during the inter-war years. Williams demonstrates the key role of churches and chapels in many areas of amateur sport in Lancashire during this period. This role was very big in women's sport; big in the two most widely played men's sports, football and cricket, as well as in the mixed sport of table tennis; much smaller in some other sports, such as rugby, golf and darts.[3] He also notes the significant place of Sunday School Leagues in youth sport.[4] The Bolton Sunday School Social League, said to be the largest of its kind in England, had in 1936 nine affiliated bodies, responsible for events in which 3,000 people participated in winter and 2,500 in summer. The sports included were football, hockey, tennis, table tennis, rounders, badminton and swimming. There were other leagues catering exclusively for cricketers, such as the Radcliffe Sunday School League with twenty-five teams in 1939. Sunday School sport was strong in other areas of England too, including London, where in 1933 the South London Sunday School Sports Association had cricket and football leagues, each with seven divisions and over sixty teams. An article of 1933 on the history of the South London Association suggests that it may have had a strategic role as the leading organizer of youth sport. The author noted that considerable numbers of street-based football and cricket teams had sought entry to the leagues, but had been told that they could only join if their members were attached to a church, Sunday School or Boys' Brigade.[5]

Sunday School teams stood, as Williams emphasizes, at the lowest level of the hierarchy of sports teams. But they served as a first rung on the ladder for many of those who subsequently climbed to the top. Bob Crompton, Blackburn and England full-back in the pre-First World War years, was first spotted while playing for a Sunday School team. Len Hutton, who in 1938 would score a record-breaking 364 against Australia, began his batting career ten years earlier by coming in at number eleven for the Moravian Sunday School in his native Fulneck.[6]

---

[2] Mike Huggins, *The Victorians and Sport* (London: Hambledon and London, 2004), pp. 41-42.

[3] Jack Williams, 'Churches, Sport and Identities in the North, 1900–1929', in Jeff Hill and Jack Williams (eds), *Sport and Identity in the North of England* (Keele: Keele University Press, 1996), pp. 114-16.

[4] Jack Williams, 'Cricket and Society in Bolton between the Wars' (PhD thesis, University of Lancaster, 1992), pp. 196, 307-308.

[5] *New Chronicle of Christian Education*, 9 February 1933.

[6] Alfred Gibson and William Pickard, *Association Football and the Men who made it* (4 vols; London: Coxton, n.d.), II, p. 52; Len Hutton, *Cricket is my Life* (London: Hutchinson, 1949), pp. 26-30.

This paper will be in two parts. In the first I discuss the ethos of Sunday School sport in the period from the 1890s to the 1930s, and will relate this to debates among historians about the relationship between religion and sport. In the second part I will look at the reasons why sport came to be a significant part of Sunday School life and the debates over sport within the Sunday School movement.

I

Although this vast amount of sport, played mainly on Saturday afternoons, has left little trace in the historical record, it was of passionate concern to many of those involved. One indication of this is provided by William Kent, a well-known writer on London history, whose autobiography was mainly concerned with his passage from evangelicalism, through liberal Christianity to secularism, and with the various Congregationalist and Wesleyan chapels, missions and Sunday Schools to which he belonged in the 1890s and 1900s. A striking feature of this account is how much of it is about sport, especially cricket. Kent recalled that 'on Saturday mornings I always included in my prayer a petition that I might do well in the match—"If it be Thy will"', and a good deal of what he remembers about the members of these institutions concerns their sporting prowess, or lack of it.[7] Another indication is the fiercely competitive atmosphere of much Sunday School sport, reflected in keen disputes over alleged breaches of league rules, and in the complaints by the South London Association about 'those who do not play a sporting game'.[8] A typical example of the disputes that plagued Sunday School Leagues, as much as Leagues of any other kind, was the football match between Tottenham and Radnor Street in the Wesleyan League on 9 November 1907. The match was stopped because of thick fog at a time when Tottenham were ahead and a replay was ordered—leading to prolonged argument and an appeal.[9] Williams notes that one of the key differences between elite and popular cricket teams was that in the former the two teams each provided an umpire and it was assumed that as gentlemen they would be scrupulously fair—or at least it would be ungentlemanly to question their impartiality. In popular cricket it was assumed that umpires would be partisan. Thus the Horwich Sunday School League asked each club to nominate an umpire, but he would be sent to a match where his own team was not playing. Williams alleges that sharp practice was not infrequent, though some of the examples he quotes

[7] William Kent, *The Testament of a Victorian Youth* (London: Heath Cranton, 1938), pp. 117-20.
[8] *New Chronicle of Christian Education*, 9 February 1933.
[9] Radnor Football Club, Minutes, 19 and 26 November 1907 (London Metropolitan Archives, N/M/17/22).

seem the stuff more of humorous anecdote than of serious cheating. For instance, he quotes stories of fielders apparently losing the ball in an overgrown outfield, only to toss the ball with alacrity to the wicket-keeper if the unwary batsmen began to run.[10]

It is unclear how far clergy and Sunday School teachers set an example by themselves playing or taking a close interest in Sunday School teams. Some certainly did. Hutton remembers his Moravian minister taking a fine catch for the Sunday School team—though he claims to have forgotten all of his sermons.[11] Active interest from 'above' was most important in the 1880s and '90s, as will be discussed later. By the 1920s and '30s it would seem that the initiative was just as likely to come from 'below'. Indeed the South London Association complained of a lack of 'leadership' in many of the affiliated teams, and called for a more active involvement by teachers and clergy.[12] Relatively few minute-books of Sunday School teams have survived. The only one that I have seen is that of the Radnor Street Wesleyan Schools Football Club in inner north London, which covers the period 1904–08. The AGM for 1904 opened with prayer but there is no indication of involvement by ministers.[13] However, those clergy who did not themselves play might still promote sport by presenting sports stars as role-models, by filling their church magazines with reports of sporting events, and by using sporting metaphors in their preaching. Thus Eric Liddell's gold medal at the Paris Olympics in 1924 and, even more, his refusal to run in an event which was scheduled on Sunday, were subjects of several approving articles in the *Sunday School Chronicle*. As one of these pointed out: 'The man who, like Mr Liddell himself, can combine Christian principles with athletics prowess, will win for himself and his faith an influence among modern youth that can be sanctified to the highest spiritual ends.' The article went on to praise the sporting enthusiasm of the present generation of Sunday School teachers which enabled the pupils to see them as human beings rather than merely authority figures.[14] Admittedly, the two sports stars most favoured as role-models in the pre-World War II period, Liddell and C.T. Studd, both moved on at a fairly early stage in their sporting careers to become missionaries. Their selection as role-models thus represented a compromise, their prowess on the cricket field or the running track being deemed likely to ensure the respect of the younger generation, while their work for the gospel in China was the main object for emulation.

---

[10] Williams, 'Cricket,' pp. 174-75, 322-23.

[11] Hutton, *Cricket*, p. 26.

[12] *New Chronicle of Christian Education*, 9 February 1933.

[13] Radnor Football Club, Minutes, 14 January 1907.

[14] *Sunday School Chronicle*, 17 and 24 July, and 7 August 1924.

The earliest example I have found of a church magazine filled with sporting news is from the 1870s. By 1900 it was commonplace. A striking, though not untypical, example is the magazine of Princes Street Baptist Church, Northampton, during the pastorate of the Rev. J.A. Roxburgh, which began in 1906. His predecessor was said by a Congregational colleague to have 'had a long innings' and to have 'played the game'. Under Roxburgh the sporting metaphors multiplied and references to actual or intended sporting events took up an increasing amount of space. In June 1907, for instance, Roxburgh called for the formation of a church swimming club and made no less than three references to cricket in his 'Pastoral Notes'. For example, he compared the church to a cricket team in which the pastor was the captain but every member of the team had a vital role. He also complained, 'Who is sufficient for preaching at his best when the man who bowled him with a wet-wicket "yorker" plants himself right under the preacher's nose the following Sunday?'[15] Even in churches with pastors less passionately committed to the gospel of sport, reports on football, cricket, cycling, and other sports, were a routine feature of the church magazines of the period.

This leads on to the question that seems to have caused most friction at the time, and which has caused dispute between historians since, namely the relationship between church-based sports teams and the church. J. Rider Smith was a leading figure in London Congregationalism in the inter-war years and was also chairman of the South London Sunday School Sports Association in 1933, which is an indication of the seriousness with which Sunday School sport was taken. In a review of the Association's history, he made a strong case for there being a mutually beneficial relationship, though he also noted some of the difficulties. Most of the members of Sunday School teams were, he stated, 'poor working-class boys' aged between fifteen and twenty-two, who had difficulty finding money for their subscriptions. He claimed that 'No other organisation enters into the life of young men and women as does the Sports Association. It touches young people outside the Church and brings them in.' However, he also noted that tensions often arose between members of these teams and the church or chapel authorities. Street teams, he suggested, were often made up of boys 'who had been turned out of the Church or Mission because of trouble or misunderstanding'.[16] The issue most commonly facing church-based teams was that of whether they could include those who played well, but seldom attended services. Other common areas of tension were bad language and gambling. The

---

[15] *Princes Street Magazine*, January 1906, July 1907 (Northamptonshire County Record Office, PSBC 24/6).

[16] *New Chronicle of Christian Education*, 9 February 1933.

Anglican University Club, a leading centre of boxing in the East End of
London, actually closed in 1902 after the managers discovered that
gambling was prevalent.[17]

This raises broader questions about relations between the Sunday
School and the surrounding community or communities. Some sports
historians posit a clear opposition between 'church' and 'chapel' on the
one hand and 'working-class community' or 'working-class values' on
the other.[18] This is often linked with a polemical agenda of trying to
establish that church involvement in working-class sport was a temporary
phase, rapidly superseded as sporting workers gained sufficient
confidence to establish their own institutions and to insist on playing in
their own way, without regard for the tenets of 'muscular Christianity' — a
subject on which enormous amounts of nonsense have been written.

This is all much too simple. It flies in the face of most of the research
on the relationship between religion and class published in the last twenty
years, which shows much more complex patterns, and highlights the
mainly working-class membership of many Nonconformist denominations. In particular, Jack Williams, one of the few historians to examine
the relationship between religion and sport in a serious way, has shown
that church-based sport had a major role at least until the 1930s, and that
most players came from the working class or lower middle class. In most
respects he plays down differences between church-based and non-
church-based teams, except that he suggests that the former had an ethos
of respectability that may have alienated keen drinkers.[19] Certainly
respectability was a consideration for some of those who first set up

---

[17] Stan Shipley, 'The Boxer as Hero: a Study of Social Class, Community and the
Professionalisation of Sport in London 1890–1905' (PhD thesis, University of London,
1986), p. 356.

[18] Thus Stuart Barlow, 'The Diffusion of "Rugby" Football in the Industrialized
Context of Rochdale, 1868–90: A Conflict of Ethical Values', *International Journal of
the History of Sport*, 10.1 (1993), pp. 61-62, 65, contrasts church-based teams with
those 'formed by ordinary people', and argues that 'the tenuous hold that "Muscular
Christianity" exerted on the "rugby" teams of Rochdale was largely replaced by the
working-class values that had developed in the streets, alleys and public houses'.

[19] Jack Williams, *Cricket and England: A Cultural and Social History of the Inter-War
Years* (London: Frank Cass, 1999), pp. 147-52. For a summary of research on religion
and class from the '70s to the '90s, see Hugh McLeod, *Religion and Society in England
1850–1914* (Basingstoke: Macmillan, 1996), pp 62-66. Major recent contributions
include S.C. Williams, *Religious Belief and Popular Culture in Southwark, c.1880–1939*
(Oxford: Oxford University Press, 1999); Richard Sykes, 'Popular Religion in Dudley and
the Gornals, c.1914–1965' (PhD thesis, University of Wolverhampton, 1999); Huw
Benyon and Terry Austrin, *Masters and Servants: Class and Patronage in the Making of
Labour Organisation* (London: Rivers Oram Press, 1994); Peter Ackers, 'West End
Chapel, Back-Street Bethel: Labour and Capital in the Wigan Churches of Christ
c.1845–1945', *Journal of Ecclesiastical History*, 47.2 (April 1996), 298-329.

Sunday School Leagues. Thus the founders of the South London Sunday School Cricket League in 1895 stated that its main object was 'to confine their matches among themselves, thus securing a felt want in associating with young men of respectable character'.[20] However, the evidence from the 1930s, cited above, suggested that the Leagues were reaching much wider sections of working-class youth. And this view is supported by Charles Booth in his *Life and Labour* (1902–03). Booth suggested that church-based sports facilities were catering for a wide range of social groups. He also noted that the same church could cater for several constituencies. He gave the example of a church in Hackney where the gym was open three nights a week and, because the subscription rates varied, three different sections of the local population were attracted on the different days.[21] At Oxford House, the High Anglican Settlement in Bethnal Green, which specialized in running clubs for boys and for working men, there was a hierarchy of organizations directed at those from different social strata. Thus the University Club drew its members very largely from the skilled working class, whereas the Repton Clubs aimed to reach a 'lower class of boys', and St Anthony's, later called the Eastbourne Club, aimed to recruit 'hooligans'. Membership statistics suggest that the clubs aimed at the upper working class attracted the biggest membership: for instance in 1922 the University Club had 500 members, as against 150 in the Repton and Eastbourne (which had apparently amalgamated).[22] As an example of a club which reached the poorer sections of the working class, Booth noted the Working Lad's Guild at the Congregationalist Christian Institute in Hoxton Market. This had about a hundred members and a programme that included gymnastics and cricket, as well as a reading room and a Bible Class. At the Lyndhurst Road Mission in Kentish Town, where membership was restricted to those living within a mile, 'Those touched are the working classes, but not, except through its charities, the lowest.' Here too there was a gym and other sporting and leisure facilities, as well as evening classes and Bible study. If these were examples of middle and upper-class philanthropy, working-class and lower middle-class districts of London also contained plenty of congregations run by local people, and with their own (probably more modest) recreational facilites.[23]

---

[20] 93rd Annual Report of the Sunday School Union (1895–96), p. 113 (Birmingham University Library, Sunday School Collection).

[21] Charles Booth, *Life and Labour of the People in London* (17 vols; London: Macmillan, 1902–03), 3rd Series, I, p. 150.

[22] *The Oxford House in Bethnal Green* (London: Oxford House, 1948), pp. 30, 42-43; *Annual Report* of Oxford House, 1922 (copies at Oxford House).

[23] Booth, *Life and Labour*, I, pp. 177-79, II, pp 120-22, III, pp. 143-44, VI, p. 25. The most thorough and nuanced study of the complete range of forms of organized

My overall conclusion is that Sunday Schools, as ubiquitous, generally familiar, and to a large extent accepted institutions, attracted all sections of the working class and lower middle class to their sports facilities—though not without tensions, which were most acute in the case of boys from 'rougher' working-class backgrounds, who frequently came into conflict with clergy and teachers.

II

The Anglicans were somewhat ahead of Nonconformists in accepting that promotion of sport was a proper task for the church.[24] At the Church Congress in 1869 'The Recreations of the People' was one of the main themes, and several speakers demanded that the clergy get more active in providing leisure facilities, including facilities for sport. This demand was especially linked with the theme of working-class alienation: it was argued that the reputation of the clergy for 'puritanism' and their failure to interest themselves in the leisure needs of their poorer parishioners was a reason why working men had left the church. Large claims were also already being made for the character-building qualities of sport. For instance, a Nottinghamshire clergyman attributed his county's high level of morality to the large number of cricket clubs in that part of England. The Rev. John Scott, vicar of St Mary's, Hull, reported that he had a gymnasium for the use of the boys in his Sunday School, and this is the earliest such reference I have seen.[25] (He also recommended gyms for girls, though he had not provided one himself.) The earliest example I have found of Sunday School cricket is the team started by the Rev. George Arbuthnot, Vicar of Arundel, in 1874. Arbuthnot, who seems to have been the first sports fanatic in that small country town, was also the team's star player. In subsequent years he also introduced football and an athletics sports day in his day school and a Sunday School swimming and diving championship. As well as filling his parish magazine with reports of matches and races, he used it to harangue his parishioners about 'manliness', and in particular to ridicule those who could not swim. Arbuthnot was a tireless controversialist, with opinions on every conceivable subject, and usually locked in dispute, whether with the People's Warden at his own church, the headmistress of a local girls'

---

religion in a working-class district of London is Alan Bartlett, 'The Churches in Bermondsey 1880–1939' (PhD thesis, University of Birmingham, 1987).

[24] Douglas Adam Reid, 'Labour, Leisure and Politics in Birmingham ca. 1800–1875' (PhD thesis, University of Birmingham, 1985), ch. 3.

[25] *Report of the Church Congress, Liverpool, 1869*, pp. 133, 141-44.

school, or representatives of the town's sizeable Catholic community.[26] But nothing seems to have been closer to his heart than sport. In June 1876 nearly half the magazine was taken up with a report on the annual Athletic Sports Day at his day school. The highlight of the report was a stride by stride account of the mile race which, because of the qualities of 'pluck and endurance' which it required, clearly operated, in Arbuthnot's eyes, on a higher moral plane than sprints or high jumps. However, something of the flavour of his rhetorical style, as well as his sporting enthusiasm, can be tasted in the following extract from his article:

> We are glad to notice that the entries were more numerous than last year, and hope that some of the old women of the school have been turned into genuine boys; but we are surprised to hear that there are some parents who still place obstacles in the way of their sons learning to be manly. For our part, we would rather have a youngster who can run and swim, and play cricket, but who is low down in his class at school, than a milksop who can do none of these things but is always first in his lessons. The combination of these two qualities, athleticism and scholarship, is the perfection of boyhood.[27]

By the 1880s numerous Sunday Schools were buying gymnastic equipment and setting up a cricket team. For instance in August 1881 the Trinity Presbyterian Sunday School in Canonbury, north London, announced that a cricket team had been formed 'by some of our teachers for the purpose of making greater friendship between the older lads and the teachers' and that they were looking for opponents. In the following years similar notices appeared frequently in the *Sunday School Chronicle*. Also in 1881 the Ragged School in Holloway, a mile further north, set up a Boys' Own Club, followed two years later by a Girls' Own Club. By 1885 they had a gymnasium, a cricket club and monthly rambles, and in 1888 they established a swimming club—apparently, like the gymnasium, restricted initially to boys.[28] Sport was now the question of the hour, debated endlessly at conferences of superintendents and in the columns of the religious press.[29] It became a symbol of innovation—a shibboleth for those who argued that the schools must move with the times and a chief target for traditionalists. Arbuthnot had promoted sport as an end in itself and a source of innocent pleasure, and also as a means towards a whole series of desirable ends deemed beneficial to the

---

[26] *Arundel Parochial Magazine*, April and June 1874, May and September 1875, June 1876, September and October 1877 (West Sussex County Record Office, Par 8 Arundel 7/1/1).

[27] *Arundel Parochial Magazine*, June 1876.

[28] *Sunday School Chronicle*, 19 August 1881, 13 October 1885, 13 November 1891.

[29] Dominic Erdozain, 'Sport and Religion in Modern Society' (PhD thesis, University of Cambridge, 2003).

community and nation, including the development of manly character (there is no suggestion that Arbuthnot was interested in sport for girls and women), the training of men who could defend their country in the event of invasion, and the inculcation of useful skills, such as the ability to rescue those who fell in the river. But many of his contemporaries had a more strictly instrumental view of Sunday School sport.

The key argument was 'The Problem of the Seniors'. From about thirteen the drift away from Sunday School began, with boys tending to leave first. Sport, it was argued, was what could persuade them to stay. The context of this debate was the late Victorian sporting boom, in which the years c.1875–85 were a key phase.[30] These were the years in which cricket and, above all, association football, became established as the two principal national sports in England, and a matter of consuming interest to a large part of the male population. It was also in these years that golf and lawn tennis established themselves as leading elite sports, and modern boxing, based on the Queensberry Rules, took the place of the unrespectable sport of prize-fighting. Proponents of 'modernisation' in the Sunday School movement argued that the current passion for playing (and indeed for watching and reading about) sport was inherently healthy, and that in any case the churches would be swept aside if they tried to stop it.

There were several key issues. First, there was the question of the relationship between 'spiritual' and 'secular'. Opponents of sport argued that it was diverting the Sunday Schools from their proper concerns. G.H. Kent of Heywood, wrote in 1882, 'This question of recreation and amusements is confronting our schools at the present day and demands an answer, nay it is the one question above all others that needs answering.' His answer was that 'Everything that is not of a strictly religious and educational character must be swept away, or at least kept at arms length.' He had nothing against football or cricket, but Sunday School teachers should have no time for such irrelevancies. Otherwise it might be more honest to put a picture of a footballer in the window and the sign 'Recreation Society' over the door.[31] On the other hand, supporters of Sunday School sport argued that our bodies, as much as our mind and spirit, have been given to us by God, that body, mind and spirit are interconnected and that the church should be concerned with all three. A comprehensive statement of this position was provided in a

---

[30] Denis D. Molyneux, 'The Development of Physical Recreation in the Birmingham District from 1871 to 1892' (MA thesis, University of Birmingham, 1957), pp. 25-26. Other major studies of the development of sport in this period include John Lowerson, *Sport and the English Middle Classes 1870–1914* (Manchester: Manchester University Press, 1993), and Tony Mason, *Association Football and English Society 1863–1915* (Brighton: Harvester Press, 1980).

[31] *Sunday School Chronicle*, 6 January 1882.

Sunday School Chronicle editorial of 1896 on 'The Saving of the Body', beginning with the claim that 'The attempted divorce of body and soul has ever been the source of the keenest woes of mankind.' Whereas the lives of medieval saints abound in examples of extreme bodily mortification, Jesus came to save the whole man. Therefore in seeking to save the souls of their children, Sunday Schools 'should be careful not to treat as of little account the culture of the body. When the religion of the gymnasium and the cricket-field is duly recognised and inculcated, we may hope for better results':

> Children should be taught that God has entrusted to them their bodies, and that He expects those bodies to be properly used and educated for His service. Let children be taught that their bodies are the most marvellous machines in the world and that their maker requires them to be kept clean and bright by proper exercise. Above all the fact that our bodies are temples of the Holy Ghost should be constantly emphasised. In thus seeking to save the body it will be found that the salvation of the soul has also been accomplished.[32]

Second, there were differing perceptions of secular amusements. On the one side it was argued that everyone needs amusement and that the church, by providing healthy amusements, could counter the influence of unhealthy amusements, such as pubs, gambling, and music-halls, or amusements provided by undesirable bodies, such as secularist clubs. For instance, when in 1889 Northampton Nonconformists organized a conference on 'Ought the Church to Provide Amusement?' the chief speaker on the affirmative side the Congregationalist, the Rev. E.W. Bremner, argued that

> Many amusements outside the Church were very bad indeed, and many good amusements were spoilt by bad associations. Mercenary motives, he pointed out, made the professional pleasure-caterer always seek to fully gratify the popular demand; but the Church, with the independence of benevolence, would be enabled to give to the people something that was a little, though not too much, above the average popular demand.[33]

On the other side it was argued that the appetite for amusement was potentially limitless, and the church should refuse to feed it. Thus G.H. Kent, whose letter in January 1882 had touched off a prolonged correspondence, later returned to the fray:

> Our teachers, especially of late years, have been so engrossed in pleasure-seeking sensationalism, such as football, cricket, boating, amateur theatricals, during the

---

[32] *Sunday School Chronicle*, 20 February 1896.

[33] *Northamptonshire Nonconformist*, December 1889 (Northamptonshire Studies Room, Northamptonshire Central Library).

whole of their spare time, that when they have come to their classes on the Sunday, instead of being refreshed and invigorated, they are completely exhausted, mind, body and soul.

There was nothing wrong, he said, with sport in itself, but the true Christian just does not have time for it. For twenty years retention of the 'Seniors' had been the main topic at every conference, and the answer always seemed to be better 'machinery'. What was really needed was prayer.[34]

Third, there were questions of physical health and its relation to moral and spiritual health. Advocates of sport believed that the two were connected. This was certainly the view taken by the editor of the *Northamptonshire Nonconformist*, who in 1889 introduced a sports column headed 'Thews and Sinews', and used it to propagandize on behalf of sport for both sexes. As the opening article declared, 'Mens sana in corpore sano. There's nothing to beat a sound mind in a sound body. Without the latter, in many cases, the former is impossible.'[35] Opponents feared that sport often fostered morally and religiously undesirable characteristics, such as the urge to win by fair means or foul. Professionalism was especially suspect. One religious magazine, *The Young Man*, published an editorial in 1889 on 'The Football Slaughter', complaining of the prevalence of violent play, leading to serious injuries and even deaths, and blaming this on the fact that 'gate-money and expensive trophies are more esteemed than fair and friendly rivalry'. A lecturer at the Sunday School Union in 1882, while not objecting to the schools providing recreation, saw problems inherent in competitive sport. Just playing cricket never seemed to be enough: there must be a club and matches, and they must win. And that led to the search for good players, who often proved to be those who might otherwise 'have been shunned because of their lack of moral principle' and to the marginalization of less talented members of the club.[36]

Fourth, there was the question of the allocation of time, including the question of Sunday. Sunday was absolutely sacrosanct to opponents of sport while some of the proponents were prepared to countenance Sunday sport, so long as worship took priority. Very few Nonconformists, other than Unitarians, would have accepted Sunday sport before the 1920s—and most opposed it even then. Among Anglicans there was a wider spectrum of opinion. Those who accepted, or even encouraged,

---

[34] *Sunday School Chronicle*, 12 May 1882.

[35] Hugh McLeod, '"Thews and Sinews": Nonconformity and Sport', in David Bebbington and Timothy Larsen (eds), *Modern Christianity and Cultural Aspirations* (Lincoln Studies in Religion and Society, 5; London: Sheffield Academic Press, 2003), p. 29.

[36] *The Young Man*, April 1889; *Sunday School Chronicle*, 22 September 1882.

Sunday recreation generally came from the High Church or Broad Church. Many Evangelicals remained strongly opposed. At the Church Congress in 1869 Archdeacon Denison of Taunton, a High Churchman, spoke strongly in favour of Sunday cricket, but he was opposed by the Rev. Nevinson Loraine of Liverpool, who approved of gymnastics, but not on Sundays.[37] Similar differences were seen in each of the subsequent debates on recreation in 1874, 1877, 1878, 1880 and 1892, and on 'The Observance of the Lord's Day' in 1877. In this latter debate the strongest opponent of sabbatarianism was the Rev. Brooke Lambert, a London Broad Churchman.[38] The opening speaker argued that Sunday should be a day first of religion and secondly of recreation. He claimed that he was trying to steer a middle path between the extremes of Scottish stringency and continental licentiousness. At this stage the majority of speakers tended towards stringency. But by the turn of the century, when Sunday cycling was widely popular, there were Anglican clergymen prepared to justify it, and indeed to practice it—so long as church-going came first. Thus Dean Farrar addressing a packed cyclists' service in Canterbury Cathedral in 1899, praised bicycles as 'a source of much innocent happiness' which 'it had taken the world some six thousand years to invent', and said that Sunday was a good day to cycle, as long as it did not replace church-going. In 1907 the Head of Oxford House was spending Sunday afternoons cycling with a large group from his Men's Club.[39]

Fifth, there was the question of how to attract outsiders. Proponents of sport often suggested that it was the best way of bringing outsiders into the orbit of the church. As was mentioned earlier, J. Rider Smith was claiming in the 1930s that this objective had been achieved. Opponents denied this. For instance, the London Baptist, the Rev. Archibald Brown in his 1889 polemic 'The Devil's Mission of Amusement' argued that the huge programme of amusements provided by some churches had not brought in converts, but had diluted the church's witness.[40]

And, finally, there was the question of how to refute the charge that religion was unmanly. 'A London Pastor' writing in 1885 in support of the introduction of gymnasia in Sunday Schools, declared that 'Of all the objections to religion that have been fabricated by its opponents, none is more absurd than the assertion that religion produces weak and effeminate habits.'[41] Charges of this kind were clearly deeply felt by those clergy and Sunday School teachers who wished to retain the good

---

[37] *Report of the Church Congress, Liverpool, 1869*, pp. 118-52.

[38] *Report of the Church Congress, Croydon, 1877*, pp. 366-406.

[39] *Sunday School Chronicle*, 20 July 1899; *Annual Report* of Oxford House, 1907.

[40] Dominic Erdozain, seminar paper, 'The Problem of Pleasure: Religion and Recreation in Nineteenth Century Britain', University of Birmingham, 10 May 2003.

[41] *Sunday School Chronicle*, 13 March 1885.

opinion of their fellow sportsmen. On the other hand the views expressed by the latter were probably written off by the opponents of sport as being those of 'worldly' or 'immoral' people, whose opinions were of little account.

III

Both inside and outside the churches, the late Victorian and Edwardian eras were an age of born-again sportsmen and, less often, sportswomen, who made far-reaching claims for the moral and religious, as well as physical, benefits of cricket, football, cycling, swimming, gymnastics, and many other sports, and who were often correspondingly dismissive of anyone who did not share their enthusiasm. By the 1920s and '30s the inclusion of some element of sport in the Sunday School programme was uncontroversial and no longer carried any symbolic significance. Yet some of the gloomy predictions of the anti-sport lobby seemed to have been borne out, as sport became an increasingly large and familiar part of national life. There were indeed still people in the 1930s who claimed that football and cricket, not to mention other sports, such as boxing, were not only enjoyable forms of recreation, but were also character-building. But by now it was harder to believe this. For instance the *Sunday School Chronicle*, while suitably appreciative of Eric Liddell's efforts on and off the running track, was in general unimpressed by the 1924 Olympics, 'where abuse, free fights, and racial bitterness sacrificed peace on the altar of international sport'. The editor was especially critical of the boxing where, he alleged, foul tactics were rife.[42]

But the biggest problem was the allocation of time, of which the Sunday question was the most conspicuous symbol. In the 1890s enthusiasts for sport had offered cogent criticisms of strict sabbatarianism and had made a persuasive case for arguing that the ideal Sunday might be a mixture of church-going with healthy recreation.[43] However, by the 1920s it was increasingly evident that there were many people for whom Sunday was a day to be devoted entirely to recreation, and for whom sport was, apart from work, the main focus of their life. An article in the *Sunday School Chronicle* clearly presented the situation as contemporary religious observers saw it. On Sunday, the writer claimed, railway carriages were 'full of young men and women clad—not in the sombre garments of respectability associated with church worship—but in white flannels and light frocks. They would be armed, not with prayer-books and Bibles, but with tennis racquets and cricket bats.' Most people's work

---

[42] *Sunday School Chronicle*, 31 July 1924.

[43] The best discussion of this issue is John Lowerson, 'Sport and the Victorian Sunday: The Beginnings of Middle Class Apostasy', *British Journal of Sports History*, 1.2 (September 1984), pp. 202-20.

offered them little fulfilment, so they looked for it in sport: 'Our congregations have largely deserted us, and have migrated to the playing-fields, the golf course, and the river.'[44]

The strict sabbatarianism to which most Dissenters and many Anglicans adhered in the 1880s and '90s, and to which some still remained faithful in the 1920s and '30s, appeared obscurantist, and often was. But it was also a way of making an important point—one which in the nineteenth century had mainly been the preserve of those arguing against a narrowly 'spiritual' agenda for the church: that the fullest life is that which balances the physical, the intellectual and the spiritual, and that no one of these should be allowed to crowd the others out.

---

[44] *Sunday School Chronicle*, 10 July 1924.

CHAPTER 7

The Lumber Merchant and the Chocolate King: The Contributions of George Hamilton Archibald and George Cadbury to the Sunday School Movement in England and Wales

Jack Priestley

A Journey of Reflection

For one of the participants the weekend did not get off to an auspicious start. It was Wednesday 19 April 1905. George Archibald was tired. For five weeks now he had been on the move, lecturing constantly, often two and sometimes three times a day, including Sundays, indeed, especially on Sundays. But respite was at hand. The conference he was about to attend would be crucial to his plans but at least he would be staying among friends in one place and in comfort for several days. Tomorrow would be Maundy Thursday and the long Easter weekend lay ahead. There was just the two-hour journey to make from London to Birmingham. He was already at the station, having booked into the Euston Station Hotel. He relaxed and went to bed early. And then :-

> When I awakened on Friday morning it was *seven minutes to ten!* I hesitated a moment, then leaped out of bed, threw on my clothes, rang the porter, paid my bill and flung myself into the train just as it was pulling out of the station. To my consternation I got into a compartment reserved for ladies... I had not shaved, my boots were unlaced, my tie was loose and my luggage was half fastened. I made all possible apologies to my fellow travellers and when I arrived I did my best to camouflage my normal appetite.[1]

Perhaps on that train journey he was able to reflect on the events which had led him, a Canadian-American lumber merchant turned Sunday School Superintendent, to this point at which he was being invited to be the guest of one of the best known and most successful businessmen and benefactors in England, George Cadbury of Bournville fame.

---

[1] E.A. Johnstone, *George Hamilton Archibald: Crusader for Youth* (Wallington: R.E. Press, 1945).

Archibald was less than a month off his forty-seventh birthday. He was descended from a long line of robust adventurers; enterprise was in the blood. The Archibalds had been among the first Scottish Presbyterian families to migrate to Ulster following the battle of the Boyne in 1690 and again, when the British ruthlessly expelled the French settlers in 1755 from what had been Acadia and re-named it Nova Scotia, a later generation of the family had been among the early pioneers, making the hazardous crossing of the Atlantic Ocean from Londonderry to Halifax. George was among the third generation of that family, not suffering the privations of his grandparents but still with plenty of wilderness around him. He was later to begin many of his lectures with the words, 'The pity is that not every boy has a primeval forest for his playground... Mine was the most wonderful boyhood a lad ever had.'[2] Besides the endless forests there were the creeks and the rivers, the fishing and the hunting, horse riding and tracking, especially in the three-month long summer holidays from school. In contrast, Sunday, as he recalled later, was 'an awful day' with narrow, straight-backed pews in the Kirk, services lasting two hours, incomprehensible sermons followed by being kept indoors all afternoon lest the children should 'commit the unpardonable sin of playing games on the Sabbath'.[3]

Catastrophe came when the logging mill had been destroyed by fire and the family had migrated to Boston, where thirteen-year old George began his working life as a cash boy earning two dollars a week. It had been a harsh transition for all the family and most members, including George, had moved back to Halifax within three years. Nevertheless, it had given the impressionable teenager a lasting sympathy for those who suffer the deprivations and street violence of growing up in the inner city. Then had followed another great family tragedy in 1873. His older brother Will had been drowned when the ship in which he had been travelling to Newfoundland to join his Uncle John in starting a new lumber mill had been sunk in a storm off the island. George had taken his brother's place and within a decade the firm had started to become very profitable. More significantly it was also during that period that George, now married, had also started Sunday School work, first as a teacher, later as superintendent.

With financial security increasingly assured it was this activity which had now begun to assume greater and greater significance for him. By the time his uncle had moved the firm to Montreal in 1888, George, the father of a daughter, had been giving his church-based work an ever-higher priority and he had soon found himself in charge of the biggest Sunday School in the English-speaking Protestant part of the city. Five

---

[2] Johnstone, *George Hamilton Archibald*, p. 11.
[3] Johnstone, *George Hamilton Archibald*, p. 24.

years later he had taken the irrevocable decision. With his fortune made he had sold out his share of the business to his uncle, become a man of independent means, and had registered at the School for Christian Workers in Springfield, Massachusetts (later to become incorporated into Hartford Theological College across the state border in Connecticut). Rejecting all suggestions that he might extend this course in order to become an ordained minister, he had found himself, within a year, back in Montreal as Provincial Secretary to the Protestant Sunday School Union for the whole of Quebec.

It was in this capacity that he had attended the large International Sunday School Convention in St Louis in 1893. There he had started to come into contact with delegates from other countries. It was also a period when new thinking about education in general was in the air. John Dewey, later to become America's most recognized educational thinker and reformer, was Archibald's contemporary, just eighteen months younger. By the mid 1880s Dewey's views on progressive education, which stressed student-centred rather than subject-centred schools, and education through activity rather than through rote learning, had already begun to permeate American day-school training institutions. Religious education, however, had remained largely untouched by them. Archibald now had the one advantage of having been a mature student: his thinking was a generation ahead of that of most of his contemporaries. Moreover, he had found himself swept along by them, for the basic ideas coincided with his own freedom-loving experiences of childhood and youth. He had started to advocate their practice in his Sunday Schools and his enthusiasm had quickly drawn him to the attention of international figures attending the great triennial international conventions. St Louis was followed by Boston in 1896 and Atlanta in 1899. In particular, certain members of the British delegation, feeling the need for some new initiative in their own schools and churches, had paid particular attention. An invitation to undertake a lecture tour of major British cities had soon followed and important names were beginning to become interested. One name had been brought to his attention above all others.

Now he was *en route* for this potentially crucial meeting which had been arranged by Frederick Taylor, the Secretary of the Friends' First-day (Sunday) School Association. It was being held in the form of an Easter Conference, at which he was to be the guest speaker at the home and in the presence of George Cadbury himself, Quaker head of the internationally famous chocolate firm and a well-known benefactor.

A Meeting of Minds

While the two men knew one another by reputation it is unlikely that they had any idea of just how much they had in common when Taylor introduced them. There was much more in their backgrounds than either could have realized. They were successful businessmen, both, in that well-worn Victorian phrase, 'self-made men', who had amassed a great deal of money early on in life, Cadbury, of course, far more than Archibald. But neither had ever seen money-making as an end in itself. For Cadbury this had been quite self-consciously so from the very beginning. His early ambition had been to become a doctor but his father had insisted that he and his older brother should follow him into the family tea business. Both had suffered major setbacks which had nearly led to failure, and both had recovered from them through their own unassisted endeavours and courage. Taking over the tea business in 1861 both Richard and George Cadbury had known, even then, that its future was in the balance. Two years later both brothers had been planning new careers as debts mounted. But they had moved into cocoa, developing a new refining and chocolate making process, so that within thirty years the Cadbury firm was using one third of the cocoa beans imported into England. Archibald had recovered from fire and deaths in the family by sheer hard grind. Neither had had any form of higher education or even apprenticeship. Now they discovered that each had lost an elder brother to whom they were deeply attached. In Cadbury's case the wound was still festering. It was just six years previously that Richard had died while travelling to the Holy Land in March 1899. A.G. Gardiner, Cadbury's first biographer, assessed the significance:

> Each was the complement of the other. George, intense, original and daring. Richard, the steadying and balancing element. Together they formed a remarkable combination, and behind the external differences there was a permanent and fundamental unity of aim. Both regarded business as the instrument of disinterested ends.[4]

And it was while the business had still been small, situated within the city and failing, that Richard and George had begun to show their practical concerns for both religion and education. They had quickly realized that many of their workers were illiterate and so they had begun classes, early each weekday to teach reading and writing. The textbook which they had used was the Bible. One thing quickly led to another and the early morning teaching session had begun to culminate in a short service of worship for those who wished to stay and join in.

Before long the brothers had moved their growing business five miles out into the Warwickshire countryside, but the practice had grown with the company until at its peak, around the turn of the century, some 2,200 women workers at Cadbury's were attending a short service of Christian

---

[4] A.G. Gardiner, *The Life of George Cadbury* (London and New York, Cassell, n.d.) p. 72.

worship every morning: the men, numbering about 1,000, for reasons not given, did so only on one morning every week.

In addition to this Cadbury continued all his life to run his own Sunday School for men and boys back in the inner city where the firm had begun. This involved him in rising at 5.30 and leaving his house in Selly Oak before 6.30 a.m. to make the four mile journey into the city either on horseback or on what was to become his famous tricycle. Always he attempted to arrive by seven o'clock, which was the time when the breakfast, which he had organized for the men, was served, giving him a chance to socialize informally for half an hour before he began the class.

Gardiner obviously found this activity difficult to characterize. It had no church or denominational connection; it was neither a temperance society nor a church but, he writes, 'the aims are distinctly religious'.[5] But if, like Gardiner, there were others who felt it was not a proper Sunday School because it had no direct denominational affiliation the Sunday School Union itself had no doubts. In the millennial year of 1901 George Cadbury had been made President of the British National Sunday School Union, a position which he had taken very seriously but with extreme modesty.

It was the custom of the weekly twenty-four page broadsheet, *The Sunday School Chronicle*, to devote the front page of the first issue of every year to a statement by the new President. However, the headline for the issue of 10 January 1901 is simply, 'A Chat With Mr George Cadbury'. He did not make statements: he conversed. Through a process of question and answer, in which it soon becomes apparent that all his achievements had to be drawn out of him, we find a seamless wholeness in his thought patterns. There is no distinction made between children and adults, but neither is there the slightest hint of condescension. His schools are for people, not just for the young or the poor; indeed they are for himself as well. For he, too, is a learner. Asked about the difficulties of combining the devotional with the commercial at his factory he replies, 'We have found the service a check on ourselves. It makes us endeavour to be absolutely just.'[6] We find too that he has little interest in teaching matters of doctrine, more on following Jesus' example of storytelling. 'We want to emphasise its spiritual character', he comments and immediately links this to political life. 'Wherever the Church has a real hold there you will find godly politicians which is what the country needs.' There is a crucial point here, however, which Cadbury, in this impromptu interview, failed to acknowledge. It is one to which both he and Archibald were to give much attention later on. For Philip Cliff gives

[5] Gardiner, *Life of George Cadbury*, p. 40.
[6] *Sunday School Chronicle* 1371 (10 January 1901), p. 1.

the basic sociological fact about Cadbury's own city when, at the beginning of his history of the Sunday School Movement, he notes that 'An examination of the Sunday School statistics indicates a less than 1% return to immediate membership of the churches over a period of fifty years.'[7] Even when, at the end of his book, he modifies that statement, it is only to state in his conclusions that it had risen to no more than 2.7% by the time of the 1957 survey and that the best that could be found in 1970 was around 4.7%.[8] By these dates, of course, overall church-going figures had begun to fall significantly in the period after Cadbury's death.

Throughout his presidential year Cadbury continued to feature in the pages of the *Chronicle*. It was noted that some 20,000 children visited his house, the Manor, at Northfield every year for services and informal Sunday School gatherings and that he had built a barn capable of holding 700 in case of inclement weather. But perhaps most significantly for the purposes of this study, his year as President showed a greater awareness than before of the need for Sunday School teachers to be trained and it is clear from an article published on 31 March 1901 that he had been making himself conversant with the wider picture. 'America is ahead of us', he commented, 'in treating the Sunday School as an educational institution, while perhaps we are ahead in the stress we lay upon the need for the deep silent work of God in the heart.'[9] While the second part of this statement can be held open to question outside of Cadbury's own Quaker tradition, there was little doubt about the first part and throughout the year the paper carried continual articles and correspondence on the topic of teacher training. And now one of the chief American exponents of the modern Sunday School had called to visit. George Cadbury and George Hamilton Archibald came face to face at the Manor House in Northfield, Birmingham.

The Child in the Midst

During that Easter weekend Cadbury listened to Archibald's lectures, which basically were the ones he had been taking round various centres in England over the previous five weeks. They were about children, about their differences of intelligence and temperament, about their thought worlds of make believe, the place of fantasy, myths and legends in their lives, and they were about teachers as teachers. What were the secrets of keeping order, of retaining interest, of using children's play for positive advantage in educational activities? Finally they were about organization

---

[7] P. Cliff, *The Rise and Development of the Sunday School Movement in England 1780–1980* (Birmingham: National Sunday School Union, 1986) p. 5.

[8] Cliff, *Rise and Development*, p. 322.

[9] *Sunday School Chronicle* 1381 (21 March, 1901) p. 1.

and about grading. What were the differences in children of varying ages and how should lessons be adapted to those differences? 'A child of twelve', Archibald constantly reiterated, 'is nearer to a person of twenty in mental outlook, than a child of six is to one of twelve.'[10]

'Nice theories', was Cadbury's immediate reported comment at the end, 'but can you really put them into practice?'[11] It was a challenge that Archibald had been expecting but it was also one which he had no difficulty in countering. He already had years of experience behind him and a reputation to support his success. Cadbury's commission was immediate. There and then he offered Archibald the use of the Ruskin Hall as a Demonstration School until the school which he was having built on his new village estate of Bournville was finished and suggested that for immediate teaching assistants he might be able to obtain the help of a group of young men and women who were training at Woodbrook to become Quaker missionaries. The full significance of this latter point was not to appear for some time, but it marked the beginning of the worldwide influence of Archibald's ideas as increasingly his general approach was taken to a growing number of countries around the world. Special attention was also given to aspects of traditional Sunday School work which had been taken for granted for years or simply never thought about. Sunday Schools were uncomfortable places for children and young people. Either they were perched on adult chairs or squashed together on benches, often in galleries, with no tables, paper or writing materials. Silence had long been explicitly regarded as a virtue. Their task as scholars was to listen but not to speak; to be inert rather than to be active, just as Archibald himself had had to be on that uncomfortable family pew in Halifax, Nova Scotia. A total revolution in the whole world of British Sunday Schools began with the acquisition of small chairs and tables, together with sand trays, blackboards, plasticine, pencils, paper and building blocks. Significantly, however, the syllabus remained the same. It was the Bible but the Bible presented as story in all its varying literary forms. Neither Archibald nor Cadbury were fundamentalists. Neither had been to a university but, as Archibald's biographer daughter recorded, all the lecturers back at Springfield had had what she termed 'the modern point of view'. 'Therefore', she added, 'lines of critical enquiry were not new to the family. So it was with satisfaction that we could follow them further at Woodbrooke.'[12] Again, in discovering Selly Oak the Archibalds had secured yet another advantage commensurate with their general outlook and philosophy. Dr Rendel Harris, a notable biblical scholar who had been offered a lectureship in Biblical Studies at the University of

---

[10] Johnstone, *George Hamilton Archibald*, p. 62.

[11] Johnstone, *George Hamilton Archibald*, p. 93.

[12] Johnstone, *George Hamilton Archibald*, p. 99.

Leyden, had turned it down in preference for the post of Director of Studies at Woodbrooke where his Monday lectures attracted great attention. Cadbury's invitation to stay, then, was to prove decisive and in the case of the Archibald family permanent, although it was to be a decade before anything like a steady state was finally arrived at in the form of substantial and permanent buildings. In the meantime a large house, bearing the nondescript name of West Hill, on the main Bristol road leading out of Birmingham, was leased, a lecture room built in the garden and a dozen students recruited for a three-month residential course. Two qualified staff, one, Emily Huntley, enticed from a Primary School headship following a regional conference at Southend, were employed under the direction of Archibald to work with his daughter Ethel, herself Froebel trained. For the first time in England, Sunday School teaching had begun to enter the world of professionalism.

Meanwhile, Archibald saw this only as a physical base. His own work as an itinerant lecturer continued. Rather like John Wesley, he seems to have regarded the whole world as his parish. He began to organize regional conferences throughout the length and breadth of the country while at the same time continuing to make international links via the missionary contacts at Woodbrooke. Very soon official figures in the major denominations began to take notice. J.H. Shakespeare, General Secretary of the Baptist Union, had already issued a warning to the Free Churches about Sunday School statistics beginning to show trends of a steep decline. At the same time a thorough investigation of the position of Sunday Schools in the Congregational churches was being undertaken by their Young People's Secretary, Melville Harris—later to become a key figure in Archibald's enterprise.

Events began to move very quickly culminating in a two-day meeting in Birmingham in November 1911 which resolved to establish a country-wide centre. It was agreed that the title should be 'The National Training Institute for Sunday School Workers' with two clear aims—'to train leaders of work in the moral and religious education of children and young people' and 'to carry on experimental research work in the study of the psychology of the unfolding life with a view to the formation of correct methods of work in schools'.[13] A major two-day conference was then arranged for the end of March 1912 under the chairmanship of Sir Joseph Rickett, with speakers from a wide range of religious organizations. Unfortunately a major railway strike coincided with the date fixed and many of the London-based delegates and speakers experienced travel difficulties. Nevertheless, three crucial resolutions were passed by this early ecumenical assembly. The first stressed the necessity

---

[13] *Westhill Minute Book 1*, 19 November 1911 (Westhill Endowment Trustees, Selly Oak, Birmingham).

of applying the best methods of work in secular education to religious education, whereby 'the spiritual life of the child may be developed and the building of Christ-like character aided'. The second resolution noted that the overall objective was to found a National Institution for the fuller development of Sunday School work, suited to the needs of children at the various stages of their development, whilst the third advocated that such intentions required a permanent base for the work, necessitating the erection of suitable buildings.[14] These resolutions were all passed unanimously by the forty-three people present which, despite the rail strike, included three Members of Parliament and well-known names such as those of the Methodists, Dr Scott Lidgett, Dr A.S. Peake, Professor James Moulton and the Baptist, Sir George Macalpine. Two other important statements for the future of Sunday School work in Britain were made at the same meeting. The first confirmed an offer from George Cadbury of a gift consisting of four acres of land for such a building as was being proposed, directly opposite Woodbrooke at Selly Oak, Birmingham. The second resolved that no building would begin until at least £8,000 had been raised.

There seems to have been just one unfortunate note: no Church of England or Roman Catholic delegates had been present. The latter had not been expected but the former had and the National Society was approached to nominate a member for the Council being set up to carry things forward. The formal reply stated, however, that the Society could not send a representative unless, 'a Church [i.e. as distinct from 'chapel'] atmosphere in the proposed Institute was guaranteed' and 'unless there were a Church Sunday School in which any students could have their practice and observation work'. This issue was discussed in full at an Executive Committee Meeting in London on 3 July. The rest of the Minute reads,

> After full consideration of the whole matter we do not see how we can guarantee either a Church atmosphere in the Institute or that a Church Sunday School will be used for practising any more than we can guarantee all other denominational facilities. To attempt such would be to split up the work into sections, instead of which we hope to lose sight of these distinctions as far as possible.[15]

Perhaps this position on both sides was to be expected. The Anglicans had already set up their own such centre at Blackheath. What does come as a surprise, however, is the immediate response of this committee in its very next Minute, following a resolution which was obviously put on the spur of the moment. It reads,

---

[14] *Westhill Minute Book 1*, 28 March 1912.
[15] *Westhill Minute Book* 1, 3 July 1912, p. 33.

> Seeing that we cannot get Church of England co-operation and that, therefore the term 'National' seems out of place, we decide to abandon the use of the word in our title.[16]

Two observations immediately spring to mind. First, this was in the period when, for the first and, perhaps, only time in British history, Nonconformists were in a majority, while the Anglicans, being the Established Church, never for one moment contemplated calling their educational organization anything other than the *National* Society. Secondly, the outcome was that this whole enterprise with its lofty, national ambitions for the new twentieth century, chose to continue its activities under the name of a suburban villa. It was to remain as 'Westhill' (albeit now one word) until the end of its existence in 2002 when its new owners, Birmingham University, immediately dropped it.

Archibald himself, however, spurned any notion of parochialism. He had a base and he never neglected it, but at the same time he remained totally committed to the national and international dimensions of his work. Among his early appointments had been an extension tutor, organizing twenty or so courses a year throughout the length and breadth of the country. When the Christian Conference Centre at Swanwick opened at Easter 1912, Archibald made the first Easter booking - for a Sunday School Teachers' Conference that was to become an annual event until 1929, with many visitors coming from overseas. Archibald, with his family, had meanwhile conducted an invitation lecture and demonstration tour in Australia and New Zealand in 1912, taking in other places *en route*. Nearer home a Westhill Kinder-kapel had been opened in the Netherlands by a former student returning from Selly Oak together with a monthly journal, which had the effect of some sixty schools following what was termed the 'Westhill method'. These were only closed down with the Nazi invasion of 1940 although, even as late as 1995, the effects were still being felt and written about.[17]

In 1913 Archibald, together with his colleagues, played a leading part among the 370 British delegates at the 2,500 strong International Convention on Sunday School work being held in Zurich, contributing a session with his team on what he termed 'atmosphere', described as a secret 'lying with the leader and in proportion to the control over self and the depth of the hidden life'.[18] 'Atmosphere' was always a key word in Archibald's vocabulary. It related to the priority of the spiritual over all else, including other recognized qualities such as scholarship. It was to remain a key expression and factor throughout Westhill's subsequent

---

[16] *Westhill Minute Book* 1, Minute 6, 3 July 1912, p. 34.

[17] See J.A. van Merlo-van Kuipers, *Westhill geschiedenis en methode* (Zoetmeer: Uitgeverij Boekencentrum, 1995).

[18] *Sunday School Chronicle,* 17 July 1913, pp. 613-15.

history, no doubt owing much to the Quaker influence of Woodbrooke across the road.

Archibald's other major contribution to the Sunday School Movement throughout the first quarter of the twentieth century lay in publications. The titles of his earliest writings, such as *Bible Lessons for Little Beginners* (published privately c.1900) sound very 'twee' to modern ears but he went on to produce, among other works, such titles as *The Power of Play in Child Culture* (Sunday School Union, 1905), a small treatise on storytelling graphically entitled *The Danger of Pointing the Moral* (Pilgrim Press, 1905), as well as a more substantive volume, *The Modern Sunday School: Its Psychology and Method* (Pilgrim Press 1926). Equally he encouraged others to write, as in the case of Carey Bonner whose *Child Songs* with its 'Foreword' by Archibald went through twenty-two editions between 1908 and 1951. In that one-page introduction Archibald spelt out his whole basic philosophy.

> We must help children to be children, not adults. The selection of words as well as music from the child's point of view is an application of a fundamental Kindergarten principle...and if the same principle be carried into all branches of our Sunday and other schools it will free the children from the trammels of adultism which have bound, and are still binding, them fast. This book is an application of that principle.[19]

The first book to come out of Westhill itself from someone other than Archibald was *The Child in the Midst*, written in 1916 by Ernest Hayes and going through seven editions up to 1953[20] Significantly, the strength of the tradition can be seen in the fact that the last book to emerge from the College before it closed was *Childhood Studies: A Reader in Perspectives of Childhood* consisting of ten essays from members of staff and associates, edited by Jean and Richard Mills.[21]

A Dying Breed

George Cadbury died on 24 October 1922. There were, of course, many tributes, including glowing ones from sections of the press which had fiercely criticized him over the years for his social and political attitudes. Few dwelt on the deep religious motivation behind all his living. His own more radical newspaper, the *Daily News* did, however, include the following notice which was duplicated in the *Sunday School Chronicle*:

---

[19] C. Bonner, *Child Songs* (London: The Pilgrim Press, 1950 [1908]).
[20] E. Hayes, *The Child in the Midst* (Wallington: Religious Education Press, 1953 [1916]).
[21] J.M. and R. Mills (eds) *Childhood Studies: A Reader in Perspectives of Childhood* (London and New York: Routledge, 2000).

The modern Sunday School Movement has lost a valuable friend and benefactor in Mr George Cadbury. From the beginning of Mr George Hamilton Archibald's work in England, Mr Cadbury realised its possibilities and gave it his unhesitating support. Few probably will ever realize all that children and teachers of our schools owe to him. He was not only generous in support of the work. He followed developments with the keenest interest.[22]

More significant, perhaps, is a simple six-page document written privately by his wife, Elizabeth Cadbury, after his death. It is discursive rather than analytical, but its significance lies in its perceived priorities over a long lifetime. There is little about prestigious projects and nothing about national events. She concentrates on the Cadbury brothers' motives and on the importance to them of the Adult Sunday School and the daily act of worship in the works. Then towards the end appears the following paragraph describing a scene shortly before George's death. It could be a commentary on the text, 'Except you come as a little child':

One morning on one of the last days that George Cadbury was able to go to his office at Bournville he was seen walking up Linden Road past the schools. It was 12 o'clock and the carillon was playing one of his favourite hymns; 'I think when I hear that sweet story of old'. He stopped and in a moment was surrounded by children coming out of school; they pressed round him and he took their hands, with a few words of blessing. Some of those present said they will never forget the impression his loving interest made on them.[23]

George Archibald continued with unabated enthusiasm for another eight years, recruiting ever more students and extending the work throughout Britain and far beyond. He finally retired in 1930 and handed over the principalship of Westhill to the Revd Dr Basil Yeaxlee, significantly, perhaps, the first ordained person to serve on the staff.[24] Archibald had one great surprise still to come. In early April 1935 he received out of the blue a telegram from Connecticut informing him that the trustees of Hartford Seminary Foundation wished to award him the honorary degree of Doctor of Divinity. His immediate reaction was to say, 'Surely not for me. I'm a businessman.' It was the first degree he had ever received and only the fourth such degree that Hartford had ever awarded in its hundred-year history. But he accepted and made what was

---

[22] *Sunday School Chronicle* (9 November 1922), p. 285.

[23] *How Did The Garden Grow?* (unpublished personal memoir of George Cadbury by Elizabeth Cadbury, Birmingham City Library, MS 466/172/1-6, undated).

[24] Equally significantly, perhaps, was the fact that Yeaxlee was also a genuine academic and scholar who, after leaving Westhill, went on to become, for fourteen years, Lecturer in Educational Psychology at Oxford University. Although ordained as a Congregational minister, Yeaxlee spent his life in education.

to be his final trip across the Atlantic. One paragraph of the full citation summarized his achievements:

> Mr Archibald, born in Canada, educated in religious education in the United States, and doing his life work in Great Britain, represents in himself an English-speaking union. Competent judges say that no one in these forty years of service has made a larger contribution to church life and work.[25]

George Archibald died at home three and a half years later, on 3 February 1938, from a heart attack. Tributes flowed in and continued to do so for some weeks. The main obituary in the *New Chronicle of Christian Education* included this assessment of his significance within the Sunday School Movement.

> During its one hundred and thirty-five years history the National Sunday School Union has good reason to be proud of the many forward movements it has initiated but it never did a finer piece of work than when it provided a platform for Dr George Hamilton Archibald when he came to England thirty-six years ago with his vision of a Sunday School Movement that placed the child in the midst. In those days the churches had not realised fully their responsibility for the nation's youth or, at any rate, they had not tackled the problem in a way that modern conditions demanded. With his vision and his enthusiasm Dr Archibald revolutionised the Sunday School Movement.[26]

Further on, a full two-page article gives a broader assessment of Archibald's significance in doing more than any other person to bring Sunday Schools and their methods into line with mainstream educational practice.[27] On his arrival in 1902 the almost universal norm had been to crowd large numbers of children of all ages together, seating them on uncomfortable backless benches and exhorting them just to listen. Archibald had begun by something as simple as changing the furniture. Then he had gone on to engage children in the activity of learning, training teachers to know both their Bibles and their child psychology. But his emphasis was never just on learning. It was primarily on spiritual growth, on learning to be, not just to know. Nor was Archibald's influence confined to Britain or even to the English-speaking world. Philip Cliff, writing his bicentennial history of the Sunday School Movement, begins his chapter on the period 1904–1939 with the statement,

> It would be true to say that this period is dominated by one man and his ideas, ideals and enthusiasms; a man who, by sheer force of wit, wisdom, common sense and

---

[25] *The New Chronicle* (6 June 1935), p. 35.

[26] *The New Chronicle* (10 February 1938), p. 86.

[27] The *New Chronicle* (10 February 1938), pp. 94-95.

candour, met a need, gave new enterprise to the Movement, and changed the face of Sunday Schools in all denominations across the country and the world.[28]

In fact, as this paper has tried to demonstrate, there were two men involved, as Archibald would have been the first to recognize. He, himself acknowledged it in his actions, if not in his recorded words. From the mid-1920s onwards the Archibalds had become regular weekly attenders at Quaker meetings and their daughter had become a full member and missionary of the Society. At the same time the records show that it was English Congregationalists who made the greatest working commitment to the new institution, providing its ministerial principals and the bulk of its predominantly lay teaching staff until 1971 after which it was led successively by a Plymouth Brother, an Anglican priest, and finally, two laymen, one a Methodist, the other a Baptist, but never by a Quaker. Their quietism, however, can easily be wrongly taken by historians to denote an absence of participation, not only in this particular story, but throughout the whole history of the Sunday School Movement. Nothing could be further from the truth. They continued right to the end to serve as governors and trustees and to be major financial benefactors, never claiming back any share of the proceeds arising from the eventual sale to the University of Birmingham in 2002, but continuing to participate fully in the new trust fund, which now carries into a new century the ideals established by Archibald and Cadbury together, stated as

the promotion of Education in a manner which reflects the principles of the Christian Religion and the tradition of the historic Free Churches and the Promotion of Dialogue and Educational Interchange between the Christian Church and persons of other living faiths.[29]

A Broader Assessment

This paper has dealt with a specific historical relationship and series of events within the Sunday School Movement. More details of it and of Westhill's subsequent history exist elsewhere.[30] However, within this particular narrative lie points of continuing significance regarding children and young people within British church life. For the truth today,

---

[28] Cliff, *Rise and Development*, p. 205.

[29] 'A Guide to Grants for Christian Education', Westhill Endowment Trust, Selly Oak, Birmingham, 2004.

[30] See, e.g., Cliff, *Rise and Development*; C.M. Parker, *Westhill: An Informal History of Seventy-Five Years* (Westhill: Westhill College, 1982); and J.G. Priestley, 'Westhill College: The Embodiment of a Religious and Educational Ideal', *Panorama: International Journal of Comparative Religious Education and Values* 14.2 (Winter, 2002), pp. 169-84.

in the first decade of the twenty-first century, is not only that the British churches face a real internal crisis as they try to look ahead towards the next generation, but also that in society at large there is probably a greater ignorance of the Bible than at any time since the Reformation. The same is not true to anything like the same extent in the United States. There, Sunday Schools continue to flourish while in Britain they have virtually disappeared for all but the children of a dwindling number of churchgoers within the concept of 'young church', itself the brainchild of one of Archibald's successors, the Revd 'Bert' Hamilton.[31] Is it possible, at least in some part, to account for this out of the story we have been telling? There are, I think, two main points for consideration.

Between them Cadbury and Archibald brought together the traditions of the North American Sunday School Movement and those of Britain. Much of the opposition which Archibald encountered through his work, especially in the early days, largely arose out of a widespread Edwardian assumption that the British had nothing to learn from the Americans and that anyway the history and cultures of the two traditions made them incompatible. That must be questioned, perhaps even more so today than a century ago.

Always there would seem to have been great similarities between the origins of the two Sunday School Movements. In North America (which includes Canada), as in Britain, Sunday Schools grew out of basic attempts to overcome poverty and deprivation. In Britain we are familiar with such names as Robert Raikes and Joseph Lancaster whose schools were committed to the need to cater, as cheaply as possible, for street children whose life prospects were severely limited. In their ragged schools irreligion and illiteracy went almost hand in hand and continued to do so right up into the twentieth century with initiatives like those of George Cadbury where the Bible served as a basic text book for learning to read. What Archibald himself experienced as a young boy in the backwoods of Nova Scotia as well as in the crowded back streets of Boston would have been very recognizable at the time to anyone involved in British Sunday School work.

But there were differences although so subtle as to be unnoticed by most historians. The main one concerned the British obsession with social class. Archibald, as a child, was a member of a poor family but the poverty he had inherited was the poverty of a settler, migrant community which did not regard it as in any way a fixed state of affairs. Sunday Schools were for everyone in such a community, not only, or even predominantly, for the poor. One of Archibald's attributes, of which he

---

[31] Rev. H.A. (Bert) Hamilton was Principal of Westhill College, 1945–54. Philip Cliff's *Rise and Development of the Sunday School Movement* is dedicated to him with the words, 'father in God to so many, soul friend and visionary'.

seems to have remained totally unaware, was his absolute classlessness in an Edwardian English environment. By contrast, the culture of the British Sunday School Movement had remained almost as class ridden as it had been through the earlier, long Victorian period. It had begun to change, but very slowly, and one reason for that was because class consciousness had actually been one of its *raisons d'être* leading to its mixed and sometimes confused motives. Cliff draws attention to this by quoting a West London Auxiliary Report of 1868, one paragraph of which reads

> Very many of the Sunday Schools have been undergoing a gradual change for some years; the class of children attending them becoming more respectable in character. While this has its advantages, at the same time *it alters to some extent the object and aims of Sunday Schools, which is mainly to look after those children wholly uncared for by their parents and who are found playing about our streets on the Sunday.*[32]

Although working so harmoniously together we see Cadbury and Archibald representing these two sides of the Sunday School Movement. Cadbury stood in the best tradition of British Christian benevolence. He had risen to great wealth, but throughout his life he had used his riches for the benefit of the poor. At the same time he remained rooted within the *mores* of a dying age. He would not, for example, employ married women in his factory: their place, he insisted, was at home. Marriage meant an automatic end to employment for any of his women workers. Meanwhile he laboured on into old age with his Sunday School work amongst the poorest men in the inner city, concerned with literacy as much as with gospel, using the latter as a primer for the former.

The Archibald reforms, by contrast, pointed to a future where basic literacy could be more and more taken for granted, but religious teaching, by which he meant Christian teaching, could not. It was to receive a tremendous boost from his initiative but, in retrospect, the American Sunday School Movement, working in a more classless society, has not been nearly as adversely affected by rising affluence and in consequence has not suffered from being left behind as part of working-class culture.

The second point for consideration lies in the relationship between Sunday Schools and day schools. Before he arrived in England Archibald had had no experience of religious education taking place anywhere else but in churches. In the United States then, as now, it was anathema to have religion taught in the state or public schools. By contrast in England and Wales, and despite the Cowper-Temple Clause insisting that 'no formulary distinctive of any one denomination may be taught', the Bible was being read daily in all elementary schools. The lessons were dull in

---

[32] Cliff, *Rise and Development*, p. 144. Italics added.

the extreme, consisting largely of reading a verse at a time round the class first thing in the morning or last thing in the afternoon, but it was there, together with the regular saying of the Lord's Prayer, and had been since 1870.

To most religious observers this must have seemed to give great advantages to the British scene over against the American one. This was especially so with developing legislation in 1918 and again in 1944 when the special restrictions were totally lifted and Religious Education was taught within the time-table like any other subject with the one exception now in its favour, that is was compulsory—the only subject by law which *must* be taught in every state school, both primary and secondary. Moreover, the churches became directly involved as partners in the Agreed Syllabus mechanism whereby the content for each local authority was determined by the agreement of four committees, those of the Church of England, other denominations, the Local Authority and the teachers through their professional organizations. As these latter two nearly always chose their representatives from church members among their professional colleagues there was rarely any dispute.

Archibald, of course, having died some nine years earlier, did not live to see this state of affairs come into being, but it is likely that he would have welcomed it, especially as it coincided with the increasing incursion into British educational thinking of many of the ideas of Dewey and others which he had helped to promote. Sixty years on, however, we can now see that it was a false dawn. Far from promoting religious education as Archibald perceived it, the subject has taken a turn that he would have been unable to imagine. Social changes in Britain have meant that it has become a vehicle for social cohesion in a multi-faith society, a way of understanding others' beliefs but not of confronting one's own. That takes place in the synagogue, the mosque, the gudwara, the temple or the church, but not in the classroom.

The problem, however, for British churches is that they are not nearly so geared up to what is termed 'children's ministry' as their American counterparts. Indeed they can be seen as more than a hundred years behind. They are now struggling to fill the gap which extends from individual churches right up into ministerial training. It is very noticeable that in American theological colleges there is a wider breadth of what is thought to constitute ministry and that 'children's ministry' has an established place alongside pastoral ministry as a professional concern. Archibald was able to choose between the two at Springfield Theological College as far back as 1895 when he elected to be commissioned for youth work in the School for Christian Workers rather than to be ordained as a pastor. Johnstone describes the principles by which such a school was established within the seminary.

> It was undenominational in the scope of its service; its teachers and managers represented various evangelical bodies; it was intended in no way to run counter to the work of the theological seminaries... The curriculum included lectures on the Bible, Christian Doctrine, Ethics, Church History, the organisation and administration of the Sunday School and methods of teaching.[33]

She goes on to comment that the course was based soundly on the teachings of the great educators. A century later it would still be difficult to find such courses of professional training available to British churches. Archibald's first courses at Westhill were revolutionary but were at most only of some eight weeks duration: most training was done at weekend conferences and that has continued to be the practice. Because of the nature of historical developments professional teachers of religious education in Britain have increasingly been trained for a different role and for a quite different ideology from that of the 1950s and 1960s. Moreover, the professional ministry within British churches has rarely recognized Sunday School leaders as colleagues. At most they are seen only as lay assistants. The historical reasons for this difference are not difficult to discern, but they have now left the British churches terribly exposed within a multi-faith environment in which the Islamic, Jewish, Muslim, Sikh and other religious groups have far more effectively co-ordinated educational policies for their children than the Christian churches. Teaching about faiths is not the same thing as teaching religion and the former is dependent on the latter. There is urgent need for a new initiative but few signs of one to come.

---

[33] Johnstone, *George Hamilton Archibald*, p. 58.

CHAPTER 8

Sir Joshua Fitch and 'The Sunday School of the Future'

Geoff Robson

The genesis of this paper lies in my contribution to the centenary celebrations of the death of Dr R.W. Dale at Carrs Lane Church, Birmingham. Unlike the papers which were published in the commemorative volume, *The Cross and the City*,[1] my paper picked up on the contemporary relevance of Dale's interest in Religious Education and, in particular, the politicizing of this subject between 1985 and 1995.[2] During these years I had served as one of Her Majesty's Inspectors of Schools[3] and subsequently as a consultant to the National Curriculum Council and its successor bodies. Re-reading Dale's biography in preparation for my contribution brought me up against the bizarre spectacle of this leader of Nonconformist theology and churchmanship banning the Bible from the curriculum of the Birmingham Board Schools in 1873 in the name of religious liberty.[4] One Nonconformist principle appeared to be contradicting another, arguably more important, namely the right of everyone to read the Scriptures for themselves.

My resulting curiosity about how this situation came about led me into the complex history of the Bible in the English elementary school and the success of the clergy, of all denominations, in claiming the sole right to its interpretation. This success had lasting and baneful effects on the place and nature of Religious Education in Day Schools during the twentieth century. One early result was the removal of Religious Education from the scrutiny of HMI by the 1870 Education Act. From then until well after 1944 no inspections of RE by HMI took place in English schools

---

[1] C. Binfield (ed.), *The Cross and the City: Essays in commemoration of Robert William Dale, 1829–1895*, *Journal of the United Reformed Church History Society*, Supplement 6.2 (Spring, 1999).

[2] G. Robson, 'Religious Education, government policy and professional practice, 1985–1995', *British Journal of Religious Education* 19.1 (Autumn, 1996) pp 13-23.

[3] Hereafter abbreviated to HMI.

[4] A.W. Dale, *Life of R.W. Dale of Birmingham* (London: Hodder and Stoughton, 1902), pp. 479-83.

and the subject ceased to be included in any official publications such as the 'Handbook of Suggestions for Teachers' which the Board of Education, relying almost entirely on HMI contributions, published regularly from 1902.[5]

In his evidence to the Cross Commission in 1887, Dale's fellow Secretary of the Central Nonconformist Committee of the National Education League, the Rev. H.W. Crosskey (by 1888 also Chairman of the School Management Committee of the Birmingham School Board) maintained that any teaching which fell short of a full exposition of denominational theology was inadequate as Religious Education. As this was not possible in schools supported by public rates then no RE ought to be given and the religious needs of the pupils left for the rival denominational Sunday Schools. Dale himself was a member of the Cross Commission and revealed his equally uncompromising position when questioning David Holdsworth, a Wesleyan teacher from Newcastle upon Tyne.[6]

Such an attitude showed great confidence in the capacity of Sunday Schools to do what Board Schools, as a result of the Cowper-Temple Clause, could not attempt, namely produce well informed and convinced members of individual Christian denominations. How far this confidence was matched by the ability of the Sunday School teachers remains a matter of debate. Whether, in the light of the nature of Sunday Schools in the later nineteenth century, they should attempt it at all was the question raised by Sir Joshua Fitch in an address entitled 'The Sunday School of the Future' given at Church House, Westminster, in the late 1890s.[7] So who was Sir Joshua Fitch and what gave him any authority on the subject of Sunday Schools?

Joshua Fitch was born in 1824 in Southwark. His father was a clerk in Somerset House. He began as a pupil-teacher in the British School at Borough Road (Joseph Lancaster's original foundation) where he rose to become a full 'assistant teacher', leaving to be head of a school in Dalston. Studying hard in what little spare time he had gained him a BA degree at London University in 1850 (with a first class in Scripture) followed by an MA (in Classics) in 1852. During that year he joined the staff of Borough Road Training College, rising to become principal in

---

[5] G.A.N. Lowndes, *The Silent Social Revolution* (Oxford: Oxford University Press, 2nd edn, 1969), pp 111-10. The 1937 edition, for example, ran to over 600 pages and covered ten subjects but made no mention of religious education.

[6] For an extended treatment of the whole issue together with detailed references to the original sources, see G. Robson, 'The Churches, the Bible and the Child: Sir Joshua Fitch and Religious Education in the English Elementary School, 1860–1902', *History of Education Society Bulletin* 69 (May, 2002), pp 365-93.

[7] J.G. Fitch, *Educational Aims and Methods* (Cambridge: Cambridge University Press, 1900), pp. 365-93.

1856. The quality of his teaching impressed Matthew Arnold when he inspected the college and Lord Granville, President of the Privy Council, who also visited Borough Road. Granville made him an HMI in 1863. He was, therefore, one of the very few members of Her Majesty's Inspectorate, before 1870, who had any real experience of teaching poor children in an elementary school.[8] Fitch was an Anglican, who for eleven years taught a Sunday School class in Southwark. A regular worshipper, he read his Greek New Testament every day, but did not belong to any party within the church. He was knighted in 1896, after his retirement from the Inspectorate, and died in 1903.[9]

The Inspectorate increased Fitch's experience, including secondary schools, as a member of the Endowed Schools Commission. In addition to inspecting elementary schools in Yorkshire he and another HMI (R.D. Fearon) investigated the total elementary education available in Birmingham, Leeds, Liverpool and Manchester in 1869. He gained a detailed knowledge of London as inspector for Lambeth (1877–83), and the rural and small town scene as Chief Inspector for the Eastern Division (all eastern counties from Lincolnshire to Essex) from 1883. A committed advocate of equal educational rights for women he was inspector of training colleges for women from 1885–94, took an active part in establishing Girton College, Cambridge, and the Girls' Public Day School Company. He was an examiner at London University and involved in the University Extension Movement. He also visited France, Belgium and America, reporting on their education and teacher training systems.

From all this it may be gathered that Fitch was an independent but committed commentator on the changes produced by the 1870 Education Act. He had experienced at first hand the bitter denominational rivalry which resulted in the removal of RE from government consideration. His own report on Yorkshire in 1869 pointed, in vain, to a middle way between sectarian indoctrination and complete secularization of the curriculum.[10] He intervened vigorously in the attempt by an Anglican lobby to introduce explicitly credal teaching into London Board schools in the 1890s[11] and was, in the last year of his life, taking issue with the promoters of the 1902 Education Act on the extent

---

[8] J.E. Dunford, 'Biographical details of Her Majesty's Inspectors of Schools appointed before 1870', *History of Education Society Bulletin* 28 (1981), pp. 8-23.

[9] A.L. Lilley, *Sir Joshua Fitch: an account of his life and work* (London: Arnold, 1906), and *DNB*.

[10] *Report of the Committee of Council on Education 1869–70* (London: HMSO, 1870), pp. 329-30.

[11] J.G. Fitch, 'Religion in the Primary Schools' and 'The Bible in Elementary Schools', *The Nineteenth Century* 36 (1894), pp. 58-66, 817-23, J.G. Fitch, 'Creeds in the Primary Schools', *The Nineteenth Century* 42 (1897), pp. 690-702.

to which it increased the scope for denominational competition in providing new schools.[12] He was a strenuous champion of the Bible as a force for liberal education rather than mere religious nurture, still less as simply a sanction for public morality.[13]

He was experienced as both a Day and a Sunday School teacher, as well as a teacher trainer and HMI, but he had no particular religious axe to grind. Rather he was concerned for the spiritual welfare of children and had thought long and hard about how this was best promoted. Although by now a septuagenarian he did not use his comments on Sunday Schools to indulge in nostalgia for a former era nor to pontificate upon the evils of the present, as compared with a past golden age. He was certainly not uncritical of the achievements of the new age of compulsory elementary education,[14] which had led to the dramatic fall in attendance at morning Sunday School sessions where the teaching of reading had predominated. So he was not out to vaunt the superiority of the qualified Day School teacher over against the volunteer teacher of the Sunday School.

What he did endeavour to communicate to both was the need to take the teaching role seriously, to be self-critical, to ask constantly, 'how can I improve my teaching and enable the pupils to learn for themselves?' The essential element in each case was the personal interaction of teacher and pupil and in this he saw that the smaller classes in the Sunday School gave their teachers a distinct advantage over those in the Day School situation. Nevertheless, there were not, in either case, any 'easy' methods, short cuts or quick solutions. Only the best was good enough for the children and this meant steady attention to every aspect of the task. What he had said to Day School teachers in his 'Lectures on Teaching' in 1880 he would not water down for the Sunday School teachers of the twentieth century.

Before outlining what he had to say and giving some telling quotations from his address it is worth reminding ourselves that all education consists in constantly re-inventing the wheel. No generation can rely on inheriting wisdom from its predecessors, all must learn afresh by experience from their own successes and failures. Hence, although many of Fitch's ideas may now seem platitudinous a hundred years or more after their enunciation, at the time they provided some very necessary stimulus for thought.

---

[12] J.G. Fitch,'The Education Problem' and 'Amendments to the Education Bill', *The Nineteenth Century and After 51* (1902), pp. 24-38, 952-65.

[13] J.G. Fitch, *Lectures on Teaching* (Cambridge: Cambridge University Press, 1881), pp. 373, 427, and 'Methods of instruction as illustrated in the Bible', in Fitch, *Educational Aims*, pp. 1-45.

[14] J.G. Fitch, 'Primary Education in the Nineteenth Century', in R.D. Roberts (ed.), *Education in the Nineteenth Century* (Cambridge: Cambridge University Press, 1901), pp. 34-58

If, as Philip Cliff has indicated, complacency rather than critical realism typified the centenary celebrations of the National Sunday School Union in 1903, the following chapter of his book shows that there were also those who were well aware of the challenges which the post-1870 situation presented to the Sunday Schools.[15] Fitch was fully alive to the context in which he was speaking.

> It is evident that the history of the present dying century has done much to alter the relative position of Sunday Schools. They are no longer needed to teach reading and writing. The law of 1870...and the subsequent legislation...have gone far to render the Sunday School in one sense superfluous. And it must be remembered too, that with very few exceptions, our public elementary schools are all impressed with a religious character... What then is the area of usefulness still left vacant, which the Sunday School of the future should be ready to occupy?... The answer to this question is not easy.[16]

He then broadens the context from the educational parallels which people would have expected from him into a consideration of the place of the Christian home in the nurture of children and the Sunday activities of a Christian family. From this vantage point he comments that

> It is very easy for those of us who are interested in a society or an institution which has done great service to overestimate it... It is a mistake to become so proud of the extension of our Sunday School system, as to think it a high triumph to record the addition of thousands to the roll of scholars year by year. It would be a much higher triumph to record that the number of instructed parents and of God-fearing households, among the working classes, had so increased that the Sunday School was becoming a superfluous institution.[17]

Recognizing that this was still far from the reality and that many parents were 'glad to be rid of the encumbrance' of children on a Sunday afternoon, 'for them it is our duty to make the Sunday School as efficient for its purpose as we can'. In doing this, however, the guiding principle should be 'that the school is rather the imperfect substitute for the home, than a supplement, or even a substitute for the day school'.[18] In fact the association of Sunday School with the experience of having to attend school during the week meant that many men and women linked leaving Day School with abandoning the church.

---

[15] Philip B. Cliff, *The Rise and Development of the Sunday School Movement in England, 1780–1980* (Birmingham: National Christian Education Council, 1986), pp. 172-75, 197-202.

[16] Fitch, *Educational Aims*, pp. 368-69.

[17] Fitch, *Educational Aims*, p. 371.

[18] Fitch, *Educational Aims*, p. 372.

> Considered as an instrument for attaching children to Christian churches and interesting them permanently in public worship, the Sunday School of the past has proved to be a failure. I once met a young workman in whom I had felt some interest, and asked him among other things whether he attended a place of worship on Sunday. 'O Sir,' he replied, 'I have left school now.' You see he associated the act of going to church with part of school discipline.'[19]

If the true parallel for the Sunday School was the Christian home rather than the day school then the teacher's prime role was that of a friend rather than an instructor.

> He derives great influence from the fact that he is not a paid professional teacher but is drawn to the children simply by good will and a desire to be useful to them. His attitude to the children should be less that of an instructor or a lecturer, than that of a friend and companion... Since the classes in a Sunday School are small there is the possibility of a closer intellectual intimacy between teacher and taught...and the character of individual scholars can be better studied.[20]

The purpose of this friendship is to share the teacher's own interests and enthusiasms with the children, including reading interesting stories to them and talking about incidents from the world around them which the teacher has noticed or heard about. 'There should be a moral meaning—an element of religious edification in it. But this meaning need not be intrusive. It should be held in solution so to speak.' The key element is to discover what interests the scholars, 'that...which the young people like and enjoy most', and use it.[21]

Fitch recognized, of course, that 'the chief *raison d'être* of a Sunday School in the minds of most persons is that it should be a place of religious instruction'. Given this function there was much to be learned from good Day Schools. Firstly, that teaching was not an easy task.[22] It required preparation, a capacity to ask questions which stimulated thought rather than simply produced stock answers, an ability to decide what could usefully be committed to memory and what was unlikely ever to have any spiritual value, and above all honesty in the selection and presentation of religious material.

> If there be Bible stories, about the historical truth or the ethical value of which you have any misgivings, do not attempt to teach them... The field thus open to you is still very wide. There are stories and parables, poetry and devotion, the narrative of our Saviour's life and teaching, the deeds of heroes and the utterances of prophets. If we can teach these things well, and if we find that teaching them interests ourselves

---

[19] Fitch, *Educational Aims*, p. 388.
[20] Fitch, *Educational Aims*, p. 374.
[21] Fitch, *Educational Aims*, p. 375.
[22] Fitch, *Educational Aims*, p. 378.

and our scholars, we may be well content to make such topics the staple of our religious instruction. But if we cannot teach doctrines *ex animo* and with the full consent both of our intelligence and of our hearts, it is better not to attempt to teach them. It is above all things necessary that we should observe perfect candour towards the children and not ask their acceptance of statements of truth which we expect them to unlearn when they grow up.[23]

Preaching, in particular, was not a model to be followed. 'To an inexperienced teacher the easiest and most obvious way of communicating knowledge is to preach. But of all methods, this is the least effective to young children. Be sure once for all that preaching in a class is not teaching.'[24] Instead teachers should be experimental, trying out all manner of approaches to discover what best suits their particular pupils. Broadening the scope of the Sunday School and making it more child-centred was the essence of Fitch's message and it may best be concluded in his own words.

There are among those who hear me, some who have serious misgivings lest in thus widening the area of Sunday School work, they should be departing from the purely religious purpose which has hitherto been understood to control that work. But such persons will do well to consider how very imperfectly even that purpose has hitherto been fulfilled, and how little it is likely to be fulfilled, so long as special religious edification or the promotion of Churchmanship, is regarded as something apart from the character and life of the child... They will also recognise the truth that after all intellectual culture is closely akin to religion and is indeed part of it. When this is considered, it will be seen that the Sunday School in the future can occupy a place in our system of public education, which the public elementary school can never fill; because its teaching is less formal, more intimate, more inspiring, and can connect itself more closely with the personal character and daily life of the child...

Here then is part of the task which lies before the Sunday School teachers of the next century. But it demands from them some freshness of mind, and some freedom from traditional ideals and methods, in order that the work may be well done.[25]

[23] Fitch, *Educational Aims*, pp. 388-89.
[24] Fitch, *Educational Aims*, p. 381.
[25] Fitch, *Educational Aims*, pp. 392-93.

CHAPTER 9

Sunday Schools and Social Change in the Twentieth Century

Doreen Rosman

On 11 June 1936 the Newark and District Sunday School Union held its annual festival and procession. Dating back to 1872, this was, according to the local newspaper, an 'ever popular event'. Banner headlines proclaimed 'SUNSHINE FAVOURS SUNDAY SCHOOL FESTIVAL', 'TWO THOUSAND SCHOLARS AND TEACHERS IN NEWARK SPECTACLE', 'NORTH END SCHOOL WINS SHIELD'. The press coverage was comprehensive, detailing every display and activity. Each school devised its own processional theme, some serious, some more light-hearted: North End Methodists depicted the people of the world as 'All One Family', while their counterparts from Charles Street dressed up as characters from 'Red Riding Hood'. Biblical tableaux, described by the local paper as 'devices', ranged from familiar gospel stories to obscure Old Testament tales, such as Nehemiah making his petition to Artaxerxes. Tableaux could also be presented on 'general' themes: the London Road Congregationalists reflected the anxiety of the times with a display on the inhumanity of warfare entitled 'Shall nation speak peace unto nation?' But the atmosphere on 11 June was far from sombre. There was a long stream of decorated wagons, each filled with excited children in fancy dress. Prizes were awarded not only for the best wagon but also for the best groomed horse and the cleanest harness. The long procession wound its way to the Sconce Hills, where in the evening further prizes could be won—for singing, for a variety of races, or for throwing a cricket ball. The reporter noted that the Salvation Army Assurance Band 'which had been specially engaged from London was an added attraction', but took care to respect local sensitivities by recording that 'the Newark number one carnival band gave an excellent performance on the hills'.[1]

The Newark festival serves as a reminder that Sunday Schools retained a high profile in local communities well into the twentieth century. Their peak in terms of attendance came in the 1880s but they remained

---

[1] *Newark Advertiser and South Notts. Gazette* 17 June 1936, p. 3.

substantial organizations long after that. Turn-of-the-century Congregationalists in Westminster Bridge Road, London, organized a total of fifteen Sunday Schools, nine in the morning and afternoon, and six in the evening, staffed by 400 teachers and catering for 5,000 students.[2] Inter-war Newark was a small market town, but the Barnbygate Methodists alone fielded 413 children in the 1936 procession.

I cite the example of Newark because my mother took part in the annual festival and like others of her generation told her own children about it. The big Sunday School jamborees were a memorable part of her childhood. But like most of the other children who participated in such activities my mother did not come from a family of regular churchgoers. From the very beginning Sunday Schools had catered primarily for children of parents who did not necessarily attend public worship and they retained this function up to and even beyond the two world wars. First World War chaplains, who compiled a report, *The Army and Religion*, noted that many of the soldiers to whom they ministered had church links in boyhood, and quoted estimates that around four out of every five children went to Sunday School.[3] Decades later a BBC poll, published in 1955, discovered that 83% of respondents born before 1939 had been involved in Sunday School or Bible class for several years as children; only 6% claimed that they had never attended.[4]

By later standards the Sunday Schools of the first half of the century with their hordes of pupils, festivals, and processions, were flourishing institutions, but church leaders of the time were more aware of failure than success. Numbers might be high but they were declining. In 1901 over three-quarters of five to fourteen year olds in England and Wales featured on Sunday School registers; by 1931 the percentage had dropped to around two-thirds.[5] This figure needs to be set in context. Eighty years earlier the proportion of children of that age in Sunday

---

[2] J. Cox, *The English Churches in a Secular Society: Lambeth, 1870–1930* (Oxford: Oxford University Press, 1982), p. 81.

[3] D. Cairns, *The Army and Religion: An Enquiry and its Bearing upon the Religious Life of the Nation* (London: Macmillan, 1919), pp. 121-22.

[4] Philip B. Cliff, *The Rise and Development of the Sunday School Movement in England, 1780–1980* (Birmingham: National Christian Education Council, 1986), p. 275

[5] My calculations, derived from B.R. Mitchell, *British Historical Statistics* (Cambridge: Cambridge University Press, 1988), pp. 15-16; R. Currie, A. Gilbert and L. Horsley, *Churches and Churchgoers: Patterns of Church Growth in the British Isles since 1700* (Oxford: Clarendon Press, 1977), pp. 167-90. The fractions are approximations, based on the assumption that pupils were predominantly aged between five and fourteen. The number of children within this age bracket has been divided by the number of Sunday School scholars. Some children, however, started Sunday School before they were five; some left before they were fourteen; others stayed on longer.

School would have been under 60%, probably well under.[6] Notwithstanding the recent decline, a larger percentage of the cohort could be found in Sunday School in 1931 than in 1851. That fact, however, would have done little to console denominational leaders, even if they were aware of it. At a time when adult church attendance was going down, churches depended on graduates from Sunday Schools to refill pews vacated by those who died. This was where Sunday Schools failed to deliver. The majority of their pupils never became regular worshippers. According to an Assistant Chaplain-General the soldiers he encountered during the First World War had been 'lost to Christ's Church at the age of adolescence'.[7] Vigorous attempts were made before, during, and after the war to improve Sunday Schools: graded classes were introduced so that children could be taught in ways appropriate to their age; new thinking about child development influenced the design of lessons, which became more child-centred; and further training for teachers was introduced.[8] But none of this induced pupils to move on from Sunday School to church. The reason for failure was simple: neither the parents, who sent their children to Sunday School with what Sarah Williams has called 'dogged determination', nor the children themselves regarded churchgoing as a logical corollary of Sunday School attendance.[9]

Sarah Williams is one of a number of historians who, in recent years, have interviewed elderly people about their childhood memories in order to ascertain what they and their parents thought about religion. Clergymen sometimes criticized parishioners, who presented their children for baptism and sent them to Sunday School but who did not go to church, for failing in their duty to God. This was not how the people themselves interpreted their behaviour. Dr Williams shows that, in the eyes of parents, having a child baptized—and sending it to Sunday School—was itself proof that they were taking their religious

---

[6] *Census of Great Britain 1851* (British Parliamentary Papers Series: Education, 11; Shannon: Irish University Press, 1970 [1854]), p. lxxi. According to the census there were 2,407,642 Sunday School scholars in 1851, 60.1% of the population aged five to fourteen. But at this time many adults attended Sunday School. Since they are included in the number of scholars, the number of children who went to Sunday School would have been well below 60%.

[7] Cairns, *Army and Religion*, p. 115.

[8] Cliff, *Rise and Development*, ch. 12; M.M.B. Bolton, 'Anglican Sunday Schools 1880–1914' (MA thesis, University of Kent, 1988); S.J.D. Green, 'The Religion of the Child in Edwardian Methodism: Institutional Reform and Pedagogical Reappraisal in the West Riding of Yorkshire', *Journal of British Studies* 30 (October, 1991), pp. 377-98; S.J.D. Green, *Religion in an Age of Decline: Organisation and Experience in Industrial Yorkshire 1870–1920* (Cambridge: Cambridge University Press, 1996), pp. 242-55.

[9] S. Williams, *Religious Belief and Popular Culture in Southwark c.1880–1939* (Oxford: Oxford University Press, 1999), p. 7.

responsibilities seriously.[10] Non-churchgoers had clearly-held views of their own about which religious observances were important and which were not. Attending church services came in the latter category. 'You don't have to go to church', one woman commented around 1930, 'I mean you can live a decent life without all that rigmarole, can't you?' But it was attendance at worship that she dismissed so peremptorily, not the basic teaching of the church: 'When I get to the pearly gates', she continued, 'he won't hold it against me, I'm sure of that. And if he does, I'll tell him straight. I was too busy on Sundays getting dinner and tea for you bloody lot to have time to sit on my arse in church!'[11] People who did not attend church sometimes followed other devotional practices. A Birmingham woman, born in 1935, recorded that her parents 'didn't have time to go to church', but noted that 'My Mom never went to bed without her prayer book by her side and saying her prayers.'[12] Going to church was not seen as a primary religious obligation, but the religious education of children was. Children from some non-churchgoing families were taught to say grace after meals and prayers at bedtime. The latter custom appears to have been particularly widespread. Geoffrey Gorer, who analysed some 5,000 responses to a questionnaire circulated in the early 1950s, noted that 'Prayers before going to bed are part of the ritual of the end of the day for most English children, almost independently of whether their parents ever say a prayer or attend a church service or no.'[13] The main way, however, in which parents satisfied their sense of responsibility for the religious training of their children was by sending them to Sunday School. Interviewee after interviewee recalled how their non-churchgoing parents had insisted that they attend. It is unduly disparaging to suggest that parents just wanted the children out of the way so that they could enjoy an uninterrupted Sunday afternoon—although that was no doubt an attractive bonus for couples with large families in tiny, cramped houses. They sent their children to Sunday School, Richard Hoggart maintains, 'because that was the right thing to do'.[14] One of Sarah Williams' interviewees, a woman born in 1915, was more explicit: she attributed her mother's insistence that the children went to Sunday

[10] S. Williams, 'Urban Popular Religion and the Rites of Passage', in H. McLeod (ed.), *European Religion in the Age of Great Cities 1830–1930* (London: Routledge, 1995), pp. 230-31.

[11] Quoted in H. McLeod, *Class and Religion in the Late Victorian City* (London: Croom Helm, 1974), p. 50.

[12] Quoted in S.G. Parker, 'Faith on the Home Front: Aspects of Church Life and Popular Religion in Birmingham 1939–45' (PhD thesis, University of Birmingham, 2003), p. 67.

[13] G. Gorer, *Exploring English Character* (New York: Criterion Books, 1955), p. 249. Cf. Williams, *Religious Belief and Popular Culture*, pp. 142-47.

[14] R. Hoggart, *The Way We Live Now* (London: Chatto and Windus, 1995), p. 4.

School, while she got on with the washing, to her belief that they should 'learn about God'.[15]

Churchmen were concerned that children who attended Sunday School did not seem to learn much about God. To the average soldier, one First World War chaplain reported, 'such doctrines as those of the Trinity, the Incarnation, the Divinity and Humanity of Christ are...mere gibberish'.[16] But this was not what the children had been sent to Sunday School to learn. Non-churchgoing parents were not on the whole bothered about the detail of dogma: children from the same family sometimes went to different Sunday Schools, even on occasions crossing the Catholic–Protestant divide, a clear sign that consumers were not unduly disturbed by theological differences.[17] They wanted their children to receive a basic religious education and some assumed that any church could supply it. Another World War I chaplain complained that 'Men who have been years in Sabbath schools have no real grasp of religion.'[18] Sunday School scholars may not have understood religion in the way that he and his colleagues hoped, but it is clear that they did acquire a generalized Christian knowledge, which those born later lacked. Writing in the 1990s, Grace Davie described the experience of a hospital chaplain who visited a gynaecological ward, filled with middle-aged and elderly women, and a maternity ward, most of whose occupants had been born after 1960. The former were familiar with Christian language and concepts; the latter were not.[19] Sunday Schools acquainted their pupils both with the language of Christian faith and with Bible stories: think of those Newark children illustrating the tale of Nehemiah and Artaxerxes. Richard Hoggart suggests that the schools also helped mould deep-seated attitudes which influenced the way people subsequently coped with life.[20] Above all Sunday School instilled a life-long familiarity with hymns. Describing a group of elderly working-class women of the 1980s, Hoggart comments, 'None of those women would know much poetry, if any, except perhaps for a few rhymes remembered from school. But their minds were full of a kind of poetry, a comforting and uplifting poetry on which they could without thinking draw, which they could hear in the backs of their heads.'[21] Women such as these may not have become the theologically literate and committed church members for whom the clergy yearned, but they retained something from their years in Sunday

---

[15] Williams, *Religious Belief and Popular Culture*, p. 138.

[16] Cairns, *Army and Religion*, p. 116.

[17] Williams, *Religious Belief and Popular Culture*, pp. 139-41.

[18] Cairns, *Army and Religion*, p. 121.

[19] G. Davie, *Religion in Britain since 1945: Believing without Belonging* (Oxford: Blackwell, 1994), pp. 123-24.

[20] Hoggart, *Way We Live Now*, pp. 268-70.

[21] Hoggart, *Way We Live Now*, p. 271.

School. It is striking that a number of people who took part in oral
history interviews recalled their teachers with affection, even remembering
the names of men and women long dead, whose kindliness and simple
piety had in some way touched their lives.[22]

For most interviewees, recollecting their time in Sunday School was an
exercise in nostalgia, but for a minority Sunday School had marked the
beginning of long-term involvement with the church. Some children
from non-churchgoing homes responded with enthusiasm to the Sunday
School ethos, and worked hard to gain credit stars, collect attendance
texts, and earn 'reward books', which were still produced in vast numbers
by the religious press in the first half of the twentieth century. Those who
chose to go a step further, however, and became church members
received little support from parents who regarded regular churchgoing as
unnecessary, excessive, sanctimonious, and hypocritical. Alan Bartlett
points out that in such a culture joining a church was an act of social
nonconformity and it is not surprising that few chose to do so. But at a
time when Protestant churches had difficulty attracting adult converts
Sunday Schools provided a steady trickle of new members. The situation
of the churches, Bartlett concludes, would have been much worse without
them.[23]

If some children positively enjoyed Sunday School, others hated it.
Faith Ogersby who was born in 1890 in Yorkshire recalled that 'Sundays
were hateful days. My mother sent us to the Primitive Methodist Sunday
School...because school began earlier and we had longer sessions and she
wanted rid of us for as long as possible. What I learned there for my good
I shall never know.' John Burnett, who reproduced her memoir in a study
of working-class autobiography, suggests that such criticism is untypical
of the writings he examined.[24] Oral history interviews indicate that for
many working-class girls Sunday provided the only opportunity of the
week to wear their best clothes. 'You had a Sunday outfit you see', a girl
born in 1914 explained, 'you only wore it on Sunday... As soon as I was
finished from the Bible class you'd take them off, hang them up and put
on your ordinary clothes. You weren't allowed to wear your Sunday best
for playing with... So...I looked forward to...Sunday just for that.'[25]
Dressing up made going to Sunday School a special occasion for girls, if
not for boys. Far from constraining the young, Sunday School often gave
them access to a wide range of social activities, sporting, dramatic, and

[22] Williams, *Religious Belief and Popular Culture*, pp. 135-36.
[23] A.B. Bartlett, 'The Churches in Bermondsey 1880–1939' (PhD thesis, University
of Birmingham, 1987), p. 196.
[24] J. Burnett, *Destiny Obscure: Autobiographies of Childhood, Education and Family
from the 1820s to the 1920s* (Harmondsworth: Penguin Books, 1984), pp. 142-43.
[25] C.G. Brown, *The Death of Christian Britain: Understanding Secularisation
1800–2000* (London: Routledge, 2001), pp. 129-30.

musical.[26] Some schools had bands, while others gave pupils the opportunity to take part in plays and sketches, concerts and comic operas. Local Sunday School Unions organized musical festivals and 'Big Sings'.[27] In the Midlands and the North there were the famous Whit Walks, and throughout the country there were anniversary celebrations and Sunday School treats. These were real treats for children who had few of the opportunities later generations take for granted. Peter Stevens who was born in Faversham in 1929 recalled the excitement of the annual outing to Sheerness by a special train chartered from the Southern Railway: 'Holidays were impossible for most folk—so what a treat it was, even if it is a pebble beach. All the Mums went, too, and the Vicar must have made special arrangements with an Island church, because we always had tea in a church hall. I have never forgotten the taste of salmon and shrimp paste sandwiches.'[28]

Accounts of treats and outings reveal what an important role Sunday Schools played in community life. The Whit Walks in northern and midland towns were major communal events, processing with bands and banners along all the main thoroughfares. Southern towns had nothing quite like this, but Alan Bartlett points out that, in Bermondsey, Sunday School excursions, which began with a march to the railway station accompanied by brass bands, had something of the flavour of the northern walks.[29] Processions such as these helped pupils identify with a particular church community. In December 1910 officials from the Sunday School at Bethel Baptist Chapel in Waterfoot, Lancashire, decided to order 'a Patent Woven Banner nine feet by eight feet in crimson and gold', and a few months later they purchased twelve new sashes to match, four blue and eight red.[30] Marching under a colourful banner, emblazoned with the school's name, or competing with rival schools in musical festivals or sports, all helped foster a powerful sense of belonging, which extended beyond the children to embrace the whole family.

---

[26] On sporting activities see Hugh McLeod's contribution to this volume, 'Sunday Schools and Sport', ch. 6 above.

[27] The North Cheshire Unitarian Sunday School Union, for example, organized picnics, rambles, musical festivals, and an 'Annual Sing'. A number of schools within the Union had their own bands, and at Gorton in 1924 thirty children took part in an operetta, 'The Gift': F. Churm, *Something Attempted: A History of the Union 1863–1963* (Mossley: North Cheshire Unitarian Sunday School Union, 1963).

[28] P. Stevens, *Childhood Memories of Abbey Street and Faversham in the 1930s and 1940s* (About Faversham, 44; Faversham: Faversham Society, 1995), p. 28.

[29] Bartlett, 'Churches in Bermondsey', p. 196.

[30] W. Arnold, *Bethel Baptist Church and Sunday School, Waterfoot: Historical Survey of the Church and the School 1839–1954* (Waterfoot, n.d.) p. 22.

Women who rarely attended services themselves regarded the church or chapel whose Sunday School their children attended as 'our church'.[31]

In the course of the twentieth century activities of this kind gradually died out. 'Big Sings', which attracted huge numbers of participants, flourished in the Victorian and Edwardian periods but became less common in subsequent years. Whit Walks continued in some places into the 1930s but seem to have ceased in their traditional form thereafter.[32] Sunday School parties, treats, and outings survived into the post-war years, but without the old sense of occasion. No longer were special trains hired, or bands employed. As increasing numbers of families enjoyed holidays away from home, children ceased to regard the annual Sunday School trip with such excitement. The Sunday School Anniversary, traditionally a major event in the chapel year, was still celebrated in the Yorkshire fishing village of Staithes as late as the mid-1970s: non-churchgoing fathers squashed into chapel to watch their children sing and recite, much as their predecessors had more than a century before.[33] But by this time celebrations of this kind, which had once been widespread, were becoming increasingly rare.

In the immediate aftermath of the Second World War few would have predicted that Sunday Schools, which had played such a prominent role in British life, were on the verge of collapse. The Second War, like the First, was followed by a drop in Sunday School attendance, but even so around 47% of five to fourteen year olds featured on Sunday School registers at the start of the 1950s.[34] Even more would have attended Sunday School, however briefly, at some point in their childhood. But from the mid 1950s Sunday Schools entered a period of terminal decline. The timing of their demise reinforces Callum Brown's claim that it was the long 1960s which sounded the death-knell of 'Christian Britain'.[35] Although attendance at Sunday School had dropped considerably in the first half of the twentieth century, it was still common in the 1950s for non-churchgoing parents to send their children to Sunday School—or to comparable non-denominational organizations such as Crusaders or

---

[31] Williams, *Religious Belief and Popular Culture*, pp. 97-98.

[32] Such processions were still held in a few post-war communities but they appear to have become events for churches at large, not just for Sunday Schools. See an account of a Whit Walk in Kingswood, Bristol, which was still held in the late 1990s, in T. Jenkins, *Religion in English Everyday Life: An Ethnographic Approach* (New York: Berghahn Books, 1999), pp. 75-220, and particularly, for the origins and nature of the walk, pp. 95-107.

[33] D. Clark, *Between Pulpit and Pew: Folk Religion in a North Yorkshire Fishing Village* (Cambridge: Cambridge University Press, 1982), pp. 95-99.

[34] My calculations, derived from Mitchell, *British Historical Statistics*, pp. 15-16; Currie, Gilbert and Horsley, *Churches and Churchgoers*, pp. 167-90.

[35] Brown, *Death of Christian Britain*, pp. 1-7.

Covenanters. In the years that followed, that practice died out entirely. By 1989 only seven out of every hundred children in England attended Sunday School.[36] An institution which had once catered for the bulk of the child population had become almost exclusively the preserve of children from churchgoing families.

The collapse of Sunday Schools both reflected and contributed to the overall decline of institutional religion. For years Sunday Schools had been the main point of contact between non-churchgoers and the churches. Indeed Sarah Williams has argued that a desire to maintain contact was part of the motivation for sending children to Sunday School: the practice was 'a conscious effort of parents to identify the family with the teachings of the church through the medium of their offspring', a process she describes as 'religion by deputy'.[37] During the 1960s that desire to identify with the churches evaporated. In an age when all existing values were being questioned and authority of all kinds was under challenge, churches lost much of their credibility, and they were increasingly regarded as out-dated and irrelevant. At the same time they suffered from a general social trend away from organized, corporate activity: life-styles became more privatized, based on home and television, and voluntary organizations of all kinds had difficulty attracting members. The churches could not hope to be exempt from this phenomenon. According to opinion polls, most people continued to profess some kind of belief in God, but they no longer saw any need to associate with a religious organization, even in the tenuous way favoured by their parents and grandparents. Once common phrases, 'our church' and 'our chapel', were replaced by the more impersonal 'the church', 'the chapel'. In Grace Davie's words, the British people were now content to believe 'without belonging'.[38]

Many parents still desired religious and moral education for their children, but they no longer looked to the churches to provide it. The 1944 Education Act had made Christian worship and religious instruction compulsory in state-supported schools for the first time in English history, and parents seem increasingly to have assumed that children would get the teaching they needed there. As in so many other areas of life, a secular institution took over a role which was once the prerogative of the churches. Late twentieth-century fathers crowded into school halls for nativity plays and harvest celebrations, instead of paying an annual visit to church to watch their children perform at the Sunday School Anniversary as their predecessors had done.

---

[36] P. Brierley, *Christian England: What the 1989 English Church Census Reveals* (London: Marc Europe, 1991) p. 100.

[37] Williams, *Religious Belief and Popular Culture*, pp 126-27.

[38] Grace Davie's book, *Religion in Britain since 1945*, is sub-titled *Believing Without Belonging*. For a summary of opinion poll evidence of belief, see pp. 77-79.

At the same time as non-churchgoers were drawing back from the churches, church leaders were re-thinking the nature of their provision for the young. In the past, schools which met on Sunday afternoons had often operated independently of other church activities, but during the middle third of the twentieth century there was growing concern to integrate Sunday School children into the wider life of the church. The church was conceived as a family, embracing both old and young. It was hoped that children would share in worship with older members of the family, get to know and feel supported by them, and so choose to retain their church links as they grew older. By the 1970s most Sunday Schools had transferred their afternoon activities to Sunday mornings so that the whole church family could meet together at the same time. The new arrangements reflected support for the idea of a 'Family Church' among church leaders, and also solved the problem of finding people willing to teach on Sunday afternoons. They did not, however, take account of the attitudes of parents who were used to sending their children to church in the afternoon, and who had no desire to accompany them to a morning service.[39] Changing the time at which Sunday Schools met did nothing to stem, and may even have exacerbated, the decline in attendance.

Church policy may have made it more difficult for Sunday Schools to retain children from non-churchgoing families, but the primary cause of the schools' demise was the changing ethos of society. In the years after the war the old consensus about what was right and proper disintegrated. In an oral history study of women and families between 1940 and 1970, Elizabeth Roberts notes that older women often accounted for their actions by saying 'It was the thing to do', a form of words which, as we have seen, was used to explain why children were sent to Sunday School. This phrase rarely, if ever, passed the lips of younger interviewees: instead of saying 'It was the right thing to do', they were much more likely to speak of 'doing your own thing'.[40] The change in terminology reflected a shift in belief away from absolute values towards a more relative value system. Even people within the churches were affected. Ian Jones, who has studied the impact of generational change in the mainstream churches, suggests that church members who became parents in the 1950s were less disappointed than their predecessors if their children failed to commit themselves to the church. Providing young people were making spiritual journeys of their own, the new generation of parents seemed content.[41]

---

[39] For the 'Family Church' concept see Cliff, *Rise and Development*, ch. 14.

[40] E. Roberts, *Women and Families: An Oral History, 1940–1970* (Oxford: Blackwell, 1995), p. 14.

[41] I. Jones, 'The "Mainstream" Churches in Birmingham c.1945–1995: The Local Church and Generational Change' (PhD thesis, University of Birmingham, 2000), p. 222.

A related development was a major alteration in the nature of parent-child relationships. In the 1950s and 1960s family life was still organized round adult agendas, and children were expected to fit in with their parents' plans. As society became more child-centred, family life focused increasingly round the activities of children, who dictated what they wanted to do to a greater extent than ever before. It ceased to be possible for non-churchgoing parents to despatch their children to Sunday School, unless the children themselves chose to go.

At the same time the range of activities available on Sundays expanded enormously. Victorian constraints on what could be done on 'the day of rest' had been losing their power at least since the 1890s, when young people started to use Sundays for bicycle rides in the country. But Sunday had retained a distinct character of its own throughout the first half of the twentieth century: it was quieter and more domestic than other days. The practice of sending children to Sunday School had fitted in well with the parental habit of treating Sunday as a day to relax at home. In the post-war period Sunday School attendance increasingly came into conflict with alternative family arrangements. It is no coincidence that the final decline of Sunday Schools coincided with the growth in car ownership: the number of private cars on the roads started to escalate around 1954, and by 1976 had increased more than four and a half times.[42] Sundays were regularly used for family outings. Activities which had once been confined to other days of the week, such as children's birthday parties, junior football leagues, and a host of other sporting events, became common on Sundays. In 1994 Sunday became a shopping day like any other. It also acquired a new function in the lives of children whose parents were separated or divorced: Sunday was 'Daddy's day', the day on which they visited the parent with whom they no longer lived.[43]

For nearly two centuries Sunday had been the obvious time for Christians to provide for the religious and educational needs of children from families which rarely attended worship. By the end of the twentieth century it was clear that schools which met on Sundays had no hope of attracting support outside church circles. Turn-of-the-century churches, which sought to appeal to children of non-churchgoers, tended to organize activities after school on week-days or during school holidays. *Sunday* Schools are thus a thing of the past. But as we mark their passing, recognizing that they have no part in the changed society of the present day, it is appropriate to acknowledge what an important role they played in the lives of children and families only a generation or two ago. For my

---

[42] Mitchell, *British Historical Statistics*, p. 558.

[43] P. Brierley, *The Tide is Running Out: What the English Church Attendance Survey Reveals* (London: Christian Research, 2000), p. 111.

mother, as for many of the elderly people interviewed by oral historians, Sunday School was a significant and memorable part of childhood experience.

Index

Studies in Christian History and Thought
(All titles uniform with this volume)
Dates in bold are of projected publication

David Bebbington
Holiness in Nineteenth-Century England
David Bebbington stresses the relationship of movements of spirituality to changes in their cultural setting, especially the legacies of the Enlightenment and Romanticism. He shows that these broad shifts in ideological mood had a profound effect on the ways in which piety was conceptualized and practised. Holiness was intimately bound up with the spirit of the age.
2000 / 0-85364-981-2 / viii + 98pp

J. William Black
Reformation Pastors
Richard Baxter and the Ideal of the Reformed Pastor
This work examines Richard Baxter's *Gildas Salvianus, The Reformed Pastor* (1656) and explores each aspect of his pastoral strategy in light of his own concern for 'reformation' and in the broader context of Edwardian, Elizabethan and early Stuart pastoral ideals and practice.
2003 / 1-84227-190-3 / xxii + 308pp

James Bruce
Prophecy, Miracles, Angels, *and* Heavenly Light?
The Eschatology, Pneumatology and Missiology of Adomnán's Life of Columba
This book surveys approaches to the marvellous in hagiography, providing the first critique of Plummer's hypothesis of Irish saga origin. It then analyses the uniquely systematized phenomena in the *Life of Columba* from Adomnán's seventh-century theological perspective, identifying the coming of the eschatological Kingdom as the key to understanding.
2004 / 1-84227-227-6 / xviii + 286pp

Colin J. Bulley
The Priesthood of Some Believers
Developments from the General to the Special Priesthood in the Christian Literature of the First Three Centuries
The first in-depth treatment of early Christian texts on the priesthood of all believers shows that the developing priesthood of the ordained related closely to the division between laity and clergy and had deleterious effects on the practice of the general priesthood.
2000 / 1-84227-034-6 / xii + 336pp

Anthony R. Cross (ed.)
Ecumenism and History
Studies in Honour of John H.Y. Briggs
This collection of essays examines the inter-relationships between the two fields in which Professor Briggs has contributed so much: history—particularly Baptist and Nonconformist—and the ecumenical movement. With contributions from colleagues and former research students from Britain, Europe and North America, *Ecumenism and History* provides wide-ranging studies in important aspects of Christian history, theology and ecumenical studies.
2002 / 1-84227-135-0 / xx + 362pp

Maggi Dawn
Confessions of an Inquiring Spirit
Form as Constitutive of Meaning in S.T. Coleridge's Theological Writing
This study of Coleridge's *Confessions* focuses on its confessional, epistolary and fragmentary form, suggesting that attention to these features significantly affects its interpretation. Bringing a close study of these three literary forms, the author suggests ways in which they nuance the text with particular understandings of the Trinity, and of a kenotic christology. Some parallels are drawn between Romantic and postmodern dilemmas concerning the authority of the biblical text.
2006 */ 1-84227-255-1 / approx. 224 pp*

Ruth Gouldbourne
The Flesh and the Feminine
Gender and Theology in the Writings of Caspar Schwenckfeld
Caspar Schwenckfeld and his movement exemplify one of the radical communities of the sixteenth century. Challenging theological and liturgical norms, they also found themselves challenging social and particularly gender assumptions. In this book, the issues of the relationship between radical theology and the understanding of gender are considered.
2005 */ 1-84227-048-6 / approx. 304pp*

Crawford Gribben
Puritan Millennialism
Literature and Theology, 1550–1682
Puritan Millennialism surveys the growth, impact and eventual decline of puritan millennialism throughout England, Scotland and Ireland, arguing that it was much more diverse than has frequently been suggested. This Paternoster edition is revised and extended from the original 2000 text.
2007 */ 1-84227-372-8 / approx. 320pp*

Galen K. Johnson
Prisoner of Conscience
John Bunyan on Self, Community and Christian Faith
This is an interdisciplinary study of John Bunyan's understanding of conscience across his autobiographical, theological and fictional writings, investigating whether conscience always deserves fidelity, and how Bunyan's view of conscience affects his relationship both to modern Western individualism and historic Christianity.

2003 / 1-84227-223-3 / xvi + 236pp

R.T. Kendall
Calvin and English Calvinism to 1649
The author's thesis is that those who formed the Westminster Confession of Faith, which is regarded as Calvinism, in fact departed from John Calvin on two points: (1) the extent of the atonement and (2) the ground of assurance of salvation.

1997 / 0-85364-827-1 / xii + 264pp

Timothy Larsen
Friends of Religious Equality
Nonconformist Politics in Mid-Victorian England
During the middle decades of the nineteenth century the English Nonconformist community developed a coherent political philosophy of its own, of which a central tenet was the principle of religious equality (in contrast to the stereotype of Evangelical Dissenters). The Dissenting community fought for the civil rights of Roman Catholics, non-Christians and even atheists on an issue of principle which had its flowering in the enthusiastic and undivided support which Nonconformity gave to the campaign for Jewish emancipation. This reissued study examines the political efforts and ideas of English Nonconformists during the period, covering the whole range of national issues raised, from state education to the Crimean War. It offers a case study of a theologically conservative group defending religious pluralism in the civic sphere, showing that the concept of religious equality was a grand vision at the centre of the political philosophy of the Dissenters.

2007 / 1-84227-402-3 / x + 300pp

Byung-Ho Moon
Christ the Mediator of the Law
Calvin's Christological Understanding of the Law as the Rule of Living and Life-Giving

This book explores the coherence between Christology and soteriology in Calvin's theology of the law, examining its intellectual origins and his position on the concept and extent of Christ's mediation of the law. A comparative study between Calvin and contemporary Reformers—Luther, Bucer, Melancthon and Bullinger—and his opponent Michael Servetus is made for the purpose of pointing out the unique feature of Calvin's Christological understanding of the law.

2005 / 1-84227-318-3 / approx. 370pp

John Eifion Morgan-Wynne
Holy Spirit and Religious Experience in Christian Writings, c.AD 90–200
This study examines how far Christians in the third to fifth generations (c.AD 90–200) attributed their sense of encounter with the divine presence, their sense of illumination in the truth or guidance in decision-making, and their sense of ethical empowerment to the activity of the Holy Spirit in their lives.

2005 / 1-84227-319-1 / approx. 350pp

James I. Packer
The Redemption and Restoration of Man in the Thought of Richard Baxter
James I. Packer provides a full and sympathetic exposition of Richard Baxter's doctrine of humanity, created and fallen; its redemption by Christ Jesus; and its restoration in the image of God through the obedience of faith by the power of the Holy Spirit.

2002 / 1-84227-147-4 / 432pp

Andrew Partington,
Church and State
The Contribution of the Church of England Bishops to the House of Lords
during the Thatcher Years

In *Church and State*, Andrew Partington argues that the contribution of the Church of England bishops to the House of Lords during the Thatcher years was overwhelmingly critical of the government; failed to have a significant influence in the public realm; was inefficient, being undertaken by a minority of those eligible to sit on the Bench of Bishops; and was insufficiently moral and spiritual in its content to be distinctive. On the basis of this, and the likely reduction of the number of places available for Church of England bishops in a fully reformed Second Chamber, the author argues for an evolution in the Church of England's approach to the service of its bishops in the House of Lords. He proposes the Church of England works to overcome the genuine obstacles which hinder busy diocesan bishops from contributing to the debates of the House of Lords and to its life more informally.
2005 / 1-84227-334-5 / approx. 324pp

Michael Pasquarello III
God's Ploughman
Hugh Latimer: A 'Preaching Life' (1490–1555)

This construction of a 'preaching life' situates Hugh Latimer within the larger religious, political and intellectual world of late medieval England. Neither biography, intellectual history, nor analysis of discrete sermon texts, this book is a work of homiletic history which draws from the details of Latimer's milieu to construct an interpretive framework for the preaching performances that formed the core of his identity as a religious reformer. Its goal is to illumine the practical wisdom embodied in the content, form and style of Latimer's preaching, and to recapture a sense of its overarching purpose, movement, and transforming force during the reform of sixteenth-century England.
2006 / 1-84227-336-1 / approx. 250pp

Alan P.F. Sell
Enlightenment, Ecumenism, Evangel
Theological Themes and Thinkers 1550–2000

This book consists of papers in which such interlocking topics as the Enlightenment, the problem of authority, the development of doctrine, spirituality, ecumenism, theological method and the heart of the gospel are discussed. Issues of significance to the church at large are explored with special reference to writers from the Reformed and Dissenting traditions.
2005 / 1-84227-330-2 / xviii + 422pp

Alan P.F. Sell
Hinterland Theology
Some Reformed and Dissenting Adjustments
Many books have been written on theology's 'giants' and significant trends, but what of those lesser-known writers who adjusted to them? In this book some hinterland theologians of the British Reformed and Dissenting traditions, who followed in the wake of toleration, the Evangelical Revival, the rise of modern biblical criticism and Karl Barth, are allowed to have their say. They include Thomas Ridgley, Ralph Wardlaw, T.V. Tymms and N.H.G. Robinson.
2006 / 1-84227-331-0 / approx. 350pp

Alan P.F. Sell and Anthony R. Cross (eds)
Protestant Nonconformity in the Twentieth Century
In this collection of essays scholars representative of a number of Nonconformist traditions reflect thematically on Nonconformists' life and witness during the twentieth century. Among the subjects reviewed are biblical studies, theology, worship, evangelism and spirituality, and ecumenism. Over and above its immediate interest, this collection provides a marker to future scholars and others wishing to know how some of their forebears assessed Nonconformity's contribution to a variety of fields during the century leading up to Christianity's third millennium.
2003 / 1-84227-221-7 / x + 398pp

Mark Smith
Religion in Industrial Society
Oldham and Saddleworth 1740–1865
This book analyses the way British churches sought to meet the challenge of industrialization and urbanization during the period 1740–1865. Working from a case-study of Oldham and Saddleworth, Mark Smith challenges the received view that the Anglican Church in the eighteenth century was characterized by complacency and inertia, and reveals Anglicanism's vigorous and creative response to the new conditions. He reassesses the significance of the centrally directed church reforms of the mid-nineteenth century, and emphasizes the importance of local energy and enthusiasm. Charting the growth of denominational pluralism in Oldham and Saddleworth, Dr Smith compares the strengths and weaknesses of the various Anglican and Nonconformist approaches to promoting church growth. He also demonstrates the extent to which all the churches participated in a common culture shaped by the influence of evangelicalism, and shows that active co-operation between the churches rather than denominational conflict dominated. This revised and updated edition of Dr Smith's challenging and original study makes an important contribution both to the social history of religion and to urban studies.
2006 / 1-84227-335-3 / approx. 300pp

Martin Sutherland
Peace, Toleration and Decay
The Ecclesiology of Later Stuart Dissent
This fresh analysis brings to light the complexity and fragility of the later Stuart Nonconformist consensus. Recent findings on wider seventeenth-century thought are incorporated into a new picture of the dynamics of Dissent and the roots of evangelicalism.
2003 / 1-84227-152-0 / xxii + 216pp

G. Michael Thomas
The Extent of the Atonement
A Dilemma for Reformed Theology from Calvin to the Consensus
A study of the way Reformed theology addressed the question, 'Did Christ die for all, or for the elect only?', commencing with John Calvin, and including debates with Lutheranism, the Synod of Dort and the teaching of Moïse Amyraut.
1997 / 0-85364-828-X / x + 278pp

David M. Thompson
Baptism, Church and Society in Britain from the Evangelical Revival to
Baptism, Eucharist and Ministry
The theology and practice of baptism have not received the attention they deserve. How important is faith? What does baptismal regeneration mean? Is baptism a bond of unity between Christians? This book discusses the theology of baptism and popular belief and practice in England and Wales from the Evangelical Revival to the publication of the World Council of Churches' consensus statement on *Baptism, Eucharist and Ministry* (1982).
2005 / 1-84227-393-0 / approx. 224pp

Mark D. Thompson
A Sure Ground on Which to Stand
The Relation of Authority and Interpretive Method of Luther's Approach to Scripture
The best interpreter of Luther is Luther himself. Unfortunately many modern studies have superimposed contemporary agendas upon this sixteenth-century Reformer's writings. This fresh study examines Luther's own words to find an explanation for his robust confidence in the Scriptures, a confidence that generated the famous 'stand' at Worms in 1521.
2004 / 1-84227-145-8 / xvi + 322pp

Carl R. Trueman and R.S. Clark (eds)
Protestant Scholasticism
Essays in Reassessment

Traditionally Protestant theology, between Luther's early reforming career and the dawn of the Enlightenment, has been seen in terms of decline and fall into the wastelands of rationalism and scholastic speculation. In this volume a number of scholars question such an interpretation. The editors argue that the development of post-Reformation Protestantism can only be understood when a proper historical model of doctrinal change is adopted. This historical concern underlies the subsequent studies of theologians such as Calvin, Beza, Olevian, Baxter, and the two Turrentini. The result is a significantly different reading of the development of Protestant Orthodoxy, one which both challenges the older scholarly interpretations and clichés about the relationship of Protestantism to, among other things, scholasticism and rationalism, and which demonstrates the fruitfulness of the new, historical approach.

1999 / 0-85364-853-0 / xx + 344pp

Shawn D. Wright
Our Sovereign Refuge
The Pastoral Theology of Theodore Beza

Our Sovereign Refuge is a study of the pastoral theology of the Protestant reformer who inherited the mantle of leadership in the Reformed church from John Calvin. Countering a common view of Beza as supremely a 'scholastic' theologian who deviated from Calvin's biblical focus, Wright uncovers a new portrait. He was not a cold and rigid academic theologian obsessed with probing the eternal decrees of God. Rather, by placing him in his pastoral context and by noting his concerns in his pastoral and biblical treatises, Wright shows that Beza was fundamentally a committed Christian who was troubled by the vicissitudes of life in the second half of the sixteenth century. He believed that the biblical truth of the supreme sovereignty of God alone could support Christians on their earthly pilgrimage to heaven. This pastoral and personal portrait forms the heart of Wright's argument.

2004 / 1-84227-252-7 / xviii + 308pp

Paternoster
9 Holdom Avenue,
Bletchley,
Milton Keynes MK1 1QR,
United Kingdom
Web: www.authenticmedia.co.uk/paternoster

July 2005